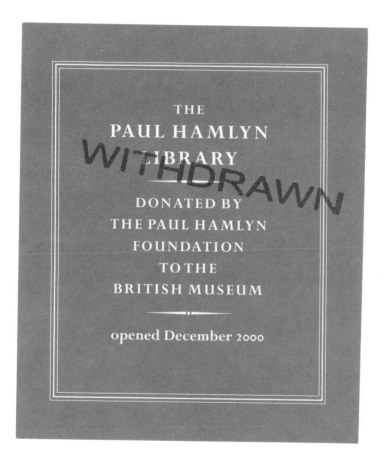

Cognitive Technologies

Oliviero Stock · Massimo Zancanaro (Eds.)

PEACH –
Intelligent Interfaces
for Museum Visits

With 101 Figures, 32 in Color, and 16 Tables

 Springer

Editors:

Oliviero Stock
Massimo Zancanaro
ITC-irst
Via Sommarive, 18
38050 Povo, Trento
Italy
stock@itc.it
zancana@itc.it

Managing Editors:

Prof. Dov M. Gabbay
Augustus De Morgan Professor of Logic
Department of Computer Science, King's College London
Strand, London WC2R 2LS, UK

Prof. Dr. Jörg Siekmann
Forschungsbereich Deduktions- und Multiagentensysteme, DFKI
Stuhlsatzenweg 3, Geb. 43, 66123 Saarbrücken, Germany

Cover image based on the "January" fresco in the Torre Aquila, Castello del Buonconsiglio, Trento, Italy

Library of Congress Control Number: 2007923181

ACM Computing Classification: H.1.2, H.5, I.2, I.3, I.4, I.7, J.5, K.3

ISSN 1611-2482
ISBN 978-3-540-68754-2 Springer Berlin Heidelberg New York

Springer is a part of Springer Science+Business Media
springer.com

© Springer-Verlag Berlin Heidelberg 2007
Printed in Germany

The use of general descriptive names, registered names, trademarks, etc. in this publication does not imply, even in the absence of a specific statement, that such names are exempt from the relevant protective laws and regulations and therefore free for general use.

Typesetting: by the editors
Production: Integra Software Services Pvt. Ltd., India
Cover Design: KünkelLopka, Heidelberg

Printed on acid-free paper   45/3100/Integra   5 4 3 2 1 0

Preface

This book reports the main results of the Personal Experience with Active Cultural Heritage (PEACH) project, whose goal was to produce intelligent tools, or, more ambitiously, an environment for making a visit to a museum a rewarding experience. PEACH was a large four year project funded by the Autonomous Province of Trento, exploring novel technologies for physical museum visits developed at ITC-irst (Institute for Scientific and Technological Research), Trento and DFKI (the German Institute for Research in Artificial Intelligence), Saarbrücken. The aim of the project was to significantly increase the quality of cultural heritage appreciation, in such a way as to transform passive objects into an active experience.

A visit to a cultural site with a friend who knows the subject well and who knows the visitor has been a precious experience for centuries. Through time, with the development of museums and the emergence of the cultural experience as a mass phenomenon, tools for museum communication have been introduced: labels illustrating exhibits, guidebooks, and guided tours. Following this, different forms of technology were introduced such as audio material on cassettes and later CDs (having the advantage of providing random access) as well as visual material through various forms of kiosks, screens, or presentation rooms. In some museums, coarse-grained localization systems have been introduced as well that let the system automatically know what room the visitor is in, so that the presentation recorded for that room can be automatically selected. In very recent times, mobile computing and wireless communication have also begun to be used in some museums.

A cultural visit is a blend of cognition, emotion, and social communication; perhaps it is the most central case of educational entertainment. The end goal is for people to enjoy the process of acquiring knowledge, to understand more about the past, to appreciate art, and, through this, to develop an interest for the site and, possibly, for a subject (archeology, history, art).

From a scientific point of view, cultural heritage appreciation is an ideal area for exploring new concepts in intelligent user interface research and dealing with a privileged educational entertainment issue. Various large themes of research are relevant. The introduction of new devices entails an interesting application and experimentation arena. This theme includes development of sensors, communication devices, novel wearable computers of various kinds, and also what we can describe as the consequences of their adoption at the system level.

A second large theme includes the higher level techniques for solving specific applied challenges. Some examples include developing artificial vision techniques appropriate for supporting a visit, or developing specific language processing techniques useful for retrieving the important information or dealing with flexible language presentations starting from retrieved information of all sorts, even designing novel infrastructural technologies with features that help realize a complex system and adapt it to the specific context smoothly.

A third even larger theme puts the visitor at centre stage. It includes issues such as novel user interfaces, intelligent multimodal presentations, and the educational and the cognitive technologies that can be developed for best serving the visitor in his or her experience. For instance, recent original work brings the affective dimension into technology for the museum experience. There are more issues to be addressed, including the dimension of the overall impact of the technology that requires novel research and most likely the introduction of novel methodologies.

Another very important theme (not directly addressed in this volume) is the even greater divide that many of the advanced technologies impose on the elderly and on individuals with disabilities. Rarely do novel devices and interfaces take into account the fact that a portion of the population is not at ease with the new offer and might simply be excluded. Flexibility and adaptability along this dimension must become an important topic of research, so that end products can incorporate disabled-friendly features without great effort. In this respect, the importance of research on multimodal interfaces cannot be overemphasized. For instance, the flexible, intelligent allocation of the message on a combination of available modalities can be a fundamental resource. In the applied scenario, a system must take into account the user's ability to function easily using the possible modalities included in the interface.

This book is an edited collection of papers describing the results achieved in PEACH. The work in the project was interdisciplinary: the technologies belong mainly to the area of intelligent user interfaces, but included other areas of artificial intelligence, microsystems and computer–human interaction. The studies conducted in PEACH resulted in the construction and evaluation of various prototypes. Together they offer an innovative applied prospect for the field of cultural heritage appreciation.

The volume is structured in six parts; each of the first five parts includes several chapters concerned with different areas of the project. A final chapter discusses directions for the future.

The first part deals with the common theme of the development of an intelligent, user-adaptive mobile guide.

The chapter 'Adaptive Multimedia Guide' presents the evolution of a multimedia adaptive, mobile guide. The museum visit is a complex experience that encompasses cognitive and emotional aspects. Visitors have different ways of elaborating background and new knowledge, and they have different interests and preferences. Designing interactive technologies to support such an experience requires effort in many aspects: the graphical interface and its usability, the adaptation mechanism and its effectiveness, and the overall satisfaction of the visitor. Moreover, technology designers need to consider the intrusiveness of the devices they propose for supporting visits. The starting idea of the work presented is that an adaptive guide that offers highly personalized information can help each visitor to accommodate and interpret the visit according to his or her own pace and interests. Hence classical audio presentations were enhanced with video documentaries—small, adaptively composed video clips—which help visitors to identify exhibit details mentioned in the audio counterpart and to show the relationship between new and previously presented information without interfering with the appreciation of the exhibit itself. In developing the guide, a user-centred design approach was adopted that includes a requirements elicitation phase and a number of iterative design steps. The results achieved at each stage are described. In particular, the evolution of the interface is in focus: its acceptability and usability after each redesign, and details on the changes required in the system backend. The main result of this process is the final prototype with an interface based on affective interaction. The prototype device, a PDA with specialized software, lets visitors express their attitudes about an exhibit using a graphical widget, the *like-o-meter*, which allows users to express preferences with four degrees of freedom. In addition, it enables them to explicitly signal their interests in order to guide the adaptation mechanism of the system. Another issue considered in this chapter is the preparation of adaptive content. Writing content for adaptive guides is a difficult task for authors, even for professional multimedia authors. The experience of involving two multimedia authors in the content preparation for the adaptive mobile guide is described, with details on how the authors were trained, how the system's adaptation mechanisms were explained to them, and, finally, the methodology (and the functionalities to be implemented in an authoring tool) for, in the future, reducing involvement of the engineers (who usually are not part of a 'standard' museum staff) during the content authoring phase.

Video documentaries are often integrated into information technology solutions that support cultural heritage exploration. However, high production costs of human authoring and lack of personalization hamper wide adoption of this technique. Automatic approaches are called for. Yet, automatically constructing a complete documentary or educational film from scattered pieces of images and knowledge is a significant challenge. Even when this information is provided in an annotated format, the problems of ordering, structuring, and animating sequences of images and of producing natural language descriptions that correspond to those images are each difficult tasks. The chapter 'Cinematographic Techniques for Automatic Documentary-Like Presentations' describes the PEACH approach to dealing with these problems. Rhetorical structures combined with narrative and film theory produce movie-like visual animations from still images. Natural language generation (NLG) techniques supply text descriptions for the animations. Rhetorical structures from NLG are used as a common denominator to assure coherence when merging work done by separate components for video creation and script generation.

The chapter 'Detecting Focus of Attention' explores different means by which the focus of attention of the visitor, i.e., the local context, can be determined and exploited in the context of intelligent systems for cultural heritage appreciation. Two different modalities of interaction of a visitor with a smart museum are considered. In the first one, the user reveals his or her interest by pointing a PDA with a camera at an exhibit. The PDA then feeds back properly contextualized information to enhance comprehension of the exhibit. Image processing techniques are used to recognize the paintings (or details thereof) viewed by the PDA camera. Once a painting is recognized, the PDA accesses relevant database information over a wireless connection. The second scenario does not require a helping device to point at the item of interest: rather, head orientation and arm gestures are directly used to determine focus of attention. The first, mediated method works well in supporting a single user in the natural exploration of museum exhibits. The system knows the layout of exhibits, permitting it to identify focus of attention by finding the intersection of the line of sight with the geometry of the environment. The second system, relying on the interpretation of deictic gestures, works well as a support to a guide who conducts and informs sightseers, but it is an unnatural way for a single visitor to interact with a museum. The smart museum can monitor the guide during his or her informative efforts, presenting additional multimedia material whenever he or she points at active spots in the exhibits.

How intelligent technologies can intervene at the end of the visit is the topic of the chapter 'Report Generation for Post-Visit Summaries in Museum Environments'. As guardians of cultural heritage, museums are interested in a continual presence within their communities for both ongoing learning and improved public awareness of their collections. Thus an additional area where the technology demonstrated in PEACH can have an important impact is the extension of the museum's influence outside the confines of the museum itself. Personalization is one key to heightening this impact, where a permanent keepsake is given to a visitor upon his or her exit from the museum which describes his or her unique experience and is immediately recognizable as such. Language technology may be used in order to accomplish this goal of continuing to educate a visitor after the museum visit is completed, and to provide the 'hook' of specific personalization leading to further visitor interest. In order to construct this personalized keepsake, the sequence of interactions with the intelligent tour guide during the visit is used to predict which exhibits the visitor was most interested in. The system then produces a page-long report summarizing the visitor's tour, the artworks he or she found most interesting as well as those he or she missed out on. The system also provides additional information linked to what he or she has already discovered and that could be used to discover new information via the Internet. The prototype described in this chapter produces written report summaries given an interest model described previously for the Torre Aquila museum, printed on demand, including colour reproductions of the referenced artworks, and in either English or Italian.

The second part deals with infrastructure and user modelling. As discussed before, context awareness is a key feature of applications for active environments, such as PEACH's automatic visitor guides. Most existing works consider context as information neutral with respect to the agents acting in the environments, thus it can be represented in some form of shared knowledge base. By contrast, in the chapter 'Delivering Services in Active Museums via Group Communication,' context is viewed as a specific perspective of each agent on its environment; what is needed is a way for agents to be systematically aware of what happens in their surroundings, i.e., they must be able to 'overhear' events and interactions. Group collaboration is possible when collaborative agents immersed in the same environment are reciprocally aware of their capabilities and their likely states as a consequence of a history of events. Such context awareness can also be obtained via overhearing. From a communication perspective, overhearing requires some form of broadcast facility, in PEACH a mechanism called 'channelled multicast' has been tested. In this chapter, the motivations for this approach are presented, the architecture for active environments based on implicit organizations is introduced, and implicit organizations can be applied in practice. A short overview of the work concerning its formalization in logic and as a design pattern is also introduced.

The chapter 'User Modelling and Adaptation for a Museum Visitors' guide' touches upon the underlying infrastructure for producing personalised information for the individual. The museum environment is rich with information that can be presented to visitors; there is more information to be delivered than time available for the visit. Supporting personalization is a particularly challenging task in the museum environment where 'nonintrusiveness' is fundamental. User modelling has to take advantage of the observation of events and behaviour, and needs integration of various techniques. Within the PEACH project, several adaptation and personalization techniques were tested, integrating a variety of technologies as sources for information about visitors' positioning data and visitors' interests. PEACH also faced the challenge of bootstrapping a user model (when no initial data is available) and the requirement for 'lean' user modelling—using whatever information is already available without additional specific information. Moreover, user modelling was exploited for two services in particular: dynamic presentation and visit summary report generation, each with different specific requirements.

The third part is dedicated to novel uses of stationary devices, in one case integrated in the mobile experience, in another as a specific application for children.

In the chapter 'Integration Between Mobile and Stationary Devices' the PEACH activities related to the integration of information presentation of the mobile tour guide, based on a PDA, and large stationary screens, the so-called virtual windows, are presented. Relevant interaction concepts as well as the software architecture that integrates both device types are discussed and experiences from two prototypical installations in the museum 'Castello del Buonconsiglio', and the 'Völklingen Old Iron Works' are presented. The accent is on the use of virtual characters, a remote-control metaphor, and a voting mechanism. Different phenotypes of the characters were designed to fit the small screen size of the PDA and, at the same time, to be able to perform communicative acts based on gestures. The remote control metaphor was used to allow visitors to individually control the presentations on the virtual windows, while the voting mechanism helps to solve conflicts in situations where more than one visitor is standing in front of the virtual window. The client–server based architecture can handle and manage several mobile devices and several virtual windows. The content is synchronized and retrieved from a common database and its presentation is driven by a script language. The architecture can also be used to collect statistical data on movement patterns of visitors. This data can then be analysed to understand more about the users' interests and to adapt the presentation of content both on the mobile and stationary device.

The next chapter reports about an innovative technology for children. For children in a museum environment, an active role is essential. It is also appropriate to stimulate shared 'cultural' activity and in particular a reflective process after the museum visit. The chapter 'Children and a Museum: an Environment for Collaborative Story Telling', describes a system called Story Table, which is aimed at supporting pairs of children in the activity of storytelling, a fundamental aspect of the reflective process. The system is based on a multiuser touchable device (the MERL DiamondTouch) and was designed with the purpose of enforcing collaboration between children. The chapter discusses how the main design choices were influenced by the paradigm of cooperative learning, and presents two observational studies to assess the effects of different design choices on storytelling activity. Finally, a study involving 70 children from a local primary school is presented. The experiment demonstrates that the use of Story Table compared to the control situation improves the quality of the interaction and, to some extent, the quality of the stories produced.

The fourth part is concerned with visual technologies for reconstruction and for simulation and control in the museum environment.

3D virtual reconstruction and modelling offer an important prospect for cultural heritage. They aim at creating highly accurate and realistic digital copies of artworks and monuments of particular cultural interest. Advances in microelectronics, microsystems, photonics and computer vision in the last decade have led to the development of faster and more reliable methods for 3D digitization of objects of nearly any shape at ever decreasing costs. The topic of photorealistic virtual 3D reconstruction of objects and architectures was approached within PEACH in two independent, different ways. The first approach, directed towards the digitization of large architectonic structures and buildings, deals with image-based modelling based on close-range photogrammetry. The second approach, directed towards the digitization of free-form objects, deals with the development of a new concept of integrated sensors for triangulation-based 3D laser scanners with improved performance in terms of dynamic range, readout speed, and multiwavelength detection. The chapter 'Photorealistic 3D Modelling Applied to Cultural Heritage' reports on the 3D modelling techniques used within PEACH, the results achieved during the project, and the challenges for the future.

Automatic monitoring of people wandering within a large, multiroom environment such as a museum provides information which supports increased security for and better planning of exhibits. The chapter 'Tracking Visitors in a Museum' describes a modular processing architecture for distributed ambient intelligence which provides a detailed reporting of people's trajectories in complex indoor environments. The design of the architecture was driven by three main principles: reliable algorithm testing, system scalability, and robust performance. The first goal was achieved through the development of Zeus, a real-time 3D rendering engine that provides simulated sensory inputs associated with automatically generated ground truth. Scalability was achieved by developing a novel modular architecture for multiplatform video grabbing, MPEG4 compression, and stream delivery and processing using a local area network as a distributed processing environment. Robust performance was attained with the introduction of a theoretically well-founded Bayesian estimation framework that allows for the effective management of uncertainty due to occlusion. The performance of the algorithms is reported for a virtual museum where groups of simulated visitors with different cultural interests move freely.

The next part deals with evaluation with users and usability issues which are, of course, of essential importance in the museum.

The chapter 'Evaluation of Cinematic Techniques in a Mobile Multimedia Museum Guide Interface' discusses the use of cinematic techniques in building mobile multimedia museum guides. The hypothesis is that a user interface that employs cinematic techniques reduces the inherent invasiveness that the PDA brings to the museum experience. The results of an initial evaluation that was conducted with 46 visitors are presented, and the evaluation supports the claim that cinematic techniques help influence the attentional behaviour of the visitor by reducing the number of eye shifts between the guide and the environment.

In PEACH, in addition to traditional evaluation performed within iterative user-centred design, attention was given to aspects not yet addressed by the community of adaptive interfaces, nor in the domain of museum guides. Two of them are discussed in 'Innovative Approaches for Evaluating Adaptive Mobile Museum Guides'. The first approach is aimed at assessing the visitors' attitudes towards several basic dimensions of adaptivity relevant for museum guides and the possible relationships between personality traits and user preferences towards those adaptivity dimensions. For this evaluation two simulated systems were used that realized an adaptive and a nonadaptive version, respectively, on each of the dimensions investigated. The study showed that the personality traits relating to the notion of control (conscientiousness, neuroticism/emotional stability, locus of control) have a selective effect on the acceptance of the adaptivity dimensions. The second approach aimed at assessing several aspects of the experience real visitors had while using an adaptive user guide during the museum visit. The data showed that a positive attitude towards technology determines greater sense of control, deeper involvement, more ease in using the guide as well as a better attitude towards its future use. Quite surprisingly, older visitors were much more favourable towards a future use of the guide than young visitors, although young visitors had generally a more positive attitude towards technology and they used the guide in a correct fashion more often.

The book ends with a chapter devoted to the future, in particular to a theme that we have just begun to address: technologies to support small groups of visitors.

To a large extent, intelligent interfaces in the museum are based on the concept of ubiquitous context-aware presentations oriented to the specific individual. Yet in most cases a museum visit is an activity performed in groups (small, like friends or families, or larger, like a class). In the chapter 'Intelligent Interfaces for Groups in the Museum' this perspective and various connected themes are introduced. Some of the main challenges are how novel technology can give a new meaning to shared presentations, how to allocate the message to members of a group, and how to foster communication within the group during and after the visit, how to favour an active intellectual attitude as a distinguished characteristic of the group experience. Related to this is the problem of how to model the group, how to take advantage of previous experiences, how to maintain the common interest in the future. Finally, a specific challenge is to go all the way to have contents emerge from contributions by a community of visitors, and to make them intelligently adaptable and expandable. The overall idea is that research on these themes will help the future experience in the museum be a radically more engaging and socially oriented experience than the one we are used to now.

Most of the experimentation in PEACH, including long evaluation sessions, was conducted at the museum of the Castello del Buonconsiglio in Trento. We would like to thank the Director Franco Marzatico for his constant support and enthusiasm. At the same time we would like to thank Meinrad Grewenig, Director of Völklinger Hütte in Saarbrücken, where various experiments were also conducted.

We are pleased to acknowledge the authorities of the Autonomous Province of Trento, who made this project possible by providing generous research funding as well as an enlightened vision of the future. We thank all the participants in PEACH. Not all were involved in this book even if they were important for the development of components and prototypes not described here. Finally we would like to thank Brian Martin for his role in revising and formatting the material for this book.

New research is continuing from the results described here: may PEACH be a tasty fruit holding the seed of larger developments in intelligent technologies for cultural heritage appreciation!

Trento, Italy, February 7, 2007   Oliviero Stock and Massimo Zancanaro

Table of Contents

Part I
Intelligent Mobile Guides

1 Adaptive Multimedia Guide

C. Rocchi, I. Graziola, D. Goren-Bar, O. Stock and M. Zancanaro

1.1 Introduction and Motivation

An important goal of museum practitioners today is to find new services that keep the museum a stimulating and up-to-date space for all visitors regardless of age (Verdaasdonk et al. 1996; Laws 1998). From this viewpoint, the information provided to museum visitors is a key component in improving their involvement and thus their attendance (Ravelli 1996). Therefore, technologies are considered a valuable resource for catching visitor attention and stimulating their involvement (Lin et al. 2005). Engineering and HCI researchers have seconded this need with several proposals consistent with this kind of environment, developing museum guides, information kiosks, web services, and progressively more intense multimedia (González-Castaño et al. 2005; Scarlatos et al. 1999). These solutions arose through considerable efforts in studying the museum environment, its communication and interaction potentialities, and interconnections with technology (Ambach et al. 1995). These studies focused on what museum audiences would like to see and learn, which visitor behaviors could be supported by technology, how to offer these technologies to visitors, and visitor attitudes towards these technologies (Silberberg 1995; Crowley et al. 2001). They demonstrated non-homogenous behaviors and interests, which provided an opening for adaptive strategies. Adaptive technologies enable visitors to get personalized information, that is, information related to their particular interest, context and path, without time pressure or the involvement of human guides. They considerably enrich what museums can offer visitors.

In this chapter, we present an adaptive mobile guide, which runs on a PDA and accompanies visitors in Torre Aquila. Communication between the visitor and the system is based on an affective interaction paradigm that allows the visitor to naturally express his or her interest in presentations regarding an artwork. The feedback is exploited by the system to adaptively select the information, according to an inferred user model built up during the visit. We investigated an interaction paradigm that allows the user to express affective attitude towards the presentations proposed by the system. We wanted to verify whether such interaction improved the efficacy of the interface, especially when technology should not hinder the "real" experience, as with museums.

The preparation of adaptive content is a difficult task for multimedia authors, even professionals. For example, writing texts for adaptive systems requires authors to exploit nonlinear writing techniques. In our case, it is even more complicated because the multimedia guide also requires experience in the mixing of text and pictures, along the lines of cinema. Moreover, authors should foster visitor engagement with artworks when organizing the exhibition, identifying communicative strategies, in particular. It is not surprising that many such professionals have a background in humanities (art, literature, and so on) and that they usually do not have knowledge of adaptive systems, and the steps necessary for preparing content for the purpose of personalized composition. In order to manage the adaptive system—and in particular to write and classify contents—the author needs to first understand the vocabulary, the concepts and definitions used by engineers to structure the adaptive system. In the last part of the Personal Experience with Active Cultural Heritage (PEACH) project, we studied this issue seriously, considering how to help authors accomplish the task of authoring adaptive multimedia content. We started from our experience in preparing content for the PEACH mobile guide, and defined a methodology to support authors in preparing the content for adaptive mobile guides. Our first goal was to identify a clear methodology to support authors in preparing "adaptivity-ready" content for a mobile guide. On this basis, we also proposed relevant functionalities of an authoring tool to help authors in writing and managing adaptive content. One of the first papers about adaptive hypermedia authoring is by Hongjing et al. (1998), which introduces a reference model for adaptive applications and which also encompasses the authoring phase. Petrelli et al. (2000) present a graphical interface for preparing content for the framework of the HIPS project. Hyper-Interaction within Physical Space (HIPS, Benelli et al. 1999) was a European funded project aimed at creating personalized presentations of museum exhibits. Recently, a series of workshops about authoring in adaptive applications was organized in conjunction with adaptive hypermedia and education-related conferences.[1]

---

[1] See http://www.win.tue.nl/~acristea/A3H/.

This chapter is structured as follows: first, we introduce the state of the art in the field of the mobile guides, illustrating the main achievements of the last 15 years. We then describe the evolution of the system—graphical interface and backend—across a set of three prototype-evaluation cycles. For each step, we illustrate the insights that drove the design of the next prototype. Finally, we provide a methodology to help museum curators organize the content of adaptive systems.

1.2   State of the Art

About 15 years ago, Weiser (1991) proposed a set of ideas about the future of computers in the next century. "Personalization" was one of the key words mentioned in that paper and later was identified as a key feature of ubiquitous computing systems (Abowd et al. 2000). In a series of attempts to port "office applications" to mobile devices, researchers realized that new features could be explored, including information sharing (Aoki et al. 2002), location and context awareness (Want et al. 1995; Cheverst et al. 1999), and adaptivity (Rocchi et al. 2004).

From the second half of the 1990s on, there have been many efforts to explore the potential of mobile systems. CyberGuide was a large project which aimed at exploring the use of a mobile, hand-held, context-aware tour guide (Long et al. 1996; Abowd et al. 1997). The authors illustrate both indoor and outdoor prototypes, explaining the issues of detecting user position and orientation, and discussing the choice of hardware, the appropriateness of communication media (audio or video), and the methodology of map representation.

The HIPS project focused on hyper-interaction (Benelli et al. 1999), which evolved from the earlier HyperAudio experience (Not et al. 1998; Petrelli and Not 2005). A novel aspect, with respect to previous projects, was the overlapping of contextual and personalized information on top of the physical space. The user experience is augmented because spatial and informational navigation occur at the same time. The system, set up in Museo Civico (Siena, Italy), used a hand-held device to support visitors in moving around, and in seeking information and guidance. Personalization was based on user position, and on interaction with the PDA and the surrounding physical space.

GUIDE is another successful mobile system (Cheverst et al. 2000). It supports tourists visiting the city of Lancaster (UK). Combining mobile technologies and wireless infrastructures, it tailors information to the user's personal and contextual situation. Its design, carried out in collaboration with experts in the field of tourism, is particularly valuable and the insights gained during evaluations brought interesting changes to the prototypes.

Survey papers have helped assess the development of research from different perspectives. For instance, Kray and Baus (2003) present a survey of mobile guides, both prototypes or commercial, whereas Raptis et al. (2005) attempt to classify current practices in the design of mobile guides for museums.

Some systems featuring mobile guides are DiscoveryPoint, the Genoa Aquarium Guide, and SottoVoce. The first is a remote control-like device that allows users to listen to short stories related to an artwork; it is installed at the Carnegie Museum of Art in Pittsburgh (Berkovich et al. 2003). It is an audio system with a special speaker which delivers pinpointed audio and can be heard near the work of art.

Another PDA application has been tested at Genoa's Costa Aquarium (Bellotti et al. 2002). The basic elements of the interface are multimedia cards, each corresponding to a presentation subject such as a particular fish or a fish tank containing several species. Each multimedia card provides users with content. Touch-screen buttons allow control of content presentation and navigation between tanks.

Grinter et al. (2002) report on an interesting study about the SottoVoce system which was designed to promote a shared experience during a visit to a historic house. The system supports shared playing of audio content between pairs of visitors, each using a PDA. The paper reports interesting findings on how this technology helps to shape the experience in the museum (shared versus individual use of the device).

Multimedia guide literature also includes research concerning the development of architectures for context-aware applications. (Dey et al. 2001) present an interesting attempt to define the notion of context and introduce a conceptual model with a set of methods to help drive the design of context-aware applications. Their proposal is a computational framework to quicken the implementation and prototyping of context-aware applications.

Efstratiou et al. (2003) introduce a new platform to support the coordination of multiple adaptive applications. Coordination can be specified in terms of policies (they also present a formal language to define them) which allow adaptive (re)actions on a system-wide level to be described. For instance, it is possible to define the level of system intrusiveness, for example, whether to notify the user of system actions.

Seamless connection between mobile devices is a recent research issue. Krüger and colleagues focused on providing user-adapted seamless services in different situations. They worked on a route planning scenario where a user is supported by a central system while using three devices: a desktop route planner, an in-car navigation system, and a pedestrian navigation service running on a PDA (Krüger et al. 2004).[2]

Evaluation studies provide insights on both design and reimplementation of prototypes. In addition to previously cited works, the added value of systematic evaluation is shown in Bohnenberger et al. (2005), which reports on improvements brought to a mobile shopping guide after an iterative evaluation cycle. In particular, the authors focus on usability issues of the PDA interface with respect to the task to be accomplished (buy items in the minimum possible time) and on the accuracy of the system in supporting the user.

1.3   History of the System

At the beginning of the project, we stated the requirements of a mobile guide. Unlike many mobile devices (e.g., cell phones) our guide had to be *wake-up-and-use* since it is not meant to be used daily. This means it had to be intuitive and clear, with almost no need for explanation. Second, it had to be nonintrusive, that is, it could not interfere with a visitor's enjoyment of artwork. Third, we wanted to experiment with a new communication paradigm based on *delegation* and *affect*. In many "information-seeking" scenarios people typically look for information (think of Web queries with search engines). We consider the museum experience as something that has more to do with entertainment than with information seeking. The system's proactiveness in delivering an appropriate presentation at the right time is essential. Therefore, we devised interaction based on delegation: visitors do not ask for information about an artwork, they rather signal liking or disliking (that is affect towards the artwork and the information presented by the system) and, almost implicitly, request information from the system. This feedback from the visitor can be seen as a sort of nonverbal backchannel gesture that the system takes into account in selecting information for that specific user. This introduces the fourth requirement: the system had to be adaptive, that is, it had to provide personalized information according to the user profile built during the visit. We also wanted to experiment with affective interaction, believing it might improve system usability and acceptability.

In the design of the system, we kept in mind four fundamental adaptive dimensions which were also used for the evaluation phase:

---

[2] See Chap. 7 on seamless presentations across devices.

- Location awareness: the system initiates interaction when it detects the visitor at a given position. This feature is enabled by means of sensors located close to each work of art.
- Follow-up: the system arranges the following presentations on the fly according to feedback received from the visitor through the interface.
- Interest: the system selects content appropriate to (estimated) user interests.
- History: the system appropriately refers to previously seen items or points to artworks closely related to the one currently visited.

From the design requirements, we moved along iteratively, through quick prototyping and small evaluations. This drove the evolution of the system—both the graphical interface and the backend—to the final prototype, which is based on a *like-o-meter* widget and a shallow semantic network for dynamically modelling visitor interests. In this section, we shed more light on the steps in this evolution.

1.3.1   First Design

The first design is based on a two-button interface, as illustrated in Fig. 1.

Fig. 1. The first prototype of the interface

Pressing the WOW button is meant to express a visitor's interest whenever she is impressed by a fresco or by a specific topic related to it. The BASTA! button, on the other hand, was to be used for lack of interest in current topic. As a side effect, the BASTA! button stops the current presentation. It is worth noting that a presentation can also be stopped by moving away from the current fresco to approach another one.[3] The central part of the screen was used to show a video presentation.

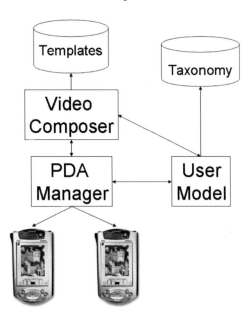

Fig. 2. Architecture underlying the first prototype

The underlying architecture that supports the first prototype consists of the following components (Fig. 2):

1. A video composer (VC) for dynamically composing presentations from a repository of templates according to the user interests stored in the user model.
2. A user interface manager (UI) for catching user location, interaction through buttons, and dispatching the presentations generated.
3. A user model for receiving the messages from the UI, for computing the current interest level of the visitor on each of the topics, and for propagating interest level according to a topic's taxonomy.

---

[3] This feature is "discovered" by the visitor during the visit.

4. A tree-based topic taxonomy which represents the contents of the pictures at three levels of abstraction (from specific content to abstract concepts such as "aristocratic leisure activities").

Templates, encoded in the XASCRIPT formalism, allow definition of a set of possible video documentaries from which user-tailored presentations are dynamically assembled (Rocchi and Zancanaro 2003). A template contains a set of instructions for image selection (or audio clips), and variable settings. By means of a merging mechanism, the system uses a single template to compose different video documentaries, conditioned by the user profile built by the user model (see Chap. 2).

1.3.2   Initial User Studies

Using the prototype described above, the first user study was set up in the real scenario, Torre Aquila, and included eight visitors. In the tower, we installed:

- A laptop, running the server side of the system.
- An access point, to allow wireless communication between devices.
- A PDA, running the interface shown in Fig. 1.
- Four infrared beacons, one for each fresco, to detect user position.

Users were "real" visitors, recruited at the entrance. They were given a short verbal introduction about the guide, followed by a real visit of four frescos (of eleven) exhibited. The experimenter observed the users during the visit. At the end of the visit, an informal interview was performed in order to assess the perception of the four adaptive dimensions: location, follow-up, interest, and history.

At the end of this evaluation cycle, both looking at interviews and considering experimenter observations, it was apparent that users did not clearly understand the graphical interface. In other words, during the experiments to investigate the effects of adaptivity on visitors, we found that the system was not usable. The WOW button was the source of many misunderstandings of the whole system. Sometimes it was pressed to initiate the interaction, although this is not needed at all.

To study usability and user perception of adaptivity in more depth, we resorted to an "action-protocol and retrospective-interview" qualitative study, targeting the expression of the affect and the delegation-of-control paradigm. The main difference of this methodology with respect to think-aloud is that the user does not provide her comments during the execution of the task, but later on, while she and the experimenter are watching a video recording of the interaction (Van Someren 1994).

The study was conducted on three subjects, in a room equipped with posters of the originals frescos, and with sensors to detect the positions of the subject with respect to the frescos. Although small, this is deemed to be a reasonable number of users for an initial investigation according to Nielsen (1993). The room was also equipped with two cameras to record both user behaviour and speech during the visit. The subjects performed a visit by using the guide; the study was limited to four frescos. At the end of the visit, each subject was interviewed by the experimenter while both were watching the video of the visit. The interview focused on the subject's understanding of the WOW button. The interview was recorded, providing important additional material for the research and design teams to discuss during the post-study phase. The results of this study revealed very interesting findings:

1. Loading the information at the beginning of each presentation takes few seconds, which was too long for visitors. In that amount of time, users get disoriented because they do not know what to expect. They do not understand their role with the system, and the WOW button is the only action they can perform during that time, probably in hope of getting information. The instructions did not prepare the users well for that situation.

2. At the end of the presentation, the system stops and shows a default screen shot, delegating the continuation of the visit to the user. This incoherence in the conceptual model confuses the user again, who presses the WOW to get some instructions but, instead, gets another presentation because the interest model was reinforced.

3. When all the content about a fresco was presented (including extended presentations retrieved by the user model) the system expects the user to move on. However, the user does not know the system status, therefore, she still expects something to occur. Again, the only available button is WOW.

4. The BASTA! button is interpreted just as a stop because it causes the system to stop the presentation. This is also incoherent with respect to the design guidelines, because the system should not enable to take an action, but just to express feelings (in this case "don't like").

In the end, the WOW button is often used as the resource of "last resort" to communicate with the system in case of problems. This shows that the intended conceptual model was not clear to the subject, and that the system often has incoherent or unexpected behaviour. In particular, the presentation should not abruptly stop. Rather, the user should be invited to move to another fresco. The system should give feedback about its own status, and inform users about its estimates of user interest; Kay (2001) calls this feature scrutability. It should skip uninteresting presentations, and focus on more interesting ones, or suggest moving to other frescos.

1.3.3   Second Redesign

Based on the results of the pilot study, we redefined the initial requirements for the new prototype:

1. The UI should clearly and intuitively enable the user to express her feelings towards the exhibits during the museum visit.
2. The UI should be coherent and consistent, reflecting the delegation of the control interaction paradigm on all four adaptivity dimensions.
3. The UI should be proactive in order to avoid user disorientation, even if users are told that the system tracks their position. For example, the system should signal when a new position is detected.
4. The UI should give visual feedback to the user, relating its understanding of user interest and its current status (such as preparing presentations for display), without disturbing user attention.
5. The information provided by the system must be structured differently, to allow different degrees of personalization.[4]
6. If the visitor does not express any feeling (that is, she never presses any button), she should receive a reasonable amount of information about the museum's exhibits.
7. Each presentation must have a title for display during the playing.

These requirements led to the prototyping of the second interface, shown in Fig. 3, which features a new widget (at the bottom), called the *like-o-meter*. It substitutes the two previous buttons and aims at better conveying the delegation paradigm. This widget allows the user to express her interest towards the current presentation, by moving the slider towards the smiley face (two degrees of liking), or state "I don't like it", by moving the slider towards the sad face on the left (two degrees of disliking). The presentation title appears close to the widget, helping the visitor to remember what she is "scoring". The feedback from the visitor is taken into account

---

[4] This requirement came from a strategic research decision and not from pilot study evidence.

by the system, which activates a propagation mechanism at the end of each presentation to update the interest model of the visitor.

Fig. 3. The second interface prototype, based on the *like-o-meter*

The propagation is performed on a network of templates, as shown in Fig. 4. In fact, in this redesign, we also made modifications to the backend of the system. We decided to drop the taxonomy of topics, in favour of a content-based classification of the templates. Instead of using a user model, reasoning on the structure of the domain at different levels of abstractions, we wanted to experiment with an explicitly linked network of contents, classified on the basis of their communicative functions (see Sect. 1.4).

The template network is organized in nodes, each having an interest value that is zero at the beginning. The interest value assigned to each template ranges from –2, meaning current lack of interest or likely future lack of interest, to +2, meaning strong interest or likely future strong interest. The links between nodes are created by the author network. Each link is a shallow semantic relation which can be paraphrased as "related to".

Nodes can be of five types:

1. Introduction: contains a general overview of an exhibit
2. Abstract: quickly describes a part of an exhibit
3. Content: extends the presentation of an abstract
4. Follow-up: describes general themes shared by two or more exhibits (e.g., hunting in the middle age)
5. Conclusion: tells the visitor that the presentation of an exhibit is over

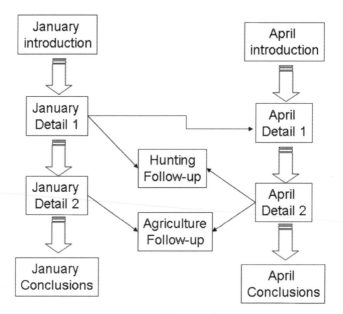

Fig. 4. An example of the template network

As feedback is received through the interface, the system updates the interest value of the current template and also propagates such information to its connected templates, according to the following dependency relations:

1. Introduction affects abstract: a positive or negative degree of interest, expressed when the system presents the general introduction to an exhibit, is propagated to all the abstracts pertaining to the same exhibit. The abstract is the basic information on an exhibit with respect to a certain topic.
2. Abstract affects content: the degree of interest towards the abstract updates the value of its related content (that is, a more detailed

description of the exhibit with respect to the abstract). When a content template has an interest value greater than zero, it is selected and presented to the visitor right after the abstract.

3. Content affects follow-up: the degree of interest towards contents affects its connected follow-ups (if any). Follow-ups are selected and proposed to the visitor when they have an interest value of +2.

4. Follow-up affects content: the degree of interest towards follow-up is propagated to all of the connected contents. Follow-ups act as bridges by propagating the interest values on one exhibit to other similar exhibits.

The selection mechanism is based on an algorithm that ensures that:

- The introduction is always the first presentation.
- Abstracts are always presented and sorted according to the interest value (from the greatest to the least).
- Contents are selected if they have a value greater than zero.
- Follow-ups are selected if they have a value greater than one.
- The conclusion is always the last presentation for an artwork.

The algorithm is iterative and starts from a skeleton, where the introduction is the first element and the conclusion is the last one. All the elements in the middle are adaptively arranged according to the visitor's interaction with the system. The overall goal of this mechanism, coupled with the visual feedback provided through the like-o-meter, is to give the visitor a clear indication that her actions do have an effect on the presentation, while avoiding the interpretation that her own actions are an explicit request for more information. As long as she remains at the same location, the system plays all the presentations, until the conclusion.

Through the widget, the system also informs the user about its own assessment of her interest on the current presentation, by presetting the like-o-meter. Thus, this widget is at the same time an input device and an output device that the system exploits to inform the visitor about the user model. This satisfies the necessity for the user to control the user model, as pointed out in Kay (2001).

The system performs another type of content adaptation with respect to the history of the interaction. The UI component keeps track of the user visit, enabling the comparison of the current presentation with previously seen ones. This is enabled by the merging mechanism, which can dynamically select presentations that explicitly refer to the visitor's history (such as "as you have seen before…").

Before making all these modifications, we created a partial mockup using Macromedia Flash to get an early evaluation of the new concepts and architecture. The mockup employs a hand-coded template network and a hand-coded propagation mechanism for one specific fresco only.

In this third study, we focused on how well the users are able to recognize and use the like-o-meter widget. Using the following questions, we investigated whether the like-o-meter properly communicates its meaning:

- Do the users recognize it as a scale with two negative and two positive values plus a neutral position?
- Do they understand that the position of the place card on the bar signals to the system their level of like or dislike of the current presentation?
- Do they understand that their expression of liking/disliking relates to the current presentation and not the whole exhibit or to a specific utterance?
- Do they notice the user model feedback on the like-o-meter bar, recognizing it as a consequence of their previous expressions of liking/disliking?
- Do they recognize that when the system provides more information this occurs because of their expression of interest?

The user study consisted again in an action protocol with retrospection. It was conducted on two users acting in the same room with the panels reproducing the original fresco exploited in the previous user study. The experimenter first presented an introduction of the museum setting and showed a copy of the fresco used in the experiment. Then, she quickly demonstrated the functioning of the system.[5] We decided to employ a task-based scenario in order to focus on the issues relevant to understanding of the metaphor. Another reason for this approach was that the new backend system was completely different from the old one (and not yet completely implemented). The task to the user was to signal interest during the presentation and a slight dislike during the description of the first detail. They had to be enthusiastic about the description of the second detail, and to stop the presentation during the description of the third detail. This task allowed us to check for proper understanding of the like-o-meter while assuring that the interaction could be handled by our partial mockup. The results of this user study were quite encouraging, showing a high degree of understanding and satisfaction by the users. The generalization of the findings to long-term effects of the expression of liking could not be reliably

---

[5] She simply explained that the like-o-meter is a way to tell the system about preferences. She did not mention any side effect caused by such interaction.

done at that time, given the limited possibility of interaction our mockup allowed.

From the responses and comments of the participants the following considerations emerged:

- The participants were able to communicate their interest to the system, correctly using the like-o-meter.
- The participants recognized that positions +1 and +2 caused more information to be provided in the general visit.
- The relationships between the standard (abstract) and the in-depth presentations (content and follow-up) were clear to the subjects. However, given the limitations of this small study, we cannot reliably conclude that the delegation metaphor was properly understood by the subjects, though this seems likely given the available evidence. In particular, we cannot reliably conclude that they fully realized that their expression of interest on the current exhibit also affected the presentations to come.
- The understanding of the meaning of the moderate disliking (i.e., position -1) is somewhat poorer than that of the liking. Apparently, the users come to expect that the expression of a moderate disliking should cause the system to provide less information. In our current system, on the other hand, the expression of a moderate dislike only changes the user model and does not affect the current presentation.
- The users did not expect that the neutral position of the like-o-meter could be selected, and expected that a single button press would have moved the slider straight from -1 to 1. Actually, we realized that the neutral position may have two distinct meanings: it communicates a degree of liking which is neither positive nor negative, while also corresponding to a lack of information about the user interest. Both of our users seemed to stick to the second meaning, expecting that only the system would be allowed to use the neutral position.
- One participant clearly noticed the feedback of the user model and understood that it was related to her previous behaviour. Both participants understood this feedback as a system initiative.

Summing up, the participants were able to properly carry out the task with a reasonable understanding of the conceptual model of the system. They both agreed that the interface was easy to use and that their expectations about the interest model were fulfilled. This encouraged us to go on with the implementation of the second prototype. In the meantime, we tried to work out the misunderstanding about the neutral position, and we restyled the interface graphics with the help of a professional designer. This led to the last interface, shown in Fig. 5. Apart from stylistic changes, the like-o-meter has been rendered with a needle, buttons have been enlarged to facilitate clicking, and the neutral position has been implemented as usable only by the system, for conveying its assumption about the user's neutral attitude towards the presentation.

Fig. 5. The last prototype of the interface

1.4 Authoring Guidelines

During the final phase of PEACH project, the museum adaptive guide was ready, but most of the content was still missing. So we hired two professional multimedia authors to prepare new content for the guide. Both authors used to work in a famous Italian publishing company. One was an expert documentary maker who also worked for the Italian national TV; the other was a multimedia designer who realized many CD-ROMs related to art. Neither is an engineer nor has a computer science background. The authors needed four months to complete the task (approximately one hour of adaptive multimedia content). During this period the authors needed several sessions of training to acquire basic skills about adaptive components. In particular, they first had to understand the vocabulary, the concepts, and the definitions used by engineers to structure the adaptive system (see the final prototype description above).

The authors were quite skilled in digging out information on artworks from the literature, but they had to structure the content as templates, for example, deciding what contents to associate with each template type. They resolved this issue by deciding that each template had to address a communicative function, as follows:

- Introduction: which exhibit is this? Who's the author?
- Detail: what are the issues or the particulars of the work-art that we would like tell?
- Abstract: what's this part?
- Content: tell more about the previous item.
- Follow-up: give a general context for this information.
- Conclusion: the presentation concerning this artwork.

In order to acquaint the author with the behaviour of the system, we explained it by examples, in a scenario-based approach, illustrating all the possible system "reactions" according to different user interaction. Authors started preparing contents from the "default" sequence, by putting together texts and images of the basic set of information for each exhibit; they would write scripts in two columns, audio and video, like cinema script-writers (Table 1).

Table 1. An excerpt of script

Video track	Audio track and voiceover
	Music, 15 sec. from CD 2, track 3.
Display whole picture of July. Focus on the blue sky and the sun.	The sun stands out of the blue sky. It is July sun, in Leo constellation,
Whole picture of July.	full of activities; almost all the fresco depicts work scenes.
Zoom on three scythe men on the left.	Peasants are busy haymaking
Zoom on four people with hay forks.	and raking up.

Further comments or instruction for synchronization were written in a third column. Once developed and tested the default sequence, authors—with our help—started implementing variations, that is, different *paths* of presentations in order to accomplish the adaptivity. We observed some difficulty for the authors in organizing adaptive variations. At this stage, a graph representation helped us to explain system behaviour in particular situations to them. For example, the graph in Fig. 6 helped us to explain the notion of fork, which can generate two different paths, e.g. *(shot1, shot2, shot4)* or *(shot1, shot3, shot4)*. The condition to choose between shot2 and shot3 relates to the profile built by the system. For instance, shot2 might contain a reference to a previously visited item (e.g., *as you have seen in …*) and shot3 might contain a suggestion (e.g., *as you will see in …*). These are simply textual variations, but authors are also allowed to modify the video part and include new or alternative visuals.

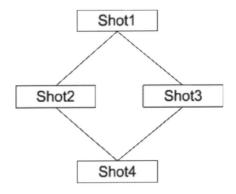

Fig. 6. A graph representing alternative paths

Images were selected from a corpus of high-resolution pictures provided by the museum. Authors were free to crop, resize, and choose the portions of picture they preferred to use in building the visual part of the shots. Texts were synthesized using a professional synthesizer, and Macromedia Flash was used to edit the presentations.[6]

After the preparation of the first exhibit, we tested the content, to find out how effective our training had been. The testing consisted in simulating different interactions with the system and its associated system output. This phase was helpful to identify possible repetitions or inconsistencies in the visual parts. The test was done on a PDA to verify how effective the choice of pictures was and to check the quality of the video on a small screen.

According to the experience described above, we proposed a set of guidelines for preparing the content of an adaptive application. For each phase, we also proposed the functionality to be implemented in the authoring tool:

---

[6] http://download.macromedia.com/pub/documentation/en/flash/mx2004/
flite1_1_authoring_guidelines.pdf.

1. Identify the salient parts of each exhibit.[7]
2. Take notes of the content of each unit. Authors should start from the "mandatory" pieces of information which have to be presented (introduction, abstracts, conclusion). Taking notes helps authors to sketch out the general structure of the content. If notes are organized by keywords, the system might help to highlight connections between exhibits.
3. Find connections between (parts of) artworks. For example, two pictures representing the same subject (or a similar one), can be connected. Each of these connections identified during this phase can potentially be a follow-up.
4. Prepare the scripts. In our experience, organization by columns proved successful and clear (Table 1); indeed, this method is also used by cinema scriptwriters. During this phase, it is also important to test possible combinations of shots to identify potential repetitions or incongruent sequences. "Debugging" came too late in the first prototype implemented.
5. Edit the presentations: assemble selected and elaborated images, and synthesize the audio.
6. Test on the PDA. The final test should be done on the PDA in the real scenario.

1.5   Conclusion

We have illustrated the evolution of an adaptive multimedia mobile guide developed in the framework of the PEACH project. We started by describing the motivations behind the requirements of an ideal adaptive guide. We introduced a new communicative tool—the video documentary—which is adaptively composed to help visitors identify exhibit details mentioned in the audio counterpart and, moreover, to ease finding the relationship between new and already presented information (Chap. 2).

Through an iterative process, we described the results achieved at each stage of the user-centered design. In particular, we focused on the evolution of the interface, and its acceptability and usability after each redesign. We also described the changes made to the system backend. The main result of the process is the final prototype, an interface based on affective interaction, graphically conveyed through the like-o-meter, that allows

---

[7] In our scenario, we identified the salient parts of each exhibit, that is, the parts that were generally described in the texts provided by the museum curators.

visitors to express their attitude towards the exhibit and explicitly signal their interests to guide the adaptation mechanism of the system.

Finally, we described our experience in training two authors to prepare adaptive content. By considering and analyzing the experience, we devised a set of guidelines aimed at helping the authors prepare and structure content for adaptive mobile guides.

1.6 Acknowledgments

The authors wish to thank Franco Dossena and Adriano Freri for their work on content preparation in relation to the Torre Aquila frescoes.

2 Cinematographic Techniques for Automatic Documentary-like Presentations

E. Not, C. Callaway, C. Rocchi, O. Stock and M. Zancanaro

2.1 Introduction

For the PEACH project, we explored how to support museum visitors who want to learn more about particular works of art seen. To do so, we created film documentaries automatically using rudimentary information about their content. Specifically, we used pictures of artworks along with a knowledge base of facts about them to automatically construct short, movie-like multimedia presentations constructing them in the same way that documentaries are made. The aim was to allow information to be personalized for each user, according to preferences and interests, as well as current and past interactions with the system. The idea of using cinematography as a paradigm for information presentation in the museum domain was initially investigated in Nardon et al. (2002), while the assessment of this approach in a mobile setting was discussed in Alfaro et al. (2004).

As an example, an automated documentary might start with a high-level sentence while showing a full-size image of the artwork (Fig. 1a). It might then focus on an important element of the art, using simultaneous discourse cues and a zoom shot to focus attention on that element (Fig. 1b). After holding the image still while the audio explanation continues, a second region of the artwork would then be highlighted with a pan motion of the camera as a voiceover explains the relationship between the two regions (Fig. 1c). After continued explanation and shot transitions, the film might conclude with a reverse zoom to the full-size image again followed by a fadeout as the audio track completes.[1]

---

[1] An example of a generated movie can be seen at
http://tcc.itc.it/i3p/research/aij05/movie.html.

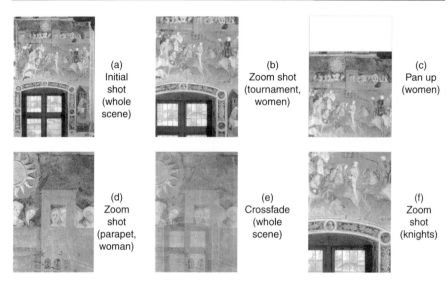

Fig. 1. An example of film sequence in the PEACH domain

Similar applications have been created in the past, although for different domains and goals, and without dynamically generated commentary or an underlying theory of film narratives. Many solutions have been developed in the field of virtual 3D animations. Virtual cameras film the behaviour of multiple characters as they interact with one another, making sure that camera movements clearly shoot the salient visual features of each event. One of the first case studies of the generation of "motion presentations" is the work of Karp and Feiner (1993), which generated scripts for animation using top-down hierarchical planning techniques. Christianson et al. (1996) presents a successful attempt to encode several of the principles of cinematography in *Declarative Camera Control Language*. Bares et al. (1998) presents a model for camera planning based on a constraint satisfaction approach: as interactive narratives unfold, a cinematic goal selector creates view constraints in order to film the most salient activities performed by the virtual characters. These constraints are then passed to a camera planner, which employs a partial constraint-based approach to compute the position and orientation of the virtual camera. Animated presentations have also successfully been employed in the illustration of technical devices (Butz 1997), in multimodal frameworks for the generation of explanations (Daniel et al. 1999), and in learning environments (Callaway et al. 1999). A camera-planning agent for polygonal graphics is described in Halper and Oliver (2000). It uses a genetic algorithm to find the optimal solution for a given set of communicative goals. A nonmonotonic reasoning approach is used in Friedman and Feldman (2004) to produce 3D animated movies from screenplays which have been encoded in a high-level formal language. Still, in the field of computer animation, Kennedy and Mercer (2002) present a planning system that transforms a description of animator intentions and character actions into a series of camera shots which portray these intentions. The planner accomplishes this portrayal by utilizing lighting, framing, camera motion, color choice and shot pacing.

Moving from the field of virtual animation to the shooting of real events, Gleicher and Masanz (2000) consider the task of creating video presentations from class lectures. They use a system and a methodology based on principles of videography to record events with minimal intrusion and then produce videos from the footage in as automated a manner as possible. In a completely different field, Mancini and Shum (2004) discuss instead how cinematography principles can be exploited to enhance coherence in structuring hypertexts.

The task of PEACH—generating video documentaries of art exhibits— shares some of the vision of previous works, but needs to solve particular problems regarding the coupling of issues related to the animation of still images and issues related to the assembly of meaningful commentary. More in detail, automatically creating a video documentary entails solving several problems: selecting salient (visual and conceptual) information from a large repository, sequencing the text and film sequences in a coherent and meaningful way, and realizing the synchronization and the playback of the intended audio and visual effects. In PEACH, we experimented with two possible approaches to generating personalized video documentaries: (1) an approach inspired by adaptive hypermedia technologies that aims at the most effective assembly of prepared chunks of audio/visual material; and (2) a generative approach that aims at the dynamic generation of commentary, starting from deep linguistic representation. To produce video sequences, the generated text is then synthesized and synchronized with dynamically animated still images.

This chapter reports on these approaches and the lessons learned. The next section introduces the principles and terminology of cinematography that underlie our automatic film production. Section 2.3 describes a template-base approach inspired by adaptive hypermedia for assembling visitor adapted video documentaries starting from manually prepared audiovisual fragments. Section 2.4 introduces an alternative generative approach that aims at the dynamic assembling of both the textual/audio commentary and visual animation for enhanced levels of flexibility and personalization. More in detail, Sect. 2.5 clarifies the natural language generation (NLG) techniques employed to create the documentary script, including text planning and realization issues. Section 2.6, instead, focuses on the algorithm used by the video planner to create the visual aspects of the film.

2.2   Cinematography for Video Documentaries

Let us first introduce the principles and terminology of cinematography that underlie film production. *Cinematography* is the art of coupling pictures and sounds in a meaningful way. Audio and video resources are tightly associated, supporting one another, creating a whole. This synergy is not a mere sum of two different communicative techniques. Audio and video continuously rely on each other to carry the message to the viewer. The construction of a movie thus involves issues ranging from the selection of the appropriate channel (visual, auditory, or both) for expressing the message, to the planning of synchronous actions (e.g., the actors or a narrator talk while a given scene is being shown), and from the correct positioning of cameras to the setting of scenes and lights.

According to Metz (1974), cinematic representation is not like a human language, which is defined by a set of grammatical rules. It is nevertheless guided by a set of *conventions* which are generally adopted by directors and expected by filmgoers. These guidelines may be considered a rich resource from which we can borrow principles, heuristics, and "rules of thumb" to develop movie-like multimedia presentations.

The steps to create a movie are many and complex: select the theme, conceive the story, write the script, shoot the video material (production), do the editing or montage (postproduction). During the first stages, the scriptwriter selects how the story will evolve, what the actors or the narrator will say and in what order. During production, the director and his team set up the scene (lights, camera positions, and movements) and film one or more takes of a piece of movie. Camera movements are typically used to emphasize the coherence relations that link the various portions of the narration, thus contributing to the overall efficacy of the presentation. For example, a camera zoom-in might help the viewer focus on a detail being described, whereas a zoom-out might help to re-establish a general view of the scene. In the second phase, editing, the filmed material is analyzed, some shots are dropped, others are cut, and transitions between scenes are selected. According to some cinema theorists (mainly Eisenstein and Layda 1969), the editing is the key step of the movie creation. Isolated shots, though well filmed and carefully planned, are only raw material. The editing gives sense to the movie, enabling the passage from photography to cinema.

Principles derived from cinematography should be considered an essential backbone for any automatic system that produces video documentaries. To enable the description of the PEACH approach to documentary generation and to present the implemented components with their underlying mechanisms we need to introduce the following technical terms.

Shots and camera movements. The shot is the basic unit of a video sequence. In the field of cinematography, a shot is defined as a continuous view from a single camera without interruption. Since we only deal with still images, we define a shot as a sequence of camera movements applied to the same image. During the shot, the camera can be fixed or move on wheels. When fixed, it can sweep horizontally or pivot up and down; if attached to a moving vehicle it can move both in the plane of the camera lens (*x*- and *y*- axes), and perpendicularly to the camera lens (*z*-axis). In this work, we refer only to movements of cameras of the wheeled type, using standard film terminology. Thus, the film term *move* is interpreted as movements along the *x*- and *y*-axes, whereas the technical term *dolly*, also called a zoom, denotes a movement along the *z*-axis.

Transition effects. Transitions between shots are considered as the punctuation symbols of cinematography; they affect the rhythm of the discourse and the message conveyed by the video. The main effects are: *display*—the first frame of the next shot immediately replaces the last frame of the shot currently on display; *cut*—the first frame of the next shot replaces the last frame of the shot currently on display after a brief audio and video blank; *fade*—a shot is gradually replaced by (fade out) or gradually replaces (fade in) a black screen or another shot; and *cross fade* (or dissolve) which is the composition of a fade out on the displayed shot and a fade in applied to the shot to be shown.

2.3   Cinematographic Templates

The first approach we experimented with for generating video documentaries consisted in giving a human author a language for composing adaptive videos. A flexible mark-up formalism was defined for writing video templates, i.e., instructions on how to compose video shots with existing audio commentaries, including choice-points to be resolved at assembly time according to visitor preferences and other user-dependent parameters (Rocchi and Zancanaro 2004a). Once a clip is requested for a given exhibit, the adaptive video engine chooses a suitable template and elaborates it according to the current user model to produce an instance of a video clip that is personalized for the given visitor in the given context (Fig. 2). There are two ways to affect the presentation with user-dependent features: (1) the actual selection of shots and (2) the choice of transition effects between shots.

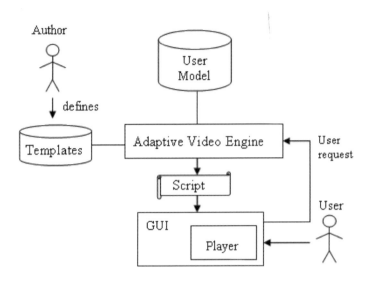

Fig. 2. Architecture for template-based video planning

Video templates are written using an XML-based language called XASCRIPT (see Fig.3 for a sample template written in XASCRIPT). In creating a template, the author first defines a shot repository (specified within `<shots>..</shots>` tags), i.e., a list of existing shots that can be used to assemble the actual video. In the second part of the template, the editing is specified, i.e., how pieces of information (shots) are presented to the visitor. The choice of transitions affects the flow of discourse and highlights the passing from one piece of information to another. In classic text-based hypermedia, transitions from one document to another might not be important for user understanding. In the case of video-based hypermedia, they are crucial, for they underline the rhythm of the presentation and signal the (semantic) "closeness" of the scenes to which they apply. For example, a short crossfade typically signals a smooth transition of the narration to a related topic.

XASCRIPT adaptation rules can be inserted in the editing section to express alternative ways in which shots should be sequenced, which transitions apply or how long transitions should last. An adaptation rule is a <condition, action> pair, where conditions include requirements for the correct firing of the rule, and actions are pieces of documentary (transitions) or other rules. XASCRIPT supports two types of resources for defining the conditions: (1) user-model features (UM-expression) and (2) editing features (EDIT-expression).

```
<movie title="Giugno - La cittadina" exhibit="june">
<shots>
  <shot id="giu-cit-abs1" file="${resources}giu-cit-abs1.swf" />
  <shot id="giu-cit-abs2" file="${resources}giu-cit-abs2.swf" />
  <shot id="giu-cit-abs3" file="${resources}giu-cit-abs3.swf" />
  <shot id="giu-mag-citta-compS" file="${resources}giu-mag-citta-
compS.swf" />
  <shot id="giu-mag-citta-compV" file="${resources}giu-mag-citta-
compV.swf" />
</shots>
<editing>
  <display shot="giu-cit-abs1" />
  <rule>
    <UM-expression>!$user.shotSeen("mag-natura-abs2")</UM-expression>
    <display shot="giu-mag-citta-compS" />
    <display shot="giu-mag-citta-compV" />
  </rule>
  <display shot="giu-cit-abs2" />
  <crossfade shot="giu-cit-abs3" />
</editing>
</movie>
```

Fig. 3. Sample XASCRIPT video template

A UM-expression amounts to a check over the set of features encoded in the user model (described in Chap. 6). For example, in the template in Fig. 3, a UM-expression checks whether the visitor has already seen the shot named "mag-natura-abs2". EDIT-expressions are instead conditions over the editing of the current movie that include dependencies among content units (e.g., when the selection of a given shot requires that another shot has already been included in the current presentation), or constraints between presentation forms (e.g., "if the last transition is not a cut, the next shot can fade in").

The combination of these two conditional resources allows us to define fine-grained templates, providing a flexible mechanism that supports both content adaptation and dynamic selection of transition effects.

The human-authored templates are organized as a network of semantically related content (Fig. 4), which is exploited by the UM component to propagate the interests of the visitor, hypothesized according to her behaviour and interaction during the visit (Chap. 6).

Templates are of different types: (1) introduction (when they contain overview information); (2) presentation of details; (3) conclusions (These are played when the system has exhausted its information about a particular exhibit; the main purpose of these templates is to suggest that the visitor move on to another exhibit.) and (iv) follow-ups (which provide insight on general topics). Follow-ups are not strictly related to a particular exhibit; rather they provide connections between different exhibits.

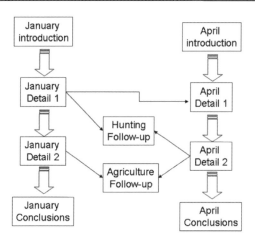

Fig. 4. A simplified network of video clip templates

The adaptive video engine component is able to customize video clips by selecting and instantiating the most appropriate template. This is accomplished by navigating through the template network (considering what the user has already heard and her assumed interests), choosing the right template and by instantiating its content using adaptation rules. An initial evaluation suggested that this type of personalization coupled with an appropriate user interface is well suited for the museum experience (Chap. 11).

2.4   Fully Automatic Documentary Generation

A more challenging approach to the generation of video documentaries for museum exhibits consists in dynamically building the video sequences by animating 2D still images. These are synchronized with synthesized audio that is generated on the fly using deep linguistic representations. Within PEACH, we experimented with an engine that takes as input a series of still images and a knowledge base containing information about those images, as well as information about their domain in general. The component selects and organizes the content to be conveyed and produces textual descriptions using standard deep NLG techniques, while a video planner submodule, taking into consideration the discourse structure of the commentary, plans film segmentations by defining shots, camera movements, and transition effects between shots. The output of the engine is a complete script of a "video presentation", with instructions for synchronizing images and camera movements accompanied by the audio commentary synthesized from the generated text. One of the chief novelties of this work is the use of rhetorical relations (Mann and Thompson 1987) to help provide structure to both the image sequences and the spoken part of the script.

As depicted in Fig. 5, the architecture of the system is based on a bipolar cascade model. The two processes, the generation of the verbal content and the planning of the video script, can be partly performed in parallel. Parallelism allows for improvements in speed (which can be very important if the generation of personalized videos is embedded in an interactive system (Rocchi and Zancanaro 2004b)) and in modularity, allowing both reusability of components and the possibility of experimenting with different approaches to cinematography or text generation.

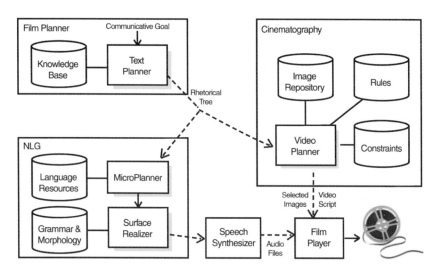

Fig. 5. System architecture for dynamic documentary generation

The NLG cascade is organized following the standard architecture proposed in (Reiter 1994). In the first phase, relevant content of the document is retrieved from the knowledge base (KB, described in detail in Chap. 6) and organized into a discourse plan structured as a rhetorical tree. Then, the microplanner applies pragmatic strategies to decide how to realize nouns (i.e., whether to use anaphora or full descriptive noun phrases, etc.) and verbs (i.e., decide the tense, the aspect, and so on). Finally, a surface realiser completes the process by selecting closed-class words and enforcing syntactic and morphological constraints according to the grammar of the target language. In our system, the cascade adds English and Italian speech synthesizers as well in order to produce verbal commentary for each video.

The video planner takes as input the rhetorical tree produced by the text planner, whose leaves represent the content facts that are to be verbalized by the NLG realiser. The video planner decides the shot segmentation, mainly according to the topic progression, and the transitions between shots, mainly according to the type of rhetorical relations between the nodes. The planner uses a database of images in which the visual details are segmented and annotated according to a similar but shallower semantic model employed in the KB (as described in Sect. 6.2).

Since the video planner works from the rhetorical tree, it is not aware of the actual duration of the final synthesized speech. This is not an important issue for synchronization between camera movements and speech since the actual timing for the chosen camera movements are expressed in terms of relative constraints. Yet, knowledge about the duration of each segment might be useful for choosing among different visual strategies. For example, it might be the case that a long elaboration is introduced by a cross-fade, while a short elaboration can simply be introduced by a cut. To allow for these high-level strategies, the text planner estimates the duration of each segment using the number of discourse facts that it contains.

This overall architecture differs from other similar works. For example, in the architecture employed by Andrè (2000), the content planner also comprises the functionalities of the video planner. A unified planner needs to include rules that contain both cinematic and linguistic conditions and actions. Thus, linguistic knowledge governing syntactic constraints is integrated, for example, with rules for determining whether two subimages are near or far away from each other, and shot-sequencing rules have to pay attention to the possible lexicalizations of discourse markers.

The architecture presented here has two advantages. First, it aids efficiency, since both main tasks can be performed in parallel. Second, it enhances the portability of the modules. For example, the verbal commentary might be realized in a simpler way than we describe in Sect. 2.5 by adopting a template composer (Reiter 1995) (obviously at the expense of text flexibility).

The hypothesis behind this architecture is that the video planner can effectively plan the video scripts starting just from the rhetorical tree, by exploiting the rhetorical relations and the basic knowledge of the topics of each discourse segment. Section 2.6 introduces our rule-based engine for mapping shots and transitions from rhetorical subtrees.

2.5   Generating Text for Documentary Descriptions

Generating text for producing documentary descriptions implies making several strategic decisions on (1) what is the most effective content to be conveyed to successfully describe the overall object in focus; (2) how information can be ordered and structured in a coherent way; (3) which lexico-grammatical patterns can be used to manifest the semantic relations between the text units and reinforce the cohesion of the text (e.g., appropriate referring expressions or cue phrases) or its naturalness (e.g., aggregation); and (4) what the final surface realization should look like.

Traditionally, steps (1) and (2) are considered part of the text planning stage, whereas step (3) accounts for microplanning and (4) for tactical generation, even though from an implementation point of view, these stages are not necessarily implemented in a pure pipeline cascade (Reiter 1994; Reiter and Dale 2000; Cahill et al. 2000). In our scenario, the requirement of generating text to be integrated in a multimedia presentation also implies that all the previous stages take into account how the final text will be rendered (i.e., via speech synthesis, subtitles, or text balloons) and synchronized with the visual track. This means that the generation system needs to build a narration around the physical and visual structure of the object, with explicit reference to its details.

It should be noted, however, that the major assumption that motivated our design choices for the overall system architecture is that the text generation component makes its strategic and tactical decisions independently from the specific media used for the visual presentation (be it still images, animations of still images, or real movie clips). The assumption for the text generation component is that there will be some visual feedback consistent with the content of the commentary. But no knowledge is required at this stage about which camera movements will be used or what shot transitions may apply, allowing for substantial modularity and flexibility.

Generally speaking, video documentaries could be readily generated using standard shallow NLG techniques such as slot-filler templates to create sentences for the audio track. In this work, however, we have adopted the use of deep NLG with a fuller linguistic representation for several reasons: (1) deep NLG allows for a finer-grained control in the generation of referring expressions and other linguistic devices that help improve the naturalness and cohesion of the text (e.g. aggregation), and facilitates the generation of personalized texts which are adapted to the current interaction context and user preferences; (2) as in many other application domains, users in the museum scenario come from many countries and speak their own native languages, making multilingual generation (a laborious task for templates) very important; (3) the underlying architecture can be shared with other application tasks over the same domain (e.g., direction giving or report generation for museum visits, as described in Chap. 4) or other projects requiring generation, reducing the intensive costs of creating deep linguistic resources and domain models; and (4), in a more general perspective, deep NLG also allows for the generation of tags, e.g., marking anaphoric references or the rhetorical structure, that direct the speech synthesizer to produce higher quality output, helping predict accent size and contours as well as accent placement (though this was outside the scope of the PEACH research plan).

2.5.1 Generation Component Overview

The architecture we adopted for the generation subsystem adheres to a fairly standard pipeline model (Reiter 1994), as previously shown in Fig. 5. (For more details on the generation component, see also Chap. 4, and Callaway et al. 2005b).

The input to the generation process is a request for text that is expressed in terms of the communicative goal to be satisfied. For the generation of documentary descriptions, the communicative goal tells the text planner to build an object description, e.g., `describe-object(exhibit1)`.

The text planner determines which information to include in the description and organizes it coherently. Information about objects resides in a domain ontology and model, the knowledge base, that collects facts and attributes about the objects to be described. For the sake of modularity and reusability, the domain representation is organized into separate partitions that contain: (1) specific domain-dependent instances that describe, for example, which characters and objects are depicted in a fresco, their relative positions, and the activities they perform; (2) domain-independent ontological concepts and relations that define how instances and relations should be semantically interpreted; and (3) lexical information required for text realization. Portions (2) and (3) are highly reusable, whereas portion (1) is strictly dependent on the objects described.

The text planner uses *discourse strategies* to access the domain representation, extract relevant facts to convey, and guarantee that the discourse plan is properly built. Discourse strategies are based on typical patterns of content organization (schemas) and on rhetorical coherence. For example, when describing complex depictions on a painter's canvas, the description (as well as the corresponding image sequence/animation) needs to reflect the spatial organization of details and their salience in motivating the painter's choices. How the content of the text is actually selected and structured obviously also depends significantly on the types of readers addressed and their specific interactions with the system (e.g., difficult terminology needs to be properly explained to children). These "patterns of appropriate ordering" (more widely known in the NLG community as *schemas* (McKeown 1985) or the *generic structure potential* (GSP) of a text (Halliday and Hasan 1985) have been adopted in many NLG systems to guide the text planner in organizing text structure. In PEACH, we implemented a schema-based text planner in which GSPs are used to declaratively describe how the text chunks should be optimally organized according to the current user profile, discourse history and object to be described.

During its decision process, the text planner accesses the *user model*. This contains information about (estimated) visitor interest, knowledge and interaction preferences (Chap. 6). The text planner also accesses the *discourse context* at this time. This stores the content conveyed in previous presentations—useful for avoiding repetition and for drawing comparisons—as well as the structure of the presentation currently being built.

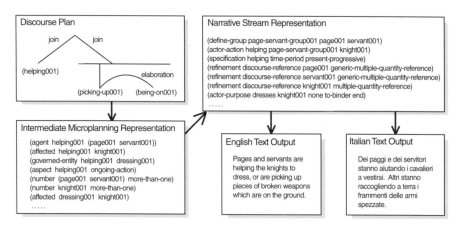

Fig. 6. Sample computation flow of internal data structures (discourse plan, intermediate microplanning representation, narrative stream representation, and final multilingual output)

The output of the text planning stage is a rhetorically annotated discourse tree whose leaves represent predicates in the domain model that must be linguistically realized. This is shown in the left upper part of Fig. 6, which shows a sample computation flow in terms of internal data structures. The intermediate rhetorical tree of domain facts is decorated with the estimated duration of the corresponding synthesized speech and is sent to the video planner to start the parallel process of video plan generation.

The rhetorical tree is then exploited by the *microplanning* stage to determine the most appropriate referring expressions and lexico-grammatical constraints required to convey the message. The output of the microplanner is a description of the linearised text plan written in the NSP formalism (Callaway and Lester 2002a), as shown in the right side of Fig. 6. The *surface realiser* maps this abstract representation onto natural text consistent with the selected output language (English or Italian). We use the *storybook* system (Callaway and Lester 2002a) for the low-level production of text. This system already includes architectural modules typically considered as part of microplanning: discourse history, pronominalisation, sentence planning, revision, and limited lexical choice.

The output of the generation process is structured commentary annotated with the visual details or concepts the text portions are meant to describe as well as the rhetorical dependencies between them. Each generated sentence is then sent to the text-to-speech synthesizer to produce corresponding audio files. Currently, we use Festival for Italian speech synthesis (Cosi et al. 2001) that produces Italian with its own specific pronunciation and prosody (Cosi et al. 2002), and the Festival Lite system (Black and Lenzo 2002) to synthesize English. The final generated commentary is written in XML notation which is compatible with standard tools for RST rhetorical structure visualization (O'Donnell 2000) (see Fig. 7). It is then passed on to the film player for the final synchronization with the video plan, produced in parallel by the video planner.

```
<segment id="01" parent="root" topic="tournament" audio="castle.mp3"
duration="3">
                At the bottom on the right is a blacksmith's workshop,
a plebeian antithesis to
                the tournament going on in the upper part of the
painting which is chiefly an
                aristocratic activity.
  </segment>
<segment id="02" parent="01" relname="elaboration" topic="castle" au-
dio="windows.mp3"
     duration="2" />
                The differences between the various styles of construc-
tion have been reproduced
                extremely carefully.
```

Fig. 7. Sample segments sent to the film player

2.6 Automatic Cinematography

The generation of video documentaries encompasses several decisions that range from selecting appropriate images to illustrate domain elements to choosing camera movements, and from selecting transition effects to synchronizing audio and video tracks. The novelty of our approach lies in the use of rhetorical structure of the accompanying audio commentary for planning the video. In particular, knowledge of rhetorical structure is extremely useful in making decisions about video "punctuation", allowing it to reflect the rhythm of the audio commentary and its communicative goals. In our view, the verbal part of the documentary always drives the generation of the visual part.

Sometimes documentary makers start from images and then try to write an appropriate accompanying text/audio commentary. If any modification is needed (e.g., for synchronization purposes), they tend to change the text since they cannot reshoot scenes. Even though we are doing documentaries, our approach is more similar to that of narrative filmmaking than documentary filmmaking, in that we start from the script just like a typical movie director: the starting point is the text, and consequently, the audio script. The video planner task is thus the generation of a video, trying to fit the audio script, with the risk that the worst result is a slide show, i.e., a sequence of pictures shown one at a time. To avoid this kind of result, the rhythm of the audio/textual script can be exploited.

We collected a small corpus of texts which illustrate a single renaissance fresco. We conducted an analysis of the text at the discourse level and then devised a fairly simple model of discourse rhythm on the basis of the rhetorical relations holding between text spans. We noticed that:

- `Elaboration` and `sequence` relations tend to connect and keep together spans. A block made up of combinations of such relations usually illustrate semantically related or spatially connected topics.

- `Background` and `circumstance` relations tend to break the rhythm of the discourse. They signal a sort of pause, a topic shift, or the introduction of a different type of information about the same topic.

The next task was to define a set of rules to fit these heuristics in order to insert consistent transition effects (e.g., a fade. See below.) when background or circumstance relations occur, or to avoid the insertion of transitions when elaborations or sequences are matched. From interviews with experts, we identified a set of tips for transition effects and constraints over the combinations of camera movements. For example, during interviews, we have found that:

- A display indicates continuity.
- Fade effects tend to underline a "passage" or a change.
- The camera should not be moved back and forth along the same path.
- A pan communicates the spatiality of a scene and tends to focus the attention on the arrival point and its adjacent space.
- A zoom in helps to focus on specific areas or details which are not usually noticeable.
- A zoom out helps to refamiliarise the viewer with the details and their position in a bigger framework.

Finally, we coupled our insights about discourse structure with the knowledge extracted from our interviews. This gave rise to implementable rules for governing camera movements and transitions.

2.6.1   The Video Planner Engine Architecture

The video planner implements a mechanism that automatically computes a full script for a video documentary. It starts from a discourse plan annotated according to an RST annotation scheme generated by the text planner, and the estimated duration of the synthesized speech. In addition, the video planner also takes as input a repository of annotated images, to which camera movements and transitions are applied. The system relies on a core of rules and constraints. They encode the rhetorical strategies that are the basic resource for:

- Selecting appropriate images.
- Designing the presentation structure.
- Completing each shot.
- Synchronizing the visual part with the audio commentary while avoiding the "seasickness" effect (back and forth motion).

The rules, fired by a forward chaining mechanism, are context sensitive. They are also dependent on: (1) the rhetorical relations among the text spans; (2) the geometric properties of images selected from the information repository, and (3) the matching of topics among segments and images. Figure 8 shows the structure of the engine.

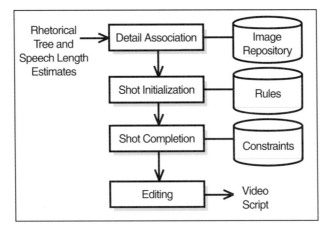

Fig. 8. Architecture of video planner component

To enable the choice of images and the planning of camera movements, the video planner needs a repository of annotated images. For each image, the relevant details depicted have to be specified both in terms of their bounding boxes and of the topics they represent. For example, Fig. 9 illustrates a portion of a 15th century fresco in Torre Aquila that depicts activities for the month of January. Alongside is its annotation.

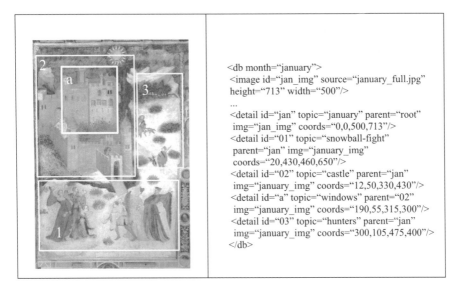

Fig. 9. An image and its annotation

This picture consists of three main details: (1) the snowball fight at the bottom, (2) the castle at the top on the right, and (3) the hunting scene beside the castle. Each detail can be decomposed into further details, as in the case of the castle, which contains further details such as the windows a. Annotation time is negligible, consisting mainly of recording the coordinates of bounding boxes and assigning a concept taken from the knowledge base to each, according to the intuition of the annotator.

The video planning consists of four phases:

- *Detail association.* A detail is associated with each segment of the commentary. In this phase, the system assigns one or more exhibit details to each segment of the commentary. This operation is performed by searching the image repository for details with the same topic as the segment. The preferred heuristic is to select the detail with exactly the same topic(s) of the segment. If this is not possible, search rules look for details which subsume the topics mentioned in the commentary.

- *Shot initialization and structure planning.* Details are grouped for inclusion in the same shot and a candidate structure for the final presentation is elaborated, starting from the rhetorical structure of the commentary. (The result of this phase can be changed because its processing is iterative.) The processing is guided by a set of rules that are fired when particular configurations of rhetorical relations are matched (see the top right of Fig. 10). For example, an elaboration or sequence relation signals a smooth transition from the current topic to new information that is strictly related to it. It is thus preferable to aggregate segments in the same shot and to exploit camera movements. Background and circumstance relations tend to highlight the introduction of new information that provides a context in which either the previous or subsequent messages can be interpreted. In addition, they tend to break the flow of the discourse. It is thus preferable to split the segments into two different shots so that, in the next phase, it is possible to exploit proper transition effects to emphasize that change of rhythm. There are cases in which the structure planned in this phase is revised during successive stages of computation. For example, to avoid the "seasickness" effect, the system can apply constraints and then modify the previously planned structure by adding new shots.

- *Shot completion.* Camera movements between details in the same shots are planned. Constraints are considered in order to avoid "inconsistencies". In this phase, the engine incrementally completes each shot by expanding and illustrating each of its segments. When a candidate move is proposed, the system verifies that it is suitable according to the list of previous camera movements and the constraints imposed over that category of movement. These constraints encode the cinematographer's expertise in selecting and applying camera movements in order to obtain "well-formed" shots (see the bottom right of Fig. 10). For instance, when a zoom-in movement is proposed where the previous movement is a zoom-out, the system discards the planned sequence as unacceptable.

- *Editing.* Transition effects among shots are selected according to the rhetorical structure of the commentary. This is the phase in which the engine chooses the "punctuation" of the presentation. In order to reflect the rhythm of the discourse, the choice of transition effects is guided by the rhetorical structure of the commentary. The system retrieves the last segment of the shot currently considered and the first segment of the shot to be presented next and plans the transition. A sample rule is "If two segments are linked by a relation of type elaboration then a short cross fade applies". The rules for editing have been defined, coupling our insights about the discourse structure with the knowledge extracted from our interviews with experts. A final tuning of the rules takes into account conventions of the typical employment of transition effects in the field of cinematography (Arijon 1976). Fade effects are fit for smooth transition when the focus of interest changes, but the new topic is related to the old one, as in the case of elaboration or background. Cut is more appropriate for abrupt and rapid changes, to emphasize the introduction of a new concept, as in the case of sequence. A special case holds when the verbal commentary enumerates a set of subjects or different aspects of the same object; in those cases a rapid sequence of cuts can be used to visually enumerate the elements described.

The output of the video planning process is a complete script for the video and audio channels encoded in an XML-based markup language, which is similar to the XASCRIPT described in Sect. 2.3. As opposed to the hand-authored templates described in Sect. 3, generated scripts do not contain conditional statements for personalization, as conditional joints have automatically been resolved by the video planner (see the left side of Fig. 10).

```
Video script:
                                              Sample rule:
<movie id="january">
  <shots>                                     (defrule split (segment)
    <shot id="shot603" image="det01">           (conditions
      <video-track>                                (or (has-relation segment back-
        <pause duration="2"/>                  ground)
      </video-track>                               (has-relation  segment  circum-
      <audio-track>                            stance)))
        <play audio="january.mp3"/>              (actions
      </audio-track>                               (init-shot shot)
    </shot>                                        (add-segment segment shot)))
    <shot id="shot605" image="det01">
      <video-track>
        <pause duration="1"/>
        <zoom duration="4" scale="4"/>
        <pause duration="2"/>
      </video-track>
      <audio-track>
        <audio-pause duration="3"/>
        <play audio="snowball-fight.mp3"/>
        <audio-pause duration="1"/>
        <play audio="castle.mp3"/>             Sample constraint:
      </audio-track>
    </shot>                                     (defconstraint zoom-in
  </shots>                                        (var mv (get-previous-movement))
  <editing>                                       (var  mv2  (get-previous-movement
  <display shot="shot603"/>                    mv))
  <crossfade shot="shot605" duration="1"/>       (and
  </editing>                                        (not (equal mv zoom-out))
</movie>                                            (not (equal mv2 zoom-out))))
```

Fig. 10. Examples of a script (*left*), a shot initialization rule, and a constraint (*right*)

A heuristic evaluation of the dynamically generated video clips was carried out with two film directors and a multimedia designer. In particular, we wanted to see if planning the cinematographic production using both the topics introduced by the verbal commentary and its rhetorical structure yielded higher quality results with respect to planning using the topics alone. Implicitly, this also leads to an evaluation of the specific cinematic rules used in our implementation, rather than an evaluation of the quality of text produced by the low-level generation component, as was, for example, examined in Callaway and Lester (2002a). Our study showed that expert evaluation in this domain might prove more useful than evaluation with naive users. Yet the experts are often biased by their particular style. In fact, even in a very specific genre such as documentaries (and even if we have camera movements on fixed images) styles can vary quite substantially. The disagreement that emerged among the experts indicates that the field needs to find an appropriate metric before larger quantitative evaluations can be undertaken. Instead, interviews proved to be a very powerful means of assessing the results and helping to improve system behaviour. From interviews, we gathered that our system, on the basis of its rich structural input, can accommodate different levels of sophistication in visual presentation. The current implementation of the rules yields a cinematic contribution that on average seems reasonably better than the default version (see Callaway et al. 2005b for more details on the evaluation experiments).

2.7 Conclusions

Video documentaries represent an effective means of presenting information about a work of art because they rely on the synergy between auditory and visual communicative channels to accompany the audience in a multi-sensorial exploration of the various physical details and the historical/artistic value of the work. Consistent with the PEACH *leitmotiv* that the exhibit remains the real protagonist of the visiting experience, camera movements can provide visual support to the audio commentary by anticipating or following details close-up, or can increase audience engagement during the information acquisition process by emphasizing the rhythm of the presentation. For the purposes of guiding and illustrating in the context of visits to a museum, multimedia applications can be delivered on both mobile and stationary devices. However, the production costs of human authoring (which are particularly high, especially when there is a strong requirement for multilinguality or for variety/personalization in the presented information) call for automatic approaches to video production.

In this chapter, we presented two approaches developed within the PEACH project for generating personalized video documentaries. The first approach, inspired to adaptive hypermedia technologies, aims at effective assembly of prepared chunks of audio/visual material. The second is a deeper, generative approach that aims at dynamically animating still images to provide video sequences synchronized with synthesized audio that is generated on the fly from deep linguistic representations. The key goal underlying both approaches is *personalization*, i.e., the dynamic adaptation of selection, organization, and rendering choices—both on the visual and on the audio sides—to the personal preferences, interests, language, interaction history, and position of the visitor. Techniques coming from the field of NLG are exploited to both guide the dynamic assembly of the audio commentary and to operationalise principles of cinematography into viable rules for shot production and editing.

Generalizing on PEACH results, there are many situations where the dynamic composition of video documentaries could be useful. Examples are the educational domain and all manner of instructional systems where specific user states and needs can be addressed by a personalized, multi-modal, dynamic presentation system. Additionally, the domain of person-alized news could benefit from advances in this area. Starting from freshly released images identified by accompanying comments, a system could produce a summary or an integration of news. On the language side of this theme, several projects are currently under development to produce textual summaries (McKeown et al. 2002). According to the view we present here, it is also possible to plan the integration of adapted video material.

3 Detecting Focus of Attention

R. Brunelli, A. Albertini, C. Andreatta, P. Chippendale, M. Ruocco,
O. Stock, F. Tobia and M. Zancanaro

3.1 Introduction

Human–computer interfaces based on the automatic recognition of gestures by means of image processing techniques are steadily gaining popularity. This is so primarily because these techniques are noninvasive and because vision is the most important of the human senses and people find it natural to interact and *interface* in ways that can be understood visually. In this chapter, we focus on the problem of delivering contextualized information to people visiting a museum. The idea is to help visitors explore museum exhibits by providing additional multimedia information on the items they find interesting. Thus the museum is expected to play a more active role, supporting user navigation of the museum's knowledge landscape, keeping track of the exhibits observed, and providing additional information based on the knowledge path followed by the visitor.

Different categories of users may need different interfaces. In particular, guided groups and single visitors are characterized by different interaction patterns. Groups are usually characterized by the presence of a guide who interfaces with the rest of the group. Because a guide must clearly identify the items she is describing, explicit deictic arm gestures are commonplace. The automatic understanding of such gestures through image processing techniques can be a valuable way of providing additional information to a group by means of wearable devices or multimedia kiosks. While arm gesturing is natural for the guide, it is probably not so for the single visitor who needs a less exposed interface based on inconspicuous portable hardware, such as a palmtop computer, or even on automatic understanding of the motion of the head or eyes. This chapter addresses both mediated and nonmediated interfaces and describes image processing algorithms which support their functionalities.

3.2   Mediated Pointing

Face analysis and gesture recognition are two techniques commonly emp-loyed to support users in controlling systems through gesturing possibly combined with speech commands. These human–computer interfaces may appear in smart environments or in conjunction with robotized system embodiments (Crowley et al. 1995; Schnadelbach et al. 2002). In both cases, the resulting interaction style supports the metaphor that human–computer interaction is similar to human–human interaction. Vision-based techniques have been used to detect the focus of attention of the user in order to augment her perception of the environment with dynamically generated overlaid presentations. While the resulting systems look quite impressive, they still require expensive hardware that may not be appro-priate for a museum visit. In this section, we investigate two different sys-tems based on visual recognition and inexpensive hardware. The first system uses a learning approach to the recognition of painting details based on low-resolution image sampling and support vector machines (SVMs). The second system is based on a fast content based image retrieval (CBIR) system that compares the image of a painting to its memory, a data-base of images of paintings.

3.2.1   Visual Learning

The investigation of simple, trainable processing architectures capable of visual competence leads to the development of low-cost robust systems and to further insight into the fundamental mechanisms underlying animal perception. This section focuses on the development of a device capable of associating a view of a known environment with the position of the obser-ving device and its viewing direction.

A system that solves this problem can be used as a *visual compass*, help-ing the user obtaining information on, for instance, the museum exhibits she is currently inspecting. Our approach is based on the characterization of world views by means of robust visual features computed for a small number of viewing directions arranged in a pseudo-random pattern around the optical axis of the sensing camera. The device is then trained to associ-ate the visual descriptors to a set of four numbers, representing the 2D posi-tions of the device and of the intersection of its viewing direction with a known painting (Fig. 1). Low-resolution image sampling strategies based on pseudo-random patterns such as those presented in this section may prove useful in other applications, most notably in the development of novel image description strategies which provide compact indexes for image retrieval in very large databases.

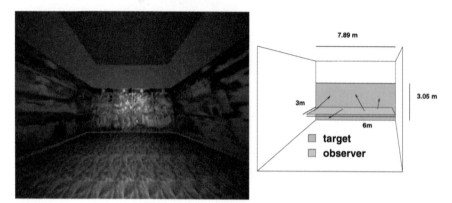

Fig. 1. A very wide angle view of the simulated environment where experiments have been performed (*left*). A ray tracing system using high-quality images of the paintings was used to render images of them as seen by a virtual camera free to move in the horizontal cyan plane while looking at different areas of the frescos in the vertical green plane (*right*)

The approach investigated is that of *learning by examples*: the system is given a set of labelled data (visual stimuli and required associated coordinates) and it is trained to recognize novel stimuli based on the knowledge of the examples provided. The key issues are: what kind of visual data are fed to the system, how they are obtained, and what learning procedure must be employed.

A major problem in the development of systems based on learning is the availability of enough training examples. We explored the possibility of training a system with synthetic data. While extensive performance evaluation was based on synthetic data, usability tests have been performed using the *same* system in the real world. In order to support this hybrid approach, a flexible graphical engine was realized. The tool supports the efficient simulation of several characteristics of real optical systems such as distortion, vignetting, digital artefacts, limited resolution, and focusing ability. This flexibility was exploited to generate synthetic images of paintings from Torre Aquila (Castello del Buonconsiglio, Trento, Italy) matching the features of the real, low-cost CMOS camera, used to test the system in the real world (Figs. 1 and 6).

The next step in the development of the system was the choice of a compact and effective representation for the visual stimuli.

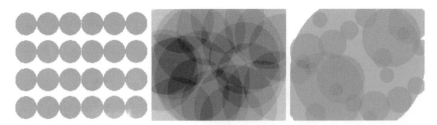

Fig. 2. The layout of the sensors in the retinas has a marked impact on the attainable performance. Several strategies were compared: a regular grid structure and progressive resolution sensors with a Sobol layout

We found a scalable solution in the use of a set of *artificial retinas*, each populated with sensors responding to different, partially correlated, image features:

- Color, the values of the red, green and blue channels.
- Hue, the tint associated to each rgb color triple.
- Luma, the overall intensity associated to a color triple.
- The energy of the first and second derivatives of luma convolved with a regularizing Gaussian kernel.

Each sensor provides two different outputs: an averaged response, given by the integral of the sensed quantity over the receptive field, and a more detailed, vector-like output, represented by a low resolution histogram (Schiele and Crowley 2000) of the values over the sensor receptive field (27 bins for color, 8 bins for the other features). For the first and second derivative descriptors, the detailed response is given by the integrated response along different directions, providing information on the local edge structure.

Another important issue that was addressed is sensor layout. While a regular grid, resembling that of digital sensors, may seem to be the most appropriate layout, features of the human visual system suggest alternative strategies. The term hyperacuity was introduced to describe the human ability of determining the position of an object with a precision that corresponds to only a fraction of the diameter of a photoreceptor. Hyperacuity implies a population code, because phase information is distributed over a number of channels. The term Vernier acuity, or positional acuity, describes the special case of hyperacuity where the observer has to visually judge the position of objects (e.g. dots, lines, edges).

Two different sensor layout strategies were compared: a traditional regular grid structure of sensors with no overlapping and a random sequence of overlapping sensors (Fig. 2). The random positions of the sensors are not generated using a uniform random number generator but according to the Sobol low discrepancy sequence (Press et al. 1992). The generated positions fill in a uniform way the two-dimensional space, providing a coarse to fine sampling: the higher the number of sensors used the more detailed the sampling. The idea of using a quasi random sequence was borrowed from the field of stochastic integration using Monte Carlo techniques. By choosing N sample points randomly in an n-dimensional space, Monte Carlo integration achieves an error term decreasing as $N^{1/2}$. If points are chosen on a Cartesian grid, the error term decreases faster as $1/N$. However, one has the problem of deciding a priori how dense the grid must be and complete coverage of the sample points is required. It is not possible to sample until some quality factor is achieved. Pseudo random sequences, of which the Sobol numbers are an example, fill the gap between a regular grid and a random choice: they provide a sequence of points that maximally avoid each other.

The characteristics of these pseudo random sequences make them particularly useful for the implementation of a progressive sampling strategy of the optical array and of the environment as well. As the amount of overlapping of the sensor fields may impact on system performance, three different variants were tested for the quasi random sequence of sensors, each one characterized by a different exponent d in

$$s = \frac{1}{2}\left(\frac{1}{i}\right)^{d}, \tag{1}$$

where i is the position of the sensor in the sequence and s is the normalized sensor size. The value $d = 0.5$ corresponds to a sensor covering one ith of the imaged area, while $d = 0.25$ and $d = 0.75$ corresponds to a slower (faster) decay of sensor size within the sequence. This corresponds to increased (decreased) overlapping of the receptive fields (Fig. 2). This strategy of progressive reduction of sensor fields is well matched to the characteristic of the Sobol sequence, realizing a *coarse to fine* sampling strategy upon which more sophisticated sensor use can be based.

Given the outputs of a set of retinas with a limited number of sensors, they must be mapped to the required coordinates. This mapping problem can be considered as a learning task. Whenever inputs and outputs are expressible as numerical vectors, the learning task corresponds to the reconstruction of an unknown function from sparse data and is equivalent to function approximation. Input data have been generated by the developed graphical engine: 10,000 low resolution, distorted, vignetted, digitally sampled images with depth of field effects at a typical lens f-stop (5.6) and focusing distance of 2 m (Fig. 3 for an example).

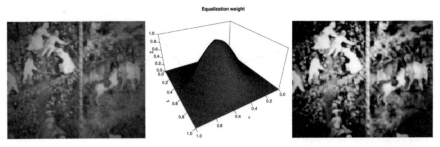

Fig. 3. Spatially weighted histogram equalization ensures robust recognition in spite of environmental changes, such as color shifts and illumination variation

Camera and target direction were chosen following a four-dimensional Sobol sequence progressively sampling the two coloured rectangles in Fig. 1. The unit of the spatial values reported in the plots is 1 m and the geometry of the synthetic environment corresponds to that of Torre Aquila in Trento. The camera was assumed to be horizontal at a fixed height (1.2 m) located in a space of a few meters in front of the longest wall looking at the painting.

Support vector machines are a modern and flexible approach to both classification and regression. They were originally introduced for pattern classification tasks. The subject is complex and a vast literature is available: for a comprehensive treatment, the reader is referred to Schlkopf and Smola (2002) and to Chang and Lin (2001) for the implementation used in the current work. One of the main characteristics of SVMs is that of representing the classification boundary in terms of a (often much smaller) subset of the training patterns: the support vectors (SVs). The complexity of the classifier is related to the cardinality of this set, and the same is true of the time necessary to compute the classification. It turns out that the underlying ideas can be generalized to the problem of function estimation while preserving the important property of sparseness provided the so-called ε-insensitive *loss function* is introduced:

$$\left| y - f(x) \right|_{\varepsilon} = \max\left\{ 0, \left| y - f(x) - \varepsilon \right| \right\}. \tag{2}$$

The ε-SVR algorithm (support vector regression) estimates linear functions

$$f(x) = \langle w, x \rangle + b, \tag{3}$$

with $\langle .,. \rangle$ an appropriate dot product, which minimize the so-called regularized risk functional

$$R[f] = \frac{1}{2}\|w\|^2 + C\frac{1}{N}\sum_{i=1}^{N}|y - f(x)|_\varepsilon \, , \qquad (4)$$

where the Eqs. (2) and (3) are used. Appropriate choices of the dot product effectively transform the linear function of Eq. (3) into a nonlinear function of the original input data, preserving all the nice computational features of the original linear approach. In our particular case, Gaussian kernels markedly outperformed the basic linear approach and were employed for all the reported experiments.

The value of ε represents the precision at which we want to approximate our function and the ε-SVR algorithm finds the *flattest* function among those providing the required accuracy. The lower the precision required for the approximation, the smaller the cardinality of the SV set. This observation is important because we can consider the number of SVs to be a measure of the complexity of the task and of the effectiveness of the feature set.

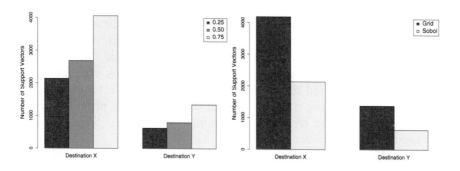

Fig. 4. The plot compares the effectiveness of the different sampling strategies considered (*left*: varying overlapping of pseudo random sensors; *right*: regular grid vs. pseudo random placement). Effectiveness is measured by the number of support vectors needed to obtain a given accuracy, kept the same for all compared strategies

Once the required precision is given, the algorithm converges to the optimal solution and does not require multiple trials as in the training of neural networks. The ε-SVR algorithm can then be used to assess the relative merits of the different feature sets, of the various retinal structure and sensor sizing strategies. The experimental results established the advantage of increased sensor overlapping and of the hyperacuity approach over the regular grid one (Fig. 4) and support the feasibility of very low resolution image recognition (Fig. 5).

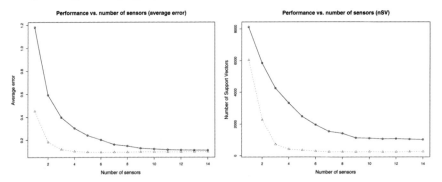

Fig. 5. Regression quality quickly saturates with the number of sensors both in terms of the number of support vectors required and in terms of resulting average error with the same trend (the *lower curve* corresponds to the y coordinate, the *upper one* to the x coordinate)

Additional experiments were performed to compare the performance obtainable with autofocus lenses over fixed focus ones. In fact, depth of field effects provide distance cues that might help to determine the observing position, but no significant differences emerged. All features, with the exception of color,[1] exhibited better performance when their vector output was used. However, joint use of all features at the scalar value provided better results, especially with respect to the number of required SVs, than the joint use of the detailed vector version.

A variation of the algorithms described, replacing SVMs with radial basis function (RBF) networks, was used to develop a prototype of a mobile museum guide (Albertini et al. 2005).

3.2.2 The First Visual Mouse Prototype

A palmtop device equipped with a small webcam allows the user to ask for informative material on painting details by pointing the camera to them (Fig. 6). The image recognition subsystem runs on a GNU/Linux machine providing its services as an HTTP server over a local wireless network. system training was performed using images of real paintings generated with a graphical engine that mimics the sensing features of the webcam used. The system was tested with real camera input from physical fresco

---

[1] This is due to the extreme quantization of color information using a 3×3×3 cube.

reproductions. The informative material database exploits an extension of mySQL which supports querying based on XML and semantic-based indexing (Alfaro et al. 2003). The graphical user interface on the palmtop device is characterized by two different operating modes. In browsing mode, the point of view of the camera is mirrored on the display and images are fed to the image processing engine every 500 ms.

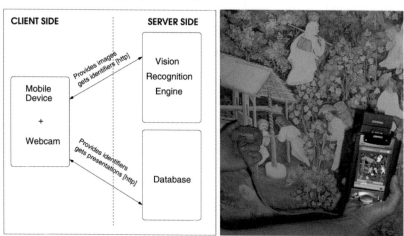

Fig. 6. The simplified architecture of the prototype system developed (*left*) and a snapshot of the interface in browsing mode

Whenever a painting detail is recognized (by means of the coordinates computed by the RBF network), the appropriate label is returned to the interface. The label may then be used to query the database for a presentation. If a presentation is available, the user is prompted with its title. If the user *clicks* on the label, the presentation is retrieved over the wireless connection and played by switching the interface to the *presenting* mode, which provides a VCR-like panel.

A small qualitative study to assess the usability of the interface was carried out in a environment that simulated the frescoed room of Torre Aquila in the Buonconsiglio Castle in Trento. The results suggested that the point-and-click style of the interaction can be mastered quickly and the automatic mode selection does not burden the user with the task of controlling the system. However, slow response may confuse the user, even if the system cues her to slow down camera motion. The scalability of such a system may be an issue due to the requirements of real-time interaction.

Anyway, the proposed interaction style does not exhaust the possibilities offered by the availability of an image recognition system. Rather then feeding a stream of images to the system, reflecting the dynamic exploration carried on by the user, a static snapshot could be provided for interpretation. While this latter strategy prevents continuous feedback from the system, it provides a more scalable solution and could be easily employed on different portable devices, such as third-generation mobile phones. The next section presents the new scenario and prototype structure. A different image recognition approach designed to support this interaction paradigm is described next.

3.2.3   The Second Visual Mouse Prototype

In this test scenario, the visitor brings a PDA equipped with a digital camera. To ask for information about a picture, the visitor simply points the PDA camera to the painting and pushes a button, in effect using the display as a viewfinder (Fig. 7). The image is then transmitted to a remote server and compared to a database of the images of the paintings in the museum (see next section for details).

Upon positive recognition, a multimedia presentation of the painting is retrieved from a semantically-indexed database of presentations (Alfaro et al. 2003). Otherwise feedback about the impossibility of analyzing the image is given to help the user learn how to use the system better. In order to reduce recognition errors due to badly framed shots, the PDA provides a grid on which the visitor is taught to align the frame of the painting.

An HP IPAQ 5550 with 128 Mb and Intel X-Scale PXA255 400 MHz processor PDA was used. It was equipped with both a wireless card that supports WiFi connectivity as well as a digital camera, the LifeView Fly-Cam CF 1.3M. The user interface was developed in C# on the Windows Pocket PC 2003 OS. All the communications among the client and the servers were based on the standard HTTP protocol.

3.2.4   A CBIR Approach[2]

The research field of content-based image retrieval has experienced sustained interest in recent years due to the need for indexing and accessing the huge amount of multimedia material being produced. Recognizing image content, in general, is still a difficult task for current systems. Nevertheless, effective systems based on low-level image description have been developed which quickly find images that are visually similar to one or more query images (Brunelli and Mich 2000; Andreatta et al. 2005).

---

[2] This work is partially funded by the European Union under the VIKEF Project.

Fig. 7. A snapshot of the interface (*left*) and a visitor using the interface in Sala Grande

These systems associate a compact signature to each query image. The query signature is then matched to signatures of images known to the system. The comparison of two signatures usually provides a measure of similarity that is used to rank all database images, the most similar being considered as an appropriate answer to the *visual* query. In our specific case (Andreatta and Leonardi 2006) the database contains images of all the required paintings, taken from different positions and under different illumination conditions. The query image is provided by the user when she takes a snapshot of the piece she is interested in. The system then recognizes the painting by comparing the snapshot to all stored images. It is important that the database be built to optimally support the *query by example* paradigm, including images as close as possible to those that will be used as queries. Several images of the museum pieces were then acquired with the palmtop camera of the prototype system (Fig. 8).

In this learning phase, the behavior of a visitor has been simulated: pictures of the paintings are taken from different angles and at different distances. The *region of interest* (ROI) for further processing is obtained by cropping the picture to ¾ of the original width and height. In order to simulate additional camera positions, the ROI is moved to 25 different positions of the original image. The ROI of the query image is centered and is assumed to contain the relevant painting in its entirety.

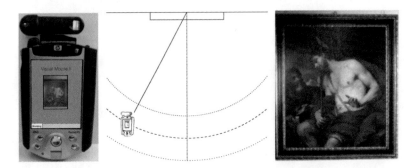

Fig. 8. During the learning phase pictures of the paintings are acquired from random positions simulating a visitor. The complete piece should be visible in the snapshot. Please note that the *left* and *right* pictures are provided only to illustrate proper framing and image quality and do not correspond to the position of the camera in the central diagram

The computation of the image signature and the retrieval itself are based on a modified version of the content based image retrieval system COM-PASS (Brunelli and Mich 2000). The ROI of the image is divided into a regular 5×5 grid and each of the resulting 25 regions is independently described by means of small histograms of low-level features (intensity, edges, hue, saturation, etc.). Histograms are represented as vectors, and the signature is obtained by taking their Cartesian product. The dissimilarity of two image regions is quantified by

$$L_1(\boldsymbol{x}, \boldsymbol{y}) = \sum_i^N |x_i - y_i|, \tag{5}$$

with N the dimension of the signature of a single region. The dissimilarity of two images X and Y can then be computed as

$$d(X, Y) = \frac{1}{K} \sum_r W_r L_1(\boldsymbol{x}_r, \boldsymbol{y}_r), \tag{6}$$

where r indexes the grid regions, W_r represent a weight for each region, and K is a normalizing factor which ensures that the value of the distance belongs to the interval $[0,1]$. The fact that each painting is represented in the database by a set of pictures can be exploited in the computation of the final similarity score by aggregating the similarity values of the query picture with the reference images on a *per painting* basis. If we denote with

$s(n) = (1\text{-}d(n))$ the similarity with the nth nearest item in the database, the score for class c representing a specific painting is given by

$$S(c) = \sum_{n_c} w(n_c)s(n_c),\tag{7}$$

where n_c is the ranking in the nearest neighbor list of class c objects and $w(n)$ is a tunable weight function. Recognition is rejected when the similarity score $S(c)$ fails to exceed a predefined threshold.

Cheap CMOS cameras, such as the one used in the experiments, have limited dynamic range and suffer from blooming effects due to the presence of *high light* areas.

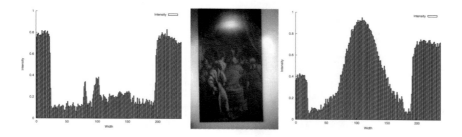

Fig. 9. Strong light sources often cause overexposure of painting areas, making recognition difficult. Overexposure effects are worsened by blooming, caused by overexposed areas bleeding into adjacent darker zones

As the descriptors used in the image retrieval system are not invariant to changes in the illumination (such as intensity or temperature), a normalizing preprocessing step is necessary. The approach chosen is based on a variant of the Gray World (GW) algorithm, using the assumption that the average world is gray. The image is normalized using a piecewise linear function whose control points are determined by inspecting the original image histograms and computing the expected gray point as in the GW method (Andreatta and Leonardi 2006).

When strong light sources are present, or the painting is not properly framed, parts of the image become overexposed. If the location of the overexposed areas varies among query and reference images, the comparison procedure outlined above produces meaningless results. The problem was solved by developing a highlight/blooming areas detector (Fig. 9). Once these areas have been detected, their weight in the comparison of image signatures can be lowered (Fig. 10), acting on the W_r factors in Eq. (6).

Only *featureful* image regions are used for the comparison, providing stable signature comparison.

Fig. 10. The pictures describe the image processing flow. From *left to right, top to bottom*: the original image, the normalized image with the description grid, the overexposed regions detected by the system and the surrounding blooming area, the weights given to the description regions (white highest, red lowest) in the retrieval process

3.2.5   Evaluation of the Second Prototype

For initial testing in Sala Grande in the Buonconsiglio Castle, a total of 13 exhibited paintings were considered. More than 500 images were stored in the recognition module database. During the testing phase, 70 snapshots were submitted by the PDA to the recognition engine, resulting in 77% correct recognition, 20% rejections, and 3% wrong results. The high rejection ratio is due to the varying illumination conditions, to the presence of spotlights over the paintings, and to the poor quality of the camera sensor.

A user evaluation was then conducted in the same environment of the first prototype: a small-scale reconstruction of Torre Aquila. Five artworks were considered, and more than 6,000 pictures composed the CBIR database. The goal of this evaluation was not only to test the recognition engine, but also to assess the usability of the interface.

Thirteen users were invited to test the system: 4 in the morning—same lighting condition of the images in the database—and 9 in the afternoon. The system was introduced as an experimental model of a new museum guide. They received short instructions on the use of the device—including the need for framing the picture before shooting—and then they were free to access the painting as they preferred. In total, 130 images were submitted to the recognition engine. The overall recognition rate was 80% in the morning session and 72% in the afternoon session. Figure 11 plots successful and failed recognition statistics, considering the attempts made by the participants. It is worth noting than nobody did more than four attempts on the same painting, yet the overall abandon rate is quite low (just six abandons in total and all in the afternoon).

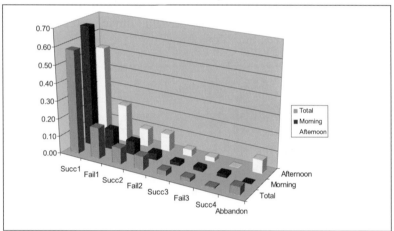

Fig. 11. Results of the user study: detailed statistics on successful and failed recognition attempts

Figure 12 shows the distribution of the types of errors. There were four different reasons why the system was not able to recognize a painting. The first reason is misrecognition due to the CBIR engine—this kind of error was quite rare, 19% in total, even if it happened more frequently in the afternoon session. In the remaining cases the system did not identify the painting for a variety of reasons. Improving the recognition algorithm or increasing the database would reduce missed identifications caused by reflections on the paintings—again this was quite infrequent, 25% of the total errors, and it happened only in the afternoon. The other cases where the system failed to identify the paintings were due to user problems in correctly using the system: shaken and badly framed images and the combination of the two. A simple solution would be improving the ergonomic grip of the PDA.

At the end of the experiment, each user was asked to fill the SUS usability questionnaire. SUS is a simple ten-item scale that gives a global view of subjective assessments of usability (Brooke 2004). Its scores range from 0 to 100; good applications are commonly considered to score in the range of 60–70 while bad applications in the range 40–50. The average SUS score of the Visual Mouse was 86.25 (stdev=6.29) for the morning session and 77.78 (stdev=15.00). If we consider the users that experienced less than 4 errors, the average was 81.67 (stdev=8.00), while for the users that experienced 4 or more errors the average was to 77.50 (stdev=23.00).

In conclusion, the second prototype of the Visual Mouse had some problems due to the difficulty of the vision task, but more than that it made evident that ergonomic features of the physical device—such as the need for firmer grip—were even more important.

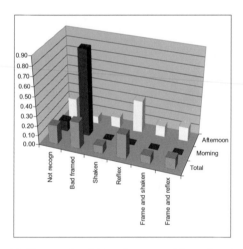

Fig. 12. Reason for failure in recognition of an image

In spite of these limitations, the users were quite satisfied by the system and the very high SUS scores—compared with the actual performance of the system—proved that in the context of a museum a natural interaction paradigm would be well accepted.

3.3   Natural Pointing

The interfaces presented so far, even if easy to master and based on wearable hardware, are not completely natural. They require the user to get accustomed to a new device which mediates her interaction with the environment. Body gestures and postures are very natural means of human to human interaction, and a human–computer interface based on the very same *devices* may be preferable.

Gesture and posture acceptability and naturalness depend on context, a dependency to be considered in the development of such interfaces. As an example, a single visitor wishing detailed information on a painting detail would probably feel uneasy in pointing to the detail with her arm. The most natural way to *select* the item of interest would be to just turn the head or eyes to look at it. The following sections present algorithms for two different scenarios: a single user *asking* the museum for information on a detail of an exhibit, and a group guide directing the visitors during the *exploration* of an exhibit.

3.3.1   Gazing

Determining the (visual) focus of attention of a visitor requires an estimation of the point where her eyes are pointing. Unfortunately, all currently available methods require cumbersome hardware or severely constrained positioning of the visitor. Given these limitations, systems based on the automatic computation of gazing do not support the development of novel, nonintrusive interfaces for museum visitors. The 3D orientation of the head—while not as precise an indicator as the direction of the eyes— provides a natural cue to the focus of attention of a person. This is even truer when the person is free to move and to change the body orientation in order to observe the environment in a relaxed way. In order to effectively and flexibly support human–computer interfaces, a system that tracks head orientation should be able to work in real time and on low-resolution/low-quality video streams. These constraints were considered in the design of a novel algorithm whose main features are:

- Efficient tracking based on a single video stream.
- Robustness to environmental conditions based on the optimization of a hybrid criterium function.
- Extended tracking coverage through the usage of multiple cameras.
- Low-resolution readiness based on reliable low-level feature extraction and robust optical flow techniques.

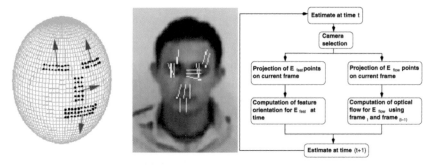

Fig. 13. *Left*: the ellipsoidal model with the points corresponding to the facial features associated to the expected edge orientation. *Middle*: locally dominant edge orientation at the model features for a real image. *Right*: the architecture of the head-pose estimation algorithm which exploits static and dynamic information to align the model to actual image data to derive accurate head-pose information

A preliminary step is the detection in the scene of the face to be tracked. Whenever color imagery is available, a computationally efficient solution can be found in the detection of skin patches as promising candidates. The resulting image regions can be further filtered using information on shape. In our case, knowledge of the environment and 3D constraints based on wide baseline stereo triangulation provide additional information. Skin color distribution is modelled using a mixture of two Gaussians, while patches in multiple camera views are associated by means of the correspondence of their centroids using relaxed epipolar constraints. Upon locating heads in image space, accurate determination of their 3D orientation as a function of time is required. The sensor set up assumed is that of a fully calibrated multi camera system (Lanz 2004a; Chippendale and Tobia 2005). The main idea of the proposed algorithm is to use a model-based approach (Fig. 13) that exploits two different information sources:

- Frame-to-frame motion of salient facial features, i.e., optical flow information, establishing head pose by aligning the motion patterns of the model to those derived from the images.
- Within frame analysis, by aligning the features of the model to those of a single image.

The specific model chosen is based on two different samplings of an ellipsoidal mesh E (Fig. 13). A first level E_{flow} comprises a set of points in proximity of the major facial features where optical flow computation is performed.

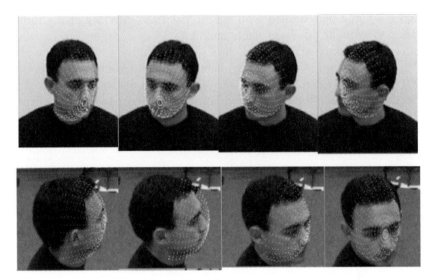

Fig. 14. The performance of the pose estimation tracking algorithm on a real sequence captured from two different cameras

A second level E_{feat} groups the points of the ellipsoidal mesh on a per feature basis (i.e., nose, left and right eye, mouth) and associates to each of the resulting groups a vector representing the direction of maximal visual discontinuity. The proposed model has the following advantages:

- It can be easily adapted to different heads.
- It can be used to focus processing on a limited image area, thereby improving tracking efficiency.

An additional feature is that of extended range tracking. As the multi-camera environment is assumed to be fully calibrated, the algorithm can easily select the video stream presenting the tracked face under the most frontal view (Fig. 14). Tracking performance is optimized and efficiency preserved by working on a single video stream.

As anticipated, the algorithm exploits the two levels of the model in two different ways (Fig. 13). Reliable computation of the optical flow is achieved by means of an efficient, hierarchical implementation of the iterative Lucas–Kanade algorithm (Lucas and Kanade 1981). Optical flow needs not be computed at all image pixels: knowledge of the current pose is used to select the appropriate points by projecting the points of E_{flow} onto the image plane. Alignment of the model using only static information is based on the extraction of reliable facial feature information at low resolution. Due to the structure of facial features, the direction of locally maximal variation (coupled with feature position) provides enough information to estimate pose accurately and in a way that is robust to variations both in illumination and contrast. An efficient solution for the computation of this information is provided by steerable filters (Adelson and Freeman 1991). They provide an efficient way to compute a stable estimate of the direction for which the intensity variation is locally maximal. The experiments performed showed that they significantly outperform traditional approaches based on the computation of a locally regularized gradient, especially for low contrast features at low resolution.

The algorithm determines head pose Ω_{t+1} at time $t+1$ by using current information on the state of the models, image I_{t+1}, and its comparison with image I_t. The new estimated pose is obtained by minimizing a three-term functional f_{err}:

$$f_{err}\left(\Omega_t, \Omega_{t+1}\right) = \lambda_1 \varepsilon_{flow} + \lambda_2 \varepsilon_{feat} + \lambda_3 d . \tag{8}$$

The first term quantifies the difference between the optical flow of the images and the optical flow of the projection of the points of E_{flow} from Ω_{t+1} to Ω_t. The second term uses a single frame and measures the misalignment of the local feature orientation at the points of E_{feat} with the information derived from the response of steerable filters at the corresponding points of image I_t. The last contribution to the functional measures the discrepancy from the position of the head as estimated by triangulation of the centroids. Minimization of the error in Eq. (8) is performed with the simplex method over a six-dimensional space corresponding to head orientation and position. The algorithm developed was applied to a typical museum scenario: close inspection of a content rich painting (Fig. 15).

The user sequentially focuses on interesting areas of the painting: the system developed is able to estimate gaze direction in real time. By intersecting the viewing direction with the known painting layout, it is possible to trigger the delivery of contextualized multimedia information to the user.

3.3.2   Pointing

Museums are often visited by groups of people following a guide who explains the exhibits. The interaction of the guide with the group typically includes deictic gestures which serve to direct the attention of the visitors to the details of the exhibits the guide is talking about. By understanding these gestures, presentations of additional multimedia material providing additional insight on the items of interest can be started automatically.

Fig. 15. Real time head orientation can support contextualized information delivery in museum environments. The *highlighted areas* on the picture represent the projection of the user viewing frustum onto the exhibit as determined automatically by the system. The user could be given audio feedback by means of wireless earphones

Pointing gestures can be complex and, for instance, two arm gestures may be used to establish relations between parts of complex exhibits. The rest of the chapter presents a system capable of such understanding with the intention of providing a rich and intuitive visual interface for the participant, offering a level of functionality beyond simple region-of-interest selection (Chippendale 2005).

Robust detection of pointing gestures is not straightforward and is open to ambiguity. Questions which need to be addressed are: When does a gesture start and finish? Which hand is pointing, left or right? And how does one define the best vector from the finger to the target object? To help reduce visual ambiguities, multiple viewpoint reconstruction was explored using a variety of techniques. Generally, in museums, it is not practical to install large numbers of cameras in every room, thus camera reuse and redeployment must be explored. To achieve this goal, active cameras with zoom capabilities must be employed. With this in mind, a means of utilizing image-streams from active cameras that are inherently subjected to re-orientation either manually or by an independent camera allocation system was implemented.

For all of the algorithms detailed here, bootstrapping parameters, such as human clothing models or a precomputed background model of the environment are not mandatory. Moreover, as our ultimate goal is to simultaneously track complex pointing-gestures using active Pan–Tilt–Zoom cameras, segmentation, detection and interpretation must operate in real time.

One of the underlying assumptions followed in this research is that motion potentially indicates the presence of a person. Moving regions (blobs) are deemed to pertain to a person through the presence of skin-coloured neighbouring pixels. Essentially, moving skin-coloured pixel regions—of sufficient density to form cohesive blobs—are assumed to be either moving heads or hands.

To derive anatomical labelling and also to say which skin blobs belong to the same entity, spatial linkages and voxelisation are explored. The first step is detecting the presence of a person, the guide, who will interface to the system. In order to obtain robust results, three different low-level filters were used:

- Frame-to-frame differencing of image luminance: only a few centimetres of movement reveal a telltale signature.
- Adaptive background modelling, introducing temporal latency for the moving objects: they do not disappear the instant they cease to move, but instead decay at a rate relative to the deemed reliability of the background model at that location.
- Skin modelling based on a mixture of two Gaussians, followed by morphological denoising.

To provide an understanding of human occupancy in the video images, the information provided by the above filters is combined by taking the largest likelihood value (the MAX image). Again morphological denoising is applied.

The next step is that of locating the hands and head of the person tracked in order to be able to extract the direction of the pointing gestures. The human model used for the purposes of understanding skin blob linkages spatially is a very simple one. Hands are connected to faces via an elliptical arc travelling through the arms and neck. Its major diameter is defined by the line connecting the two centroids (or nodes) and the minor radius is defined by the perpendicular distance from the major's bisect to the elbow. The strength, S, of an arc linkage is calculated by looking at the pixel values from the MAX image at the coordinates of each point along the arc.

Fig. 16. *Left*: Elliptical linkage test arcs used to associate hands to heads. *Right*: Clustering head and hand skin hypothesis represented as voxels in 3D space provides more robust results

As is apparent, the head is the common node for both left and right hands. This node commonality is the indicator employed for recognising which blobs are heads and which are hands. However, a single snapshot in time is insufficient to guarantee correct labelling; hence a stage of temporal linkage examination follows. To understand what is happening in the current scene, a triplane motion history image (MHI, containing hand, arm, and face planes) is created from the stream of spatial linkages. A hypothesis as to whether a skin blob is a hand, face, or something inconclusive is made upon the observation of "Λ" shape patterns in localised areas of the arm-plane MHI. In each frame, the contents of the arm-plane MHI are updated by incrementing the values of pixels that lay under spatial linkages and decrementing those that do not. In the event that a calibrated camera network is available and the same scene is being observed by multiple cameras, it is possible to combine the information from the various 2D views to create a 3D interpretation of the scene. To achieve this, first the 3D position of all of the heads in the room is calculated. Virtual rays are projected from each camera through the centroids of each 2D skin-blob labelled as a "head" into 3D space. Next, using an SVD algorithm the minimum distances between each "head-ray" and the head-rays from the other cameras are computed. Providing that the closest ray intersection distance is small (say, less than 30 cm) and the hypothesised position of the 3D head is inside the room and less than 2m high, a 3D head position is created. This process is repeated until all of the 2D heads from all of the cameras have been accounted for. Once the head skin-blobs have been processed, the left and right hands are reconstructed in the same manner. To improve the robustness of human segmentation an additional approach was explored. This involves the quantisation of the entire room volume into 3D voxels, in our case, each measures 4×4×4 cm^3 and involves at least two calibrated cameras. From each of the skin pixels from Camera 1, project a virtual 3D ray into space using the projection matrix furnished by the calibrated camera network. The first pixel encountered (in Camera 2) by the projected ray from Camera 1 is taken to be the intersection point. If a pixel correspondence is found (i.e., the projected ray encounters a skin pixel in Camera2), a virtual ray is projected from this pixel in Camera2 and a 3D point in space appears where both rays intersect. At the point of intersection, the corresponding voxel in the room is tagged as skin. These voxels are then clustered into cohesive 3D blobs.

To understand when a pointing gesture is present and how stable it is, two different metrics are employed:

- Frame-to-frame spatial stability of a hand.
- Height of the hand above the floor plane.

Figure 17 illustrates the spatial interframe stability of the left and right hands during the sequence shown in brief in Fig. 16. The two traces represent the frame-to-frame Euclidean distance movements of the hands, measured in millimetres. The position of the hand at any instant in time is calculated through the formation of a 3D bounding box around all of the voxels in a hand-cluster. The 3D hand position is then taken to be the centroid of this box. Using this centroid, the height of the hand above the floor plane is also assessed. The horizontal bars in Fig. 17 indicate the hand is more than 1 m from the floor and also that it has moved less than 10 cm between frames, hence a pointing gesture is taking place. As the data clearly show, the protagonist is right-handed, exemplified by a dominance of isolated right-hand gestures. The direction of the pointing gesture is calculated during the phases of hand stability and sufficient elevation (i.e., during the periods marked by the bars). The pointing ray is defined by joining the head centroid to the furthermost voxel contained within the hand voxel-cluster. This ray is then projected onto the exhibit and, at the point of intersection, a box of radius 15 cm is drawn around it. Such an intersection can be seen in Fig. 18. To verify the performance of the voxel algorithm, a further sequence was created in which the protagonist pointed to various targets on a wall mounted poster. A snapshot from the video sequence is visible in Fig. 18. At this particular instant in time, the subject was asked to point at the sun and at the lady crouching in the bottom-right of the poster as if he was giving a request to the system: "Give me information linking these two portions".

The accuracy of the pointing segmentation algorithm can be clearly seen in the image. Considering the fact that the protagonist was standing over 2 m away from the poster, the accuracy of the pointing gesture segmentation is high enough to provide a useful input for a human–computer interface which understands visitor interests.

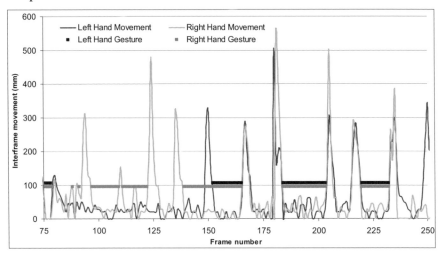

Fig. 17. A critical issue is detecting when a pointing gesture is actually present. The strategy adopted is based on the spatial stability of the hand position and on its height above the floor. Pointing gestures can be *segmented* using appropriate thresholds

Fig. 18. Two hands used to links different parts of the exhibit. Assuming that each *hot spot* (boxes) on the painting is given a numerical index i, a two-hand gesture like the one detected in the picture may be used to address an element in a two-dimensional matrix $\mathbf{M}_{ij}$. Each such element may be associated to a multimedia presentation that provides in depth information on the relation between the two selected hot spots

3.4 Conclusions

Human–computer interfaces based on vision are becoming increasingly appealing due to their unobtrusiveness and to the increased set of functionalities that novel image processing techniques support. In this chapter, we focused on supporting interfaces between humans and smart environments. Specifically, we focused on the interaction of single and group visitors within a responsive museum environment able to provide contextualized information on demand. Two different classes of human–computer interactions were investigated: those mediated by portable devices and those based on free body gesturing. Regarding the latter, both single-visitor and guided-group needs were addressed. Novel image processing algorithms supporting real-time user interaction were designed and tested for all the scenarios considered. The experimental results obtained, while still limited, are very promising and open the way to the adoption of novel ways to interface people with smart environments.

4 Report Generation for Postvisit Summaries in Museum Environments

C. Callaway, E. Not and O. Stock

4.1 The Museum Mission

As guardians of cultural heritage, museums are interested in a continual presence in their communities for both ongoing learning and for extending public awareness of their collections (Stock 2001). One way for museums to have an important impact is to extend their influence outside of the confines of the physical museum itself (Callaway et al. 2005a). But continued education will not take place if visitors simply take home their admission ticket and put it into a box as a simple keepsake, or buy a book from the gift shop and put it on their bookshelf. Such items are not likely to be shared with family and friends, or taken out and viewed very often.

Personalization can be one key to furthering the impact of a museum visit, whereupon exiting the museum the visitor is given a permanent item as a keepsake that describes her unique experience during the visit and is immediately recognizable as such. Rather than an item which is an exact copy of what every other visitor can obtain, something obviously personal and unique is likely to be eagerly shown to visitors in the home and discussed at length with family, friends, and work colleagues. Personalization thus leverages experiences familiar to everyone, whether through home videos of the family in front of a famous monument instead of the official DVD version, book and travel recommendations from Web sites over simple lists, or Web forums and blogs rather than traditional media outlets.

But a personalized item representing an entire museum tour is not easy to create. It must be dynamically produced immediately at the end of the visit; it cannot be prefabricated or later sent to the visitor's home weeks after their visit when they have already forgotten all but a few memories. It must be obviously personal and unique so as not to be immediately discarded: the text itself, associated images, and suggestions for further visits and additional material are all candidates for personalization that will also help to improve a museum's "brand awareness". To be able to learn lessons on what personalization strategies work from a prototype, it must be implementable with available and current technology, which excludes dynamic video or animated 3D movies, even though in the future this will also be possible (Chap. 2). Written text is a medium that can satisfy these requirements, and research on this topic in general has been studied for many years in the field of natural language generation (NLG).

4.1.1   Museum Postvisit Reports

As a first step to explore postvisit museum interactions, we were thus interested in using language technology to produce a text-based artefact that would continue to educate a visitor after the museum visit was concluded, and personalization of the text as the "hook" leading to further visitor interest. In this scenario, a museum-goer's visit to a museum is intermediated by a hand-held PDA (Benelli et al. 1999; Cheverst et al. 2000; Chap. 1), which is logged and used to determine that visitor's individual interests (Chap. 6). Immediately at the end of the visit to the Torre Aquila museum, the project's test site described in earlier chapters, a custom report is printed and given to the visitor, including an overview of which frescos and themes were seen, additional information about specific topics they were interested in, nonobvious relationships between elements in the eleven frescos, interesting ties to other similar topics they did not have time to see, and follow-up Web links to locations of Trentino art to continue exploring these topics at home. The knowledge base (KB) and inference methods described in (Chap. 6) are used to produce the text of the report in either English or Italian using NLG techniques.

NLG attempts to provide adaptive text across a variety of domains and applications. Museum applications using NLG typically describe historical, functional, and physical data about objects in museum collections (Oberlander et al. 1998; Calder et al. 2005). However, extended explanations or descriptions of individual museum exhibits are not the only possible application of NLG technology in cultural settings. The introduction of mobile computing devices with localization and orientation information allows for a range of dynamic interactions.

The prototype report generator described below produces page-long personalized reports given the interest model (Chap. 6) for the Torre Aquila museum, printed on demand with colour reproductions of the referenced artworks and in either English or Italian. (An example is shown at the end of the chapter.) The written report includes a basic narration of their visit, the items and relationships they found most interesting with images of exhibits placed near the text describing them to let visitors remember the artworks as they read, and links to additional information on the Internet related to their favourite items. It also includes the date and time of the visit, the name of the visitor, and, at the bottom of the page, links and pictures to additional tourist locations in the region surrounding the Torre Aquila.

The narration itself is derived from two distinct types of information: (i) factual aspects of the visit such as exhibits visited, the visit sequence and amount of time spent at different locations, the presentations that were shown to the user, and user actions such as clicking to stop an animated presentation; and (ii) the specific interests of individual visitors, which are computed by taking this data and running an inference algorithm with it over the contents of the KB (Chap. 6). The resulting personalized report is produced automatically by the NLG system using HTML markup, allowing for the easy combination of text and graphics, and which can either be printed immediately or sent to the visitor's e-mail address.

4.1.2   Design Methodology for Postvisit Reports

Before devoting the significant amount of time needed to implement a prototype, we needed to know exactly what constituted an interesting report that museum visitors would want to see and continue to read after they left the museum. We created sample reports for fictitious visitors and exhibits using a variety of organizational styles, facts, and layouts. These samples were then iteratively critiqued as a group, as is common practice in design-based paradigms. Various interesting features and problems were identified, leading to newer rounds of higher quality and more interesting reports. We finally settled on three example reports to be produced as prototypes with the main distinction between them being the organizational style.

The first type was a sequential, linear narrative following the particular sequence of visited exhibits, preserving the visit path and recording events in a chronological order. This approach was the simplest to implement as it required very little inference capability or sophisticated organizational rules. However, it was also the least interesting and required filtering redundant data to ensure a minimum of repetitions in the text. A report organized around the sequential method could, for instance, describe the five frescos where the visitor spent the most time, ignoring the remaining frescos. Personalization in this case would thus consist of assuming that the visitor actually spent more time in front of these exhibits expressly because they were interesting, although it is equally possible she was talking on a mobile phone in front of some random fresco. Also, without access to visitor interests, links between artworks could not be established based on its constituent elements but rather on a predetermined theme for that particular artwork. In summary, sequential visit reports were very helpful for implementing the basic infrastructure of the prototype, but not very satisfactory for the visitors to read.

The second type was a thematically organized narrative, developing each paragraph around one of the central themes the user was interested in. This approach requires more extensive inference over the interest model as the themes themselves are not contained in any specific fresco and some ordering over themes must also be computed. Links to artworks elsewhere, whether in the same museum or nearby ones, are easily related in the narrative as long as those artworks are indexed thematically. Here, however, specific details of the visit must be included for two reasons: (1) the visitor may not be able to immediately associate broad themes with the mental images retained from her visit, and (2) generalizations are more likely to lead to less variation and thus less personalization since multiple artworks may be clustered together under a common theme and thus result in a more abstract, but also more narrow search space.

Finally, a third type combines both sequential and thematic approaches, and is intended to solve some of the problems inherent in each approach above used alone. While combining sequential and thematic narratives generally yielded lower quality text than thematic-only, it provided for a greater amount of variation. We briefly looked at two different methods for combining: an overall sequential organization with extended interludes describing the most important theme at each stage in the sequence (but only taking the longest three artworks in the sequence in order to stay under the one-page limit), and an overall thematic organization where the major artwork in each theme was explicitly mentioned along with details about its position in the visit sequence.

In addition to the organization and layout of the report, the content (what actually gets printed) is also vitally important. We found that reports should draw from a wide array of possibilities: an overall description of the artwork, details of what is visible in each artwork, relationships between different elements within a single artwork, historical notes about the painter, origin and current state of the artwork, details related to the visitor's requests for information, interesting connections between seemingly unrelated exhibits, comparisons between the exhibits the visitor found interesting, and descriptions of and suggestions for related exhibits they would probably have been interested in but did not have a chance to see. The content should also allow for some flexibility and variation, so that two visitors touring together and walking on the same paths would still get different reports, strengthening the visitors' perception of personalization. Variability should be present as soon as possible in the wording of the report (we generated only a single sentence as a welcome message that was identical in all reports) and images of each piece of art mentioned should be placed as close as possible to its written description.

From the museum's perspective on continuing education, the report should always be correct and make the visitor want to continue to study the topics depicted in the exhibits. It should make this study as easy as possible for the visitor by suggesting relevant links to follow up at a later date, additional items to visit in the future, and possible additional related exhibits in nearby museums. Because museum visitors typically come from all over the globe, it is desirable to provide them with the report in their native language (although we did not explore culture-based adaptation, but solely the equivalent of language translation). Reports can be produced as a printed hardcopy that is then handed to the visitor as they leave, emailed as a Web page with hyperlinks generated inline within the text that point to additional information, or potentially a complete multimedia show at an available museum kiosk that combines their interests into a dynamically produced film (Chap. 2).

Museums are also interested in *visitor fidelisation* (similar perhaps to brand loyalty) where visitors repeatedly return to the museum when travelling exhibits arrive or when cultural or entertainment events are held in conjunction with the museum (for instance, a yearly concert series held in a castle's courtyard). Personalization can reinforce these events and keep them in the mind of visitors even when they are not at the museum. Suggestions for further visits and additional material, personalized Web links, and the use of images known to appeal to certain stereotypes can increase this.

4.2   Resources Needed for Producing Report Summaries

Dynamically creating unique, written summaries of a museum visit is a resource-intensive process. Collections of such reports do not exist in books or on the Web, where the computer could choose a prewritten report that most closely matches a particular visitor's path. And while the fragments of information that go into a report can be found, they are typically in printed, rather than digital form, and in any case automatically rearranging pieces of text (Not and Zancanaro 2000) into a useful whole is a challenging and unsolved problem. The frescos of the Torre Aquila museum, for example, are described by several books, but while these contain a large amount of factual detail, they are not cross-referenced across all possible themes. Writing out a large enough number of pieces of text to cover the billions of possible combinations would require a superhuman effort for one museum, let alone for thousands of museums around the world.

Rather than creating adaptivity through reassembly of surface text, for the visit-summarization task we would thus prefer a more conceptual approach that produces the text of the report by combining semantic, fact-based content with separate methods for selecting, ordering, and converting this content into text as final stage after all inferencing has been completed. This process requires a significant number of resources in digital form, including semantic and linguistic data that, while difficult to create with current methods, have been extensively studied in the literature. Static resources which are either dependent or independent of the application domain (museum reports) and particular data required (Torre Aquila museum) are:

- The KB: a taxonomically related listing of all concepts, instances and relations that exist in the domain, plus the facts consisting of these elements; in our case, for the Torre Aquila museum that contains 11 renaissance frescos.
- The lexicon: a pairing of words and their associated grammatical information which can be used to piece together the text of the reports after all semantic knowledge has been properly selected and organized.
- Links to real world sources: hyperlinks for the Web and descriptions of the contents of nearby museums or local cultural events that can be used as recommendations for further exploration. Also, images of the art to include.
- Spatial layout of museum: geometrical description of the rooms and each exhibits, such as which artworks are adjacent.

Other resources are dynamically created when the system is called upon to guide the visitor through the museum or to produce a report at the end of the visit:

- The user history: the list of events that were involved in the visitor's tour.
- The interest model: a subset of the concepts and instances contained in the KB ranked according to inferred interest as determined by inference over the user history for a visit (Chap. 6).

- Layout of the report itself: where the title goes, how many paragraphs to include, locations for artwork images, etc.

The user history and interest model are described in Chap. 6, whereas links to Web sources, the museum's spatial layout and the layout of the report itself are self-explanatory. We thus now describe the interaction between the KB and the lexicon that allows the system to recombine facts proposed by the user history (sequential report) or interest model (thematic report) to produce the text rather than arranging snippets of text directly.

4.2.1   Knowledge Base and Multilingual Lexicon

The KB underlies not only the natural language generation system that produces written postvisit reports, but has also been used directly by other related applications such as automatic cinematography (Chap. 2) and direction giving within the museum grounds, as well as indirectly by other elements of the architecture that support nonlanguage applications such as user modelling (Chap. 6).

Similar to a database, a KB is a network of semantic entities (either generic *concepts* or unique *instances*) and relations that hold between them. Concepts in the Torre Aquila museum domain include *fresco*, *castle*, and *peasant*, while their respective instances might include *april-fresco001*, *stenico-castle001*, and *peasant001*. Examples of relations holding between pairs of concepts and instances are *to-the-left-of*, *depicting*, and *harvesting*. The actual content of the KB, the semantic network itself, is expressed as a set of facts, which are triples of the form (*entity relation entity*), for instance (*april-fresco001 containing hunting-scene004*), or (*peasant001 to-the-right-of stenico-castle001*). Because knowledge about the domain is stored as conceptual knowledge rather than as text strings, it can be used for inference by other elements of the PEACH system as well as for generating written text for the report generator or spoken narration for the automatic cinematography system.

A large amount of the work needed to support inference and text generation was devoted to creating the KB and customizing it for the particular applications supporting PEACH. The KB for the Torre Aquila currently consists of about 4,000 concepts and facts that fall into four main categories:

- An *upper level ontology* of very generic concepts like *physical-object*, *movement*, *colour*, *activity*, and *profession*. The ontology is a taxonomic grouping where very abstract entities such as *physical-object* are further subdivided into categories like *building*, *person,* and *tool*, forming a large Web of interconnected concepts.

- Concepts, instances, and facts which are specific to individual frescos, allowing the system to determine the content of a particular artwork in order to compute what interests it might support or to be able to generate descriptions of its contents when needed.
- Concepts and facts which interrelate the various frescos, allowing the system to provide recommendations on what artworks to see as well as how they are spatially related in the museum's physical space.
- Annotations on images of artworks and the relationships between them that can be used to support two types of personalization: choosing one image over another and deciding whether to choose an entire image or just a particular subregion.
- Language-based concepts, instances and facts that are needed to generate the text for reports or films, but which are not necessarily specific to the domain itself. For instance, *stenico-museum001* is a proper, neuter noun while *peasant001* is a common, masculine noun. This lexicon also includes encodings for entities and relations in both English and Italian.

Because the user modelling component in the PEACH project must communicate which topics from the interest model should be included in a given report the construction of the KB was coordinated by agreeing on a scheme for uniquely addressing names of semantic concepts.

4.3   Producing the Text of the Report

The input to the text generation process is a request for a particular style of report along with the necessary user and interest model data. As stated previously, the report style can be either sequential, thematic, or mixed. The decision of what style to use can be proposed based on the number of exhibits seen, the amount of time spent interacting with the mobile presentation system, the size of the inferred interest model, or even randomly. The report style, user history, and interest model (if a thematic or mixed report was chosen) are then passed to the first NLG module: the text planner.

The NLG system is organized as a pipeline architecture (Reiter 1994). In the first phase, relevant content for the document is selected from the user/interest model and the KB and is organized into a discourse plan structured as a rhetorical tree. Then, the microplanner applies a number of discourse strategies to decide how to realize elements of the text so that it will be linguistically coherent and properly convey the desired information. Finally, a surface realiser completes the process by converting the entities and relations in the rhetorical tree into lexical strings and enforcing syntactic and morphology constraints according to the grammar of the target language.

The process of generating text from conceptual representations has been well-studied (Reiter and Dale 2000) in the literature. Because museums receive a large number of international visitors, it is also necessary to explore techniques for generating text in multiple languages from a single conceptual representation (Bateman 1995; Stede 1996; Scott 1999; Novello and Callaway, 2003a).

4.3.1 Text Planning

The text planner determines the most relevant information to be included in the description and its coherent organization. Information about artworks is extracted from the KB, representing facts and attributes collected from the domain about the objects to be described (e.g., which characters and objects are depicted in a fresco, their relative positions, and what activities they are involved in). Discourse strategies based on typical patterns of content organization and rhetorical coherence as observed in our corpus of example reports are used to guarantee that the discourse plan is properly built.

During its decision process, the text planner accesses the user model, which contains information about (estimated) user interest, knowledge, and interaction preferences, and the discourse context which stores the content conveyed in earlier presentations—useful to avoid repetitions and to draw comparisons—and the structure of the presentation currently being built. It uses this information to help determine what content should be extracted from the KB and how it should be ordered (for instance, put all facts about a particular artwork in the same paragraph). The text planner thus ensures coherence across paragraphs and between sentences within a single paragraph, and ensures that enough content is present in each paragraph to prevent them from being too large or small.

The content selection and organization approach adopted in our text planner is based on the assumption that in descriptive texts, the conventions on how information is typically presented play a major role. For example, when describing complex depictions in a fresco, the text should first include an overview of the artwork before describing the various elements that comprise it, or describe the most important elements before the least important, with more detail on the former.

How the content of the text is actually structured depends significantly on the type of readers addressed and their specific interactions with the system (e.g., visitors who see only one wing of a museum should get recommendations rather than descriptions for artworks in another wing, and difficult terminology often needs to be properly explained to children). These "patterns of appropriate ordering" (more widely known in the NLG community as schemas (McKeown 1985) or the Generic Structure Potential (Halliday and Hasan 1985) of a text) have been adopted in many NLG systems to guide the text planner in organizing the text structure.

For the report generator we have implemented a schema-based text planner in which schemas (which we call generic structure potential or GSP, consistent with the Halliday and Hasan terminology) are used to declaratively describe how the text chunks should be optimally organized according to the current user profile, user and interest models, discourse history and artwork to be described. GSPs can be defined at different levels of abstraction and may contain calls to other finer-grained GSPs. For instance, GSPs may block thematic introductory passages when they have been explained previously.

Each GSP is composed of the following:

- Name: Identifies the communicative goal the GSP is meant to satisfy. Many GSPs may share the same name, if they represent alternative ways to convey the same communicative goal. Sample names currently used in the various PEACH application tasks include `describe-object`, `refer-event-in-scene`, `summarize-visit`, `introduce-report`, `direction-to-next-door`.
- Parameters: Variables appearing in the body of the GSP which will be instantiated with specific entities or entity types at run time, before the GSP is expanded. For example, a variable `Exhibit` might be instantiated with the value *january-month001*, the instance in the PEACH KB that indicates the January fresco in the Torre Aquila.
- Condition: A series of nested conjunctions or disjunctions of applicability tests over the discourse context, the user model, and the domain model. For example, a condition may require that an object be taxonomically under the *FRESCO-ART* concept in the KB when the text structure associated with the GSP concerns descriptions of artwork. Other entities failing this condition are thus prohibited from using that GSP.
- Local variable: This field contains the definition of a local variable, i.e., a variable appearing in the body of the schema but not in the input parameters. The definition specifies the name of the new variable and an expression (e.g., a query to the domain model), whose computed value will be assigned to the variable at GSP-instantiation time. For example,

a variable named `FrescoDepiction` could be instantiated at run-time with a fact retrieved from the KB which tells whether it is the representation of the exhibit currently being described.

- Element: Specifies one of the substructures into which the current GSP will be decomposed. It can identify:
  - A `Leaf` of the text planning tree, i.e., a set of facts to be passed to the microplanning stage for eventual verbalization as text or audio
  - A `schema` call to be further expanded. The schema call is composed of the name of the child GSP to be called and one or more input parameters, either expressed with variables or with queries to the KB. In our example, the GSP `describe-object` is recursively called to describe the scenes depicted in the fresco.
- Schema: Provides for the actual order and optionality of the elements (described above) for which the schema will be expanded, together with rhetorical relations holding between them that express meaningful relations between portions of the discourse tree.
- Root: This field specifies which of (possibly) multiple elements plays the main role in conveying the message structured by the GSP.

The output of the text planning stage is a rhetorically annotated discourse tree whose leaves represent predicates in the domain model that must be linguistically realized. This preliminary discourse tree then goes under a reduction phase that compacts long branches without siblings produced by the GSP expansion process and merges leaves with the same topic for the sake of efficacy of the subsequent stages of text realization. The reduced discourse tree is then passed to the microplanning engine described next.

4.3.2 Referring Expression Generation

While the structure that results from the text planning stage above predicates grouped into paragraphs, it does not contain a specification within each paragraph for the ordering of individual facts relative to each other, the partitioning of facts into groups which could represent sentences, the description of the facts in relation to the KB, or in fact a proper format for the next module in the pipeline which determines referring expressions. The rhetorical tree when it arrives is a mixture of atomic triples as described earlier (Sect. 4.3.1) and predicates with arguments that can be further decomposed into triples, all bound together by discourse relations.

There are thus two main functions to be provided by the referring expression algorithm: to expand predicate/argument structures into sequences of facts in order to arrive at a uniform specification (which we term a *fact list*), and then followed by a discourse-oriented phase where discourse information based on the semantics of the facts and additional information from the KB are used to produce the structures that can be further processed linguistically. The fact list is thus for us an interlingual representation which is the boundary between the conceptual and the linguistic, and should be able to be converted to text in any language.

The preliminary expansion phase takes the leaf nodes of the discourse tree, which represents events or entities in the domain model, and looks in the KB for the semantic roles that are worth being mentioned in the text to correctly describe the event or entity. For events, this consists of retrieving the corresponding thematic roles (agent, patient, instrument, etc.) that are fundamentally involved in the event, together with the modifiers that help refine the event description and its position within the spatio-temporal framework of the discourse. For this task, we selected a list of (domain-independent) semantic relations from the ontology to guide access of semantic concepts in the KB.

For producing nominal expressions, work on referring expression generation (Dale 1990; Claassen 1992) has studied how to correctly produce noun phrases (whether full description, definite description, deixis, pronoun, or reduced noun phrase) that will enable a reader to mentally select the intended referent from the set of possible referents (Reiter and Dale, 2000). Many referring expression algorithms focus even more particularly on the production of distinguishing expressions, namely the minimal noun phrase necessary to distinguish the intended referent from all other referents. Although not all domains need such specificity, the Torre Aquila is such a domain due to the large number of similar objects and people found in the frescos. If, for example, the report generation application wishes to refer to a particular couple in a fresco such as May that has nine such couples, it could create a distinguishing expression such as "the couple wearing red and white" or "the couple to the left of the castle tower". Without the creation of such distinguishing expressions, a generated report may be misleading.

Once all the events have been expanded and the entities to be mentioned in the text have been explicitly listed, the first stage of the referring expressions algorithm goes on to determine any additional KB content that appropriately describes each entity. From the representation of the entity in the KB, the algorithm extracts those semantic roles that contribute to its unique identification (as in "the women behind the parapet" when there are multiple women in a scene) and presents the descriptive features that characterize its visual appearance (as in "20 young women"). This double goal of introducing distinguishing and also descriptive features is motivated by our application task of producing descriptions that help the visitor understand and appreciate the details of each artwork.

Once the content has been completely determined, the second referring expression component must then determine potential discourse-level properties (called *discourse references*) that might eventually have linguistic ramifications for each concrete concept, but which are related to the linguistic environment and rather than to lexical information stored directly in the KB. There are four main types of discourse references we have identified in our domain, which are influenced by the fact that the text will be coupled with a visual feedback of what is currently described:

- Visually available: Objects that we can assume the reader is currently looking at (i.e., in their field of view in an image of the artwork included in the report). Thus if we know the reader can see a farming scene in some fresco, we can say "the peasant farmer" instead of "a peasant farmer" because we can assume the reader can identify the particular person we are describing.

- Mentally available: Objects which have not yet been mentioned or are not visible, but which are conceptually very closely related to an already mentioned concept. For example, describing a church building allows us to say "the bells" instead of "bells", because we can assume the reader knows that bells are contained in churches even if they were not explicitly painted on that particular church in the fresco.

- Unique: Objects marked in the KB as being exclusively one value of a finite set. In this case, we can refer to "the top side of the painting", as the fact that it is unique means we cannot say "a top side of the painting" (although this might be different in other languages).

- Generic: Used when making an example out of a generic entity. For instance, "A fresco is painted on a plaster wall while it is still wet." refers to frescos and plaster in general, not to a particular instance the visitor has seen in a museum.

Additionally, this second phase of the referring generator component converts the fact list, now augmented with discourse information, into the input form expected by the following stage: the NSP formalism described in Callaway and Lester (2002a), which is used by the StoryBook low-level generator. This is accomplished by querying the semantic type of the actors, relations, and modifier details in the KB. Depending on the relationship between these elements, different NSPs are chosen and their appropriate arguments filled. The resulting list of NSPs is then given immediately to StoryBook to produce text, along with related global discourse information such as time period, language (English or Italian), and formatting type.

4.3.3   Discourse and Linguistic Processing

StoryBook (Callaway and Lester 2002a) is a dedicated system for creating text from narrative-based representations. Given speech-act-based structures augmented with the linguistic data described in Sect. 3.2, it employs strategies to account for the following linguistically-motivated discourse-level phenomena found in the type of descriptive text needed for report generation:

- Pronominalisation: converting repeated entities in the fact list into pronouns. For instance, in the sentence "The knights put on the knights' armour", the second occurrence of the word *knight* should be replaced by *their*.
- Revision: combining multiple short sentences into a single, longer sentence. For example, "The hunting dogs are chasing the badgers" and "The hunting dogs are from the castle" can be joined together as "The hunting dogs from the castle are chasing the badgers."
- Discourse Markers: indicating the relationship between two units of text. For instance, if the sentences "The bears are searching for food" and "Winter is approaching" are in a causal relationship, we can insert the discourse marker because: "The bears are searching for food because winter is approaching."

Pronominalisation is a pervasive phenomenon in multiparagraph text. Authors routinely and necessarily use pronouns in texts spanning all types of genres in discourse and dialogue. Without pronouns, texts quickly become confusing as readers must pay attention to the incongruous writing style than to the content that makes the text informative or enjoyable. StoryBook uses a Pronominalisation algorithm based on recency, entity distance and sentence distance of the repeated entities from the fact list (Callaway and Lester 2002b). The algorithm has access to detailed information about the underlying discourse structure which is initiated in the text planner and carried through the referring generator, allowing it to achieve a high degree of accuracy. To produce multilingual reports, we also implemented an Italian version of the Pronominalisation algorithm (Novello and Callaway 2003b), which can reproduce pronoun phenomena from Italian, such as zero-pronouns, which are not present in English.

Revision is another strategy for producing more natural prose when generating descriptions from conceptual representations. Because the content in a discourse plan is represented at such a fine level of granularity, the most natural method to convert that content to text results in a large number of very small sentences containing multiple redundancies. This produces a choppy, repetitive writing style that is often annoying to readers. Work in revision (Callaway and Lester 1997; Harvey and Carberry

1998; Shaw 1998) has developed techniques to appropriately combine similar sentences. As for Pronominalisation, access to the entire discourse plan provides a wealth of knowledge that can be used to ensure sentences are combined in an effective way.

Multiparagraph text (such as report generation) is also characterized by the linguistic use of discourse markers at appropriate points in a text (Grote and Stede 1999; Power et al. 1999; Yang et al. 2000; Callaway 2003). Revision involves the syntactic joining of two simple sentences into a more complex sentence by deleting redundant elements. Discourse markers instead link two sentences semantically while not necessarily joining them syntactically, and involve a limited subset of words to specify the relationship between them. These words, called *discourse markers* or *cue words*, mark specific semantic relations between adjacent sentences or small groups of sentences in a text. Typical examples include words like *however*, *then*, and *because*. Discourse markers pose a problem for both the parsing and generation of clauses in a way similar to the problems that referring expressions pose to noun phrases: changing the lexicalization of a discourse marker can change the semantic interpretation of the nearby clauses. The StoryBook system correctly handles both linguistic phenomena, and for both English and Italian.

The final stage is surface realization (Elhadad 1992; Bateman 1995; Lavoie and Rambow 1997; White and Caldwell 1998), which is the process responsible for converting a linguistic (rather than conceptual) representation of a sentence produced by the series of previous components into the actual text seen by the reader. Given the linguistic representation for a particular sentence, the surface realiser checks its validity against a grammar, adds morphological endings to words, and ensures that each phrase and word is produced in the correct order. StoryBook employs the FUF/SURGE surface realiser (Elhadad 1992) which has been extended to generate HTML as well as plain text. This allows the report generator to produce images inline with the text and thus generate Web pages which can be printed out with pictures of the exhibits placed near its textual descriptions as well as similar reports sent by e-mail. An Italian version of FUF/SURGE (Novello and Callaway 2003b) has also been created that allows the report generator to produce reports in Italian when paired with Italian versions of the previous linguistic components.

4.4 Personalization

Personalization in the report generator is driven at all levels by the user history and the interest model. As described in Chap. 6, the user history gathers timing, location, and interaction information throughout the visit. The interest model draws from this data along with the domain KB to infer visitor interests based on their behaviour. The goal of personalization in our domain is to ensure that a report's content is substantially different than reports for other visitors. When possible, this should also be visibly reflected in the images chosen to be included, since noticing variability derived only from the text requires reading two different reports, something that museum visitors are not likely to do as their life experiences have not included previous examples of this new type of technology but rather of reading brochures which are identical for everyone.

While supporting adaptive presentation generation during the visit mainly requires recording interaction events and abstracting and inferring information about user interests, the report generator requires much more detailed information to be able to produce the types of details found in the text than is available in the user history and interest model alone (e.g., details of scenes appearing in paintings, relationships between two frescos or between elements in a fresco and real-world objects, or comments on the current physical state of a fresco). Thus another primary source of personalization is the amount of information available in the KB which can be drawn upon to produce the report. Small KBs offer little chance to gather different details for different visitors as the user history and interest model are both connected to the KB. Well-structured knowledge is also important, as a large number of simplistic or random facts will not improve the quality of the report.

In a large museum, another element of variability is the selection of artworks to include in the report. Because our test domain consisted of only 11 frescos, we were able to simplify this problem by, for instance, deciding to talk extensively about those frescos which the visitor either spent the most time standing in front of or else requested the most information about. In larger museums with multiple categories of artworks or artworks across large ranges of time period or painting method, greater variability can be achieved by choosing which categories to include as well as which artworks fall within each category. For instance, a report mentioning a Roman sword, a modern abstract painting, and a Renaissance marble sculpture will seem significantly different compared to another visitor's report if the second visitor spent most of her time in the Egyptian wing.

The more artefacts and thematic content a museum has, the greater the likelihood that two visitors will choose very different paths.

Given a smaller museum with a more restricted set of artefacts and themes, personalization will be much more easily obtained through the text of the report, and can occur at several different levels: paragraphs, sentences and words, although we have not explored the latter in the PEACH project. To achieve variability at the paragraph level, the text planner queries the user history for the log of the user interactions and initiates inference over this data to obtain the interest model. The first decision is to pick either a sequential, thematic or mixed report style, which strongly impacts variability at the paragraph level. For instance, to sequentially describe what the visitor saw, the text planner extracts from the log the list of visited artworks and accesses the KB to get a shallow description of the main contents of each artwork to be included in the summary as a reminder of what was seen. A refinement strategy chooses the order to present these artworks, such as by viewing duration. Alternatively, the text planner can retrieve a list of ranked topics from the inferred interest model. Thus the corresponding thematic report may consist of a series of paragraphs iteratively describing the top items in the interest model. Additional aids for variability include:

- Perspective (artistic, historical, etc.).
- Knowledge from only within the museum or also external.

At the sentence level, variability is determined by which details from the KB are included, in which order they appear, what sentence types are used, and how those sentences are related to each other. The first two are conceptually determined and derive directly from the interest model, while the latter two are linguistic. For a given topic, there are a number of ways to vary the text for that topic, including:

- Ordering via focus: "At the top, there is a bear and her cubs" vs. "There is a bear and her cubs at the top."
- Sentence type: "There are many knights jousting" vs. "Many knights can be seen jousting."
- Point of view: "The hunters and their hawks are searching for rabbits" vs. "Rabbits are running away from the hunters."

These examples are in addition to a number of means of grammatical and lexical variation such as active vs. passive, or "searching for" vs. "looking for", which do promote variation, but not the type likely to engage museum visitors. Finally, additional variation can be derived by changing the types of revision rules described in Sect. 3.3, which would then combine sentences in different ways for different visitors.

In the end, the greatest amount of variation derives from the interest model itself. The interest model is initialized with an unordered or semiordered list of interests extracted from the KB and each element is annotated with levels of interest such as *very high*. Because the KB is the source of these elements, the list can include both very specific concepts as well as highly abstract concepts. For dynamic presentation generation, all that is needed is a list of concepts and a level of user interest in each and every one of them, so that the user model can respond to queries such as what is the level of interest the user has in some concept X (in addition to queries like whether the user has seen a concept X or did the visitor visit some exhibit X). Such a list is ill-suited for direct processing by a report generator, which needs rhetorical and discourse motivations to produce text. Processing the interests to determine which to include requires a number of basic functions whose parameters include the semiordered topic list, the KB, and fundamental user parameters:

- Filtering: removing or retaining particular interests that satisfy a filter condition, such as all artwork elements containing animals or farm implements.
- Clustering: grouping similar interests under more abstract hierarchies (which may need to be constructed on the fly), such as aristocrats from a set of interests including lords, ladies, and knights, to avoid repetition in the report.
- Sorting: placing a series of interests in some logical order, so that the report does not result in a sense of random order.
- Splitting: separating similar items into groups depending on an external element, such as when they are distributed across adjacent artworks, and especially for incorporating rhetorical effects like comparison and contrast.
- Searching: looking through the KB for items similar to a given interest, which can be used to populate the text with additional details.

Such functions are required for the system to group together the individual concepts in a semantically meaningful way. Such a grouping allows the system to focus on concepts that were the most interesting for the visitor and for later elaborating specific concepts of interest by querying the KB for more details.

The end goal of personalization is to present a generated report that is both visibly and scrutinably different from other examples of reports from the same museum. While this can be concretely realized through variations in the text itself, the choice and placement of images, and the types of dynamic links to the outside world, the most important element for improving visitor fidelisation is through recommendations: suggestions for what activities to do and exhibits to pay more attention to in future visits and suggestions for additional material that can be examined at the visitor's leisure when away from the museum. Having knowledge of characteristics of each visitor is vital to making such suggestions relevant as well as to increasing variability in the text of the report.

4.5 Implementation Methodology

Because report generation and the interest model constituted a large software project, we first created a prototype version of the system to ensure we had the right basic data which we could combine to produce a basic report. As a first step, we added the knowledge required for the background facts of proposed sentences for a report into the KB along with its associated lexical information. We also added other facts that could serve as the raw information for potentially similar sentences about topics that are depicted in the frescos but that were not included in the sample reports we had written, enabling us to add a section at the end of the report containing links to additional information on the Web.

At this point, we created fictitious logs of simulated visitors and simulated inferences over the user model created from the logs in order to test the organizational capabilities of the higher-level text generation system. The first stage was to test sequential report organization by adding text planning rules that could examine the user model and produce paragraphs corresponding to the order that the frescos were visited. Later, we added additional text planning rules that could implement additional ways of ordering sequential paragraphs as well as rules that could examine the interest model and order different types of paragraphs appropriately.

Next, we implemented an interface between the text planner and the StoryBook text generator, allowing the full system to produce actual reports as HTML pages. In addition to solving linguistic problems as described earlier throughout Sect. 3, we were also able at this point to add a method to select images of artworks associated with each paragraph and add them via HTML code produced by the StoryBook generator itself adjacent to the intended text.

The final step was to ensure that the interaction of the user modelling module with the log of visitor interactions with the mobile devices would actually lead to the production of full-page reports with interesting and relevant content. This process involved a significant amount of trial and error to obtain a page's worth of content without going either over-length or significantly under, plus keeping the conclusions of the inferences interesting and nontrivial.

One important issue we noticed during the prototyping phase was that the formatting of the report is contingent on the media in which the report is given. For instance, on a printed page, we assumed we could insert URLs directing the museum visitor to online Web resources as text directly into the report so that visitors could type them in upon arriving at home. However, we discovered that many museums use modern HTML techniques such as pages constructed dynamically from databases and session codes unique to the URL environment, and printing out those URLs could consume up to three lines of text. If the same report is sent as an e-mail message to the visitor, however, then such details can be hidden. This necessitates taking into account the modality of the report prior to the surface realization phase. Email also permits the use of video and Flash animations, which would be impossible in the printed version of a report.

4.5.1   Report Generation Walk-Through

In a typical scenario, a visitor to the Torre Aquila wanders around the exhibit space with the mobile information presentation device described in Chap. 1, requesting presentations when she is curious about the frescos. When finished, she returns the mobile device to the museum desk, while the system calculates the interest model from the user history and proceeds to print out a custom report that is then handed to her as she leaves. If she has supplied an e-mail address, the electronic version of the report is also mailed to her.

At the point where she returns the mobile device, the report generator first builds the interest model representing the visitor's interest in the different visual elements of each artwork. In our case, these consist of various scenes in narrative frescoes and the more abstract interests. For example, from the fact that the user enjoyed the hunting scene of January fresco and the tournament of February fresco, it might be inferred that the visitor is interested in winter aristocratic leisure activities. Low interest in collocated activities involving peasants, for instance, would also help infer the same thing. The text planner clusters the interests to produce abstract topics such as "aristocratic activities" (in case they were not already directly discovered by the user model) rather than "knights" and "ladies" individually. If well-defined clusters of interests can be created, the text planner then chooses a thematic report centred on the top clusters in the list. Otherwise, the system chooses a sequential report that describes what the visitor saw in order, pulling details from the interest model. In either case, variation in the report text is ensured at the organizational level, depending on the visitor's path through the museum and their requests for further details. The text planner relies on its GSPs to structure visit reports, extract from the interest model the list of visited frescoes, and access the KB to get a shallow description of the main contents of each artwork to be included in the summary as a reminder of what was seen.

The example report (Fig. 1) presents a full-page report for a mixed thematic and sequential summary report from a museum visit. The title and first paragraph are standard text strings to introduce the report. The following two paragraphs are sequential in nature, describing two frescos the visitor liked in the sequence in which they were visited. It is impossible to tell from this report whether the visitor had seen another fresco before these two, but if so, she did not find it interesting. These two paragraphs summarize the most interesting topics from the point of view of "winter leisure activities" as inferred by the system. The description corresponds to a visitor who started at the January fresco that included scenes of a castle, a snowball fight, and hunters in the snow. She requested a follow-up presentation describing the snowball fight, followed by more detailed presentations of its participants and later about the hunting scene and one of its hunters. Later, she moved to the February fresco, where she saw an overview about a tournament with knights along with a blacksmith working in his shop. She requested a large number of additional detailed presentations, one about a specific knight taking part in the tournament, another about the blacksmith, and a third about the servants helping the knights put on their armour. The presentation on the blacksmith was halted, presumably indicating a lack of interest in the various themes with which it is associated. The enormous amount of interest in February causes the report to then include an additional paragraph about the themes it contains.

From there the visitor proceeded to various other frescos before stopping at November, where again she showed great interest. The KB entries describing the November fresco contain links between the daily activities of medieval life and those of today, and due to mixed interest in the November fresco (i.e., overall great interest, but no single topic more interesting than others), the report generator instead includes Web links to local festivals (indicated in blue) which, in the case where the report is emailed, can take the visitor directly on their browser to information about those festivals from the local tourist board. Finally, the system takes the most interesting item over the entire visit and recommends similar themes in the Trentino region (places to see art representing knights and tournaments) and castles where such frescos might be located. The printed version of the report is then handed to the visitor as he or she leaves the museum.

Visit to the Buonconsiglio Museum

For Joan Smith, Tuesday, February 24, 2004

  This report is a summary of your visit to the **Buonconsiglio Museum**. Your visit was dedicated to the Cycle of Months in the Torre Aquila.

When you entered you first looked at a **fresco** which represents the month of January. The main theme of this fresco is a snowball fight in the foreground between two aristocratic groups wearing colorful robes. The whole scene is set in a snow-covered landscape, the first such representation of this type in the history of Western painting.

 Then you moved to the fresco which represents the month of February. The main theme of this fresco is a tournament. Four **knights** are jousting against four other knights below the curtain walls. About twenty young ladies are watching from atop the castle walls. Squires are running between the horses collecting broken weapons.

The choice of a tournament for the month of February is related to jousts and revelries that took place in Carnival time. You seemed very interested in this fresco and asked for additional information about **aristocracy**. Only the nobility and landholders were allowed to become knights and thus participate in jousts.

 You also seemed to greatly enjoy the fresco which represents the month of November. Here the main themes are the varied Autumn activities. For instance, swineherds are driving pigs through the town gates to market, and hunters are busily looking for bears. **Trento** is host to many autumn events, such as the **Polenta Festival**, and many nearby towns have **Wine Festivals**.

For further information about knights and tournaments see:

 The frescos of knights at the **Castello Rodengo**

 Battle scenes at the **Castello Avio**

Other castles in the Trentino region like the Buonconsiglio:

Castello Beseno   **Castello Madruzzo**   **Castel Ivano**

Fig. 1. Example report

Part II
Infrastructure and User Modelling

5 Delivering Services in Active Museums via Group Communication

P. Busetta, P. Bresciani, L. Penserini, S. Rossi, T. Kuflik, A. Albertini
and A. Cappelletti

5.1 Motivations

Active environments have some characteristics that make them substantially different from traditional computing and human–computer interfaces. For instance, multiple users may be in a single place, interacting with different applications simultaneously. The set of users changes dynamically over time. Users are unaware (and uninterested in the fact) that the environment is formed by many physically and logically distributed components. Therefore, they interact with the environment as if it was a single, monolithic system. They expect it to take note of choices, preferences, and events concerning their presence. They expect it to adapt to them silently, in other words, to be "context aware". However, services are provided to users by set of variable components that join and leave the environment (e.g., on mobile devices or on stationary objects that may be busy or not working) or that may even be running on some remote, back-end computer. Services provided by these components sometimes overlap (e.g., there may be multiple data sources, or different devices for delivering information); therefore, they need to coordinate in order to decide. An example is deciding, for instance, which component will look after a specific service request and how. These considerations lead to a *multiagent system* (MAS) (Wooldridge 2002) approach to the development of active environments.

PEACH aimed at creating an interactive museum where users are provided with personalized information about exhibits through a variety of information sources of different media types and delivered by several available clients. Visitor position and resource availability may impose constraints on the generation and display of information. Information, sources, and agents change rapidly over time as visitors move around. In the background, user modelling agents should silently record histories of visitor interactions and build profiles by observing their behaviour with the goal of customizing presentations. Furthermore, future extensions of PEACH to consider might include services oriented towards groups of museum visitors (Chapter 13).

The requisites outlined above imply intensive communication among the agents collaborating to provide services. At present such services are not well catered to by current communication architectures and service composition techniques. These are commonly based on a pattern of service discovery, selection of a specific provider, and direct, point-to-point communication between client and server. (This is typical of Web services, for instance.) Publish/subscribe services partially alleviate the inflexibility inherent in this approach by making communication indirect and allowing multiple, anonymous receivers. Our objective is to support a highly distributed and dynamic environment whose main functionality is known, but where the number and capabilities of service-providing agents continuously varies. Moreover, we want services to be context-aware, in the sense mentioned above. Context awareness is considered a key feature of applications for active environments. Most existing works define "context" as a continuously updated collection of data that is neutral with respect to the agents acting in the environment. Thus, it can be represented in some form of shared knowledge base. By contrast, we view context as a specific perspective of each agent on its environment, which is thus largely dependent on its design goals and execution history. What is needed is a way for agents to systematically perceive whatever happens in their surroundings. In other words, they must be able to "overhear" events and interactions and process them to extract data useful for their purposes.

Our approach relies on the ability to *send* messages to *roles* within a team of service-providing agents rather than to its individual components, and to *overhear* conversations happening among any components within the system. This allows us to aggregate service-providing agents into *implicit organizations*, i.e., subteams that do not require an explicit formation phase nor brokers or middleagents for their functioning, and that continuously renegotiate how to coordinate as the situation evolves. To this end, we adopt a form of group communication that we call *channelled multicast*; this is basically a form of unrestricted broadcast on thematic channels, where messages are addressed to their intended destinations, but are received by all listeners. Our approach enables context-sensitive behaviour to be built into objects embedded in the environment, freeing high-level applications (concerned, for instance, with supporting knowledge sharing within a group) from issues concerning service composition and delivery in a specific environment. Channelled multicast does not impose any technological constraint; our implementation is in Java and C#, but the underlying communication infrastructure is based on standard technology (TCP/IP and XML).

We have elaborated our experience with implicit organizations into a *design pattern* for active environments. This pattern tackles some limitations shown by traditional patterns for group collaboration in multiagent systems when context-awareness is required or groups change very dynamically. Indeed, we eliminated middle agents (e.g., *matchmakers* and *brokers*), simplifying the application logic and moving context-specific decision-making from high-level applications and middle agents down to the agents called to achieve a goal. The resulting pattern allows for dynamic and collective schemata (Bresciani et al. 2004a; Penserini et al. 2005), as well as collaborative reconfiguration of service provisioning.

In this chapter, we do not elaborate on how agents can be context-aware via overhearing in general nor on the technology that can be applied since this would far exceed the scope of this work. (An example, based on an ontology-based filter able to elaborate XML messages of any type, can be found in Aiello et al. (2001)). Rather, we mostly focus on communication aspects, and in particular on the management protocols of implicit organizations; these are designed such that, by means of overhearing, awareness of the state of the organizations is straightforward.

The rest of this chapter is organized as follows. We first provide a short background and the state of the art concerning group communication in multiagent systems. We then introduce our group communication infrastructure. We briefly present a logic formalization that accompanied this work. We discuss the internal workings of implicit organizations. Finally, we show how the infrastructure supporting implicit organizations should be used for application development by introducing a design pattern, a few examples, and briefly presenting the Buonconsiglio Castle software architecture.

5.2   Group Communication in Multiagent Systems: the State of the Art

Group communication, in traditional distributed systems, is available at different levels of abstraction, from low-level networking, where IP multicast (a group extension of UDP/IP) is very popular and widely used, to event-driven enterprise buses based on XML and publish/subscribe systems, e.g., WS-Notification in the Web services world. By contrast, the major agent communication languages have either no provision or no well-defined semantics for group communication. For instance, in the Foundation for Intelligent Physical Agents (FIPA) agent communication language (ACL) (FIPA 2002), the only way to inform a set of agents is to inform them individually, one at a time.

The reason for this limitation is that standard theories of speech acts (Searle 1969) require that the speaker knows to whom he is addressing his illocutionary act. Consequently, there is no way to send messages to unknown agents. Thus, one of the problems with standard theories of communicative acts is that when a conversation involves more than two parties, there can be the case in which one person can "speak to" the others without knowing which of them he is addressing (Clark and Carlson 1982). For instance, the sentence: *Authorized personnel only*, is addressed to whoever reads the message, from who ever wrote the message (some authorized role), and the intended actors of the sentence are a subset of intended addressees. Addressing an utterance to more than one recipient is more than a convenient way to refer to many people simultaneously. There are also many occasions in which there is an explicit address of an utterance but the goal of our sentence is to inform other people of what we are saying. This is the case of television or newspaper communication, for example, where, while we can address the speech to a specific person—for example, the editor of the journal—we are communicating with all the readers or listeners.

Initial work towards semantics for group communication with agents was provided by Kumar et al. (2000). As they state, an agent communication language should be able to properly convey these nuances of requester intentions about the performers of an action. Artificial agents should be able to communicate with groups as well as individuals, where group communication is not only intended as the possibility to address messages to many addresses, but also as the possibility to address messages to groups without knowing who the potential recipients are. A typical scenario is broadcast communication, but current mainstream agent communication languages lack adequate support for broadcasting. Publish/subscribe services move in that direction, but imply the presence of specialized middleware, require additional operations such as registration to a server, and are typically implemented as pairwise communication (event producer to server, server to each event consumer), thus partially missing the advantages of specialized group communication protocols.

One of the consequences of this situation is that coordinated behaviour by a group of agents, e.g., to react to a request for service, is typically obtained by means of "middle agents", such as brokers and matchmakers (Klusch and Sycara 2001; Sycara et al. 2002), which introduces dependencies and single points of failure.

5.3   Channelled Multicast and LoudVoice

We propose a form of group communication, called channelled multicast (Busetta et al. 2002), as the main technique for agent coordination in *active museums* (Kuflik et al. 2004) and other smart environments. Channels are identified by their *theme*, i.e., an expression in some application-specific language which defines an interest group, and are reminiscent of chat rooms in that messages sent on a channel are received by all agents tuned to it. Channelled multicast often reduces the amount of communication needed when more than two agents are involved in a task, and allows overhearing (i.e., the ability to listen to messages addressed to others). Overhearing, in turn, enables the collection of contextual information (e.g., (Aiello et al. 2001)), proactive assistance (Busetta et al. 2001), monitoring (Kaminka et al. 2002), and even partial recovery of message losses in specific situations (Rossi and Busetta 2004).

We implemented LoudVoice, a channelled multicast library in Java and C#, within our experimental communication infrastructure. LoudVoice uses IP multicast, which is fast but inherently unreliable. This limitation does not worsen problems in active museums, since the communication media in use (which include wireless links to mobile devices) are unreliable by their own nature. Indeed, we had to deal with message loss and temporary network partitions in real time by carefully crafting application-level protocols and using time-based mechanisms to ensure consistency of mutual beliefs within organizations.

Messages in LoudVoice are encoded in XML, and thus can be manipulated in any language. LoudVoice allows senders to address messages either to specific agents or to *roles*, i.e., to all agents that at the time of delivery offer a certain service on a channel. For instance, messages exchanged during an auction are sent to the *bidder* or to the *auctioneer*, without ever explicitly mentioning which agents are currently playing either role. Of course, an agent may play more than one role, simultaneously or at different times, depending on its capabilities and the context.

Our approach to active museums exploits role-based communication by modelling individual components of an environment (hardware such as sensors and actuators, as well as software such as groupware applications) as *organizations* of agents, and having them communicating via Loud-Voice rather than using point-to-point connections.

An agent can discover what channels exist in its current environment, "tune" to as many as it pleases, and listen to all messages exchanged on them, no matter their destination. It is left to the receivers (that is, everybody tuned on a specific LoudVoice channel) to decide whether a message is intended for them at the time and in the context of reception; some filtering functions are provided by LoudVoice to simplify this task. An appropriate definition of topics and arguments for conversation headers and communication channels simplifies the problem of addressing the correct audience. In particular, the current channel discovery mechanisms within Loudvoice supports matching with respect to taxonomies of topics.

Thanks to this approach, we solved the problem of service discovery in highly dynamic environments where services can be provided by more than one agent in a way quite different from the common lookup/bind logic of service-oriented environments. First, clients need to discover channels rather than specific service providers; second, it is left to the implicit organization of service providers to decide, by means of the protocols described later, who responds and how to a specific request at the time and in the context the request is issued.

5.4   Modelling Group Communication

Given an infrastructure for group communication, such as channelled multicast and LoudVoice, we needed a way to model interactions to be able to reason on the semantics of messages and the properties of protocols. As mentioned in the state of the art, an appropriate formalization was still lacking at the time our work began since most of the related research still focused on modelling multiparty communication as conversations between two parties at a time. In this section, we provide a short overview of the research that was performed within PEACH on logic for group communications that we used to model implicit organizations. The reader can skip this section if not interested, since we avoided logic formulas in the rest of this chapter.

To formalize group interactions on channelled multicast, we started from the work of Kumar et al. (Kumar et al. 2000), which modelled group "REQUEST" communicative acts based on an attempt-based semantics of communicative acts (Cohen and Levesque 1990). According to them, it is possible to define a semantics for group communicative acts that takes into account the problem that potential recipients of a message can be unknown (making it possible to address messages to roles), and that the semantics has to include potential overhearers and third parties that can be indirectly involved in a conversation (enabling a formal specification of overhearing).

The work of Kumar is based on the Joint Intention Theory (JIT) (Cohen and Levesque 1991). JIT is expressed in a modal language with the usual

connectives of a first-order logic with equality and operators for proposi-
tional attitudes and event sequences. Joint action by a team does not consist merely of simultaneous and coordinated individual actions; to act
together, a team must be aware of, and care about, the status of the group
effort as a whole (Cohen and Levesque 1990). In the JIT model, agents
perform teamwork when they have a *joint intention* towards an action,
which means that there is a joint commitment to achieve its expected
effects and that the agents share mutual beliefs concerning the joint action
itself (e.g., that the action is starting, has been completed, has become
impossible to perform, or is irrelevant with respect to the joint commitment). In other words, the key property that distinguishes joint or collaborative action from coordinated action is the joint mental state of the
participants. In order to prevent teamwork breakdowns that may be caused
by belief divergence in individual agents, joint commitments extend individual commitments to include an additional concept, namely the weak
achievement goal, to ensure that a mutual belief about the team goal is
believed by all team members. A very important element of this formulation is that it provides criteria with which team members can evaluate their
ongoing problem solving activity or coordination activity. The reason behind robust behaviour exhibited by teams is that the members of a team are
committed not only to the success of their portion of the joint action, but
also to the success of the team as a whole. A team will try to recover from
problems and will abandon the joint goal only when it is mutually believed
by team members that the goal is no longer possible. Moreover, when an
agent comes to believe privately that the joint act is untenable (or completed) it must ensure that all its fellow team members are made aware of
this fact. These specifications ensure there is a clear path which is necessary and which defines how the agent should behave in both normal and
unanticipated circumstances. At the least, multiagent conversation can be
described by joint action expressions. Such joint actions are actions that
the agents perform while in the state of having a joint intention.

We have provided an extension of the JIT formulas that takes into account the notion of group within the logic. Details of such extensions can
be found in (Busetta et al. 2003; Rossi et al. 2005; Rossi 2006). In (Rossi
2006), we extended the defeasible rules for communication presented by
Kumar and collegues in (Kumar et al. 2002b), and we added some new
ones to be able to reason about the concept of *intended recipients* of an
utterance, but also about *third parties* that may be, voluntarily or not,
involved in the communication. In particular, in the definition of group
communicative acts, we introduced the possibility of a *referential* or *attributive* way of addressing groups. With the attributive way of referring to
groups, it is possible to define a semantics for group communicative acts

which deals with the problem that potential recipients of a message can be unknown (making it possible to address messages to roles).

5.5   Implicit Organizations

We call *implicit organization* a set of agents that play the *same* role on a given channel who are willing to coordinate their actions for service delivery. The word "implicit" highlights the fact that there is no need for a group formation phase (joining an organization is just a matter of tuning to a channel), and no name for it: the role and the channel uniquely identify the group. We adopt the term "organization" from (Tidhar 1999) to refer to teams where explicit *command, control*, and *communication* (C3) relationships are established among subteams about goals, courses of action, and ongoing information concerning organization activity. Note that we do not make any assumption about the sophistication of agents, e.g., their inferential capabilities. The only requirement is that an agent be able to coordinate with others by following common syntax and protocols, as described below.

For implicit organizations, the main *command* relationship is straightforward since goals are established by external agents whenever they send a service request to the role of the organization. By contrast, *control* and related *communication* are internal matters which we discuss in Sect. 5.6.2.

Implicit organizations are formed by agents that can all support the same role; however, they may do it in different ways. Traditionally, this situation is managed by putting a broker or some other form of middle agent. By contrast, our objective is to explore advantages and disadvantages of an approach based on unreliable group communication, and moreover, in a situation where agents can come and go fairly quickly, their capabilities change or evolve over time, and where it is not necessarily known a priori which agent can achieve a specific goal without first trying it out. For instance, in our museum setting, a "Presentation Composer" role on a channel concerning "presentations" can be played by many agents, which may be added or removed on-the-fly, depending on the number of simultaneous users and the availability of local or remote knowledge bases. These agents usually have different specializations (e.g., different contents and schema of their knowledge bases), but they may also be redundant in order to allow prompt reaction to simultaneous requests.

In the rest of this section, we show how implicit organizations automatically decide their own control policy at run-time, discuss how they provide a service when a request arrives, and present a few basic coordination policies that are in use within our active museums. A formalization, using the logic mentioned in the previous section, can be found in Busetta et al. (2003).

5.5.1   Establishing How to Coordinate

An implicit organization is in charge of defining its own "control policy": (1) how a subteam is formed within the organization in order to achieve a specific goal, that is, who must react to a service request sent on the organization's channel; and, (2) how this subteam pursues its goal, that is, how its members coordinate to serve the request. This control policy can change over time, depending on the number of users, the capabilities of the agents in the organization, the current workload, user preferences, feedback from a profiling tool or network manager, and so on. Thus, establishing the "right" control policy for serving a request at a given time is the main mechanism by which an organization as a whole shows context-aware behaviour. Driven by the requirements of our application domain (the active museum), we have made some specific design choices concerning the control policy which are formalized in (Busetta et al. 2003) by means of the JIT (Cohen and Levesque 1991) and the landmark-based diagrams derived from it (Kumar et al. 2002a).

As mentioned above, part of the control policy is deciding how a subteam pursues its goals. This is decided beforehand. The organization establishes a *coordination policy*, which is applied by subteams to decide who actually works towards achieving goals and how to coordinate if more than one agent is involved in goal achievement. To this end, whenever a new agent joins an environment, a protocol is run on a dedicated *control channel* to negotiate the coordination policy of the organization the agent wants to be part of. The same happens when an agent leaves, or whenever somebody detects an inconsistency (due, for instance, to network partitioning or agent crashes, or simply to changes in the environment). This allows each member to propose the coordination techniques (chosen within a set known to the agent) and the related parameters it deems most appropriate to the current context and to its own capabilities. Here, we do not discuss how each agent elaborates its proposals, but it is worth stressing that this may have a significant impact on the context-awareness and overall effectiveness shown by the system. The negotiation, also formalized and described in detail in Busetta et al. (2003), was designed to work as efficiently as possible. The protocol was designed to allow an external entity (such as a network administration tool) to participate and influence its results.

In summary, the negotiation protocol works in two phases: first, the set of *policy instances* common to all agents is computed; then, one is selected. A policy instance is, conceptually, a tuple with the name of a policy (chosen within a vocabulary defined by an application designer) and ground values for all its parameters. For example, <*auction, Euro*> represents an "auction" policy whose first parameter (presumably the currency) is "Euro". A potential issue is that an agent may support a very large (even infinite) or undetermined number of policy instances. This happens, for instance, when a parameter may take any integer value, or has to be set to the name of one of the agents of the organization. To this end, we have designed a language for expressing sets of policy instances in a compact way by means of constraints on parameters and preferences. For instance, *"param = BidTimeout constraint = (in 100..2000) suggested = (1000)"* means that the BidTimeout parameter can take any value within the range of 100 to 2000, and the preferred value is 1000.

In the first step of the protocol, triggered by a query message concerning the organization's policy by any agent, a mutual belief about the policy instances common to the entire organization is established. This is done by having each agent repeatedly notifying (by means of an informational message addressed to the role and sent on the control channel) the intersection of the policy instances it supports with those already notified by others. These messages should be repeated until a fixpoint is reached, i.e., everybody agrees on the policy instances supported by the group; two parameters, concerning the maximum number and period of repetitions, avoid going on forever. In the second step of the protocol, an agent called the *oracle* picks the policy instance to be selected as coordination policy for the organization. The oracle can be anybody, a member of the organization as well as an external agent (the latter can overhear the negotiation protocol, thus it knows the common policies). A very simple default mechanism selects an oracle if none appears within a short time: it is the agent of the organization with the lowest agent identifier.[1] The oracle can apply whatever decision criteria it deems more appropriate: from a random choice, to a configuration rule, to inferring on previous policies based on machine learning, and so on. Its decision is communicated to the organization with an informational message on the control channel.

In addition to the parameters mentioned above, a couple of other simple mechanisms (a sequence number and a periodic reminder) prevent the negotiation from being continually restarted, or inconsistencies from going

---

[1] Note that agents get to know who else is part of the organization during the first part of the negotiation, simply because every message contains the identifier of its sender.

undetected because of communication and timing issues (message loss, network partitioning, agents joining during a negotiations, multiple oracles, etc.). In our experiments on a wired LAN, we were able to tune the parameters in such a way that some 20 agents reliably negotiate an organization policy in less than 2 seconds; in a loss-prone wireless environment, this time goes up to around 3 seconds.

5.5.2   Providing Services

Once that the coordination policy has been established, the organization is ready to serve requests from its clients. Group communication and overhearing are exploited to avoid an explicit subteam formation phase and to minimize internal communications.

A client sends its request to the role of the organization over the appropriate channel. At this time, not all agents of the organization may be available to work on this request because they are busy or unable to handle on the specific request and so on. A subteam then needs to be established, composed by only those members of the organization that are available to service the request. Its goal is to satisfy the request of the client. Rather than running an ad hoc protocol to determine who is part of this goal-specific subteam, we exploit the fact that, thanks to group communication, there is no real need for each agent of the subteam to know who the others are. Indeed, all the messages are addressed to roles, and it is a matter for their receivers to decide whether they are relevant or not. Thus, by convention, the subteam serving a specific goal is silently established by enrolling all agents of the organization that—at the time the request message is received—are immediately available to serve it. The coordination policy of the organization is now applied to coordinate the work of the members of the subteam and to decide who responds to the client when the request has been serviced. As in the case of policy negotiation, internal coordination is performed on a dedicated control channel different from the application channel where clients request services to the organization.

In reality, the interactions between clients and implicit organizations are a bit more complicated than it may look from above because of the unreliability of the communication channels and the dynamicity of the organizations themselves. Figure 1 is a finite state machine that captures, with some simplifications, the possible evolutions of the protocol between a client and an organization. The events on the top half represent the normal case: no message loss and a goal-specific subteam achieves the goal. The events in brackets on the lower half represent degraded situations.

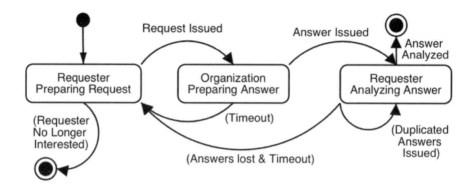

Fig. 1. Interaction between client and implicit organization

Consider, for instance, the cases where a request or its answer is lost, or no goal-specific subteam can be formed. A timeout forces the client to reconsider whether its request is still relevant—e.g., the user's context has not changed—and, if so, whether to resend the original message. It follows that an implicit organization must be able to deal with message repetitions. This implies that agents should discard repeated messages or reissue any answer already sent; also, the coordination policies should contain mechanisms that prevent confusion in the cases of partial deliveries or new agents joining the organization between two repetitions.

Similarly, a client has to deal with repeated answers, possibly caused by its own repeated requests. In the worse case, these repeated answers may even be different because something has changed in the environment, a new agent has joined the organization, and so on. Rather than introducing middleagents or making the organizational coordination protocols overly complicated to prevent this from happening (which is likely to be impossible to achieve anyway, according to Halpern and Moses (1990), our current choice is to have the requester consider whatever answer it receives first as the valid one, and ignore all others.

Of course, the protocol mentioned above can only be used in applications that are not safety-critical or in situations where some degree of uncertainty can be tolerated. This is definitely the case of an active museum, where communications quality is fairly high and the objective is nothing more critical than providing some guidance and context-sensitive cultural information to visitors of museums. Partial solutions to communication problems may be offered by overhearing on a channel (Rossi and Busetta 2004), making the interaction with implicit organizations much more robust, e.g., by detecting message loss, or by identifying whether a goal-specific subteam has been established.

5.5.3   Basic Coordination Policies

Four general-purpose coordination policies which exploit overhearing for their functioning have been formalized so far (see Busetta et al. 2003); we will show some examples of their use in the next section. Many other variants and alternatives can be designed to meet different requirements, such as quality of service objectives, efficiency, and so on. All policies have to follow a straightforward, abstract three-phase schema, summarized in the figure below. Before doing anything, the subteam coordinates to form a joint intention on how to achieve the goal (*Prework Coordination*). The agents in charge perform whatever action is required, including any necessary ongoing coordination (*Working*). When everybody finally finishes, a *Postwork Coordination* phase collects results and replies to the requester (which corresponds to the *Answer Issued* event of the previous figure).

Fig. 2. Abstract policy state machine

The *Plain Competition* policy is nothing more than "everybody races against everybody else, and the first to finish wins". It is by far the easiest policy of all: no prework nor postwork coordination is required, while the ongoing coordination consists in overhearing the reply sent by who ever finishes first. In summary, *Plain Competition* works as follows: when a role receives a request, any agent able to react starts working on the job immediately. When an agent finishes, it sends back its results. The other agents overhear this answer and stop working on that job.

A race condition is possible: two or more agents finish at the same time and send their answers. This is not a problem, as explained in the previous section, since the requester accepts whatever answer comes first and ignores the others.

The *Simple Collaboration* policy consists of a collaboration among all participants for synthesizing a common answer from the results obtained by each agent independently. This policy does not require any prework co-ordination; the ongoing coordination consists in declaring the results achieved, or what work is still ongoing. Finally, postwork coordination consists in having one agent (the first to finish) collect answers from everybody else and send a synthesis to the requester.

Simple Collaboration works as follows. As in *Plain Competition*, all agents able to react start working on the job as soon as the request is received. The first agent that finishes advertises his results with a message to the role, and moves to the postwork phase. Within a short timeout (a parameter negotiated with the policy, usually around half a second), any other members of the subteam must react either by sending to the role its own results or by stating that it is still working, eventually followed by the result when done. The first agent collects all these messages and synthesizes the common result in a goal-dependent way. Let us stress that, to support this policy, an agent must have the capabilities both to achieve the requested goal, and to synthesize the results.

As in the previous case, a race condition is possible among agents finishing at the same time, such that more than one may be collecting the same results. As mentioned above, multiple answers are not a problem for the requester, and generally imply a minor waste of computational resources because of the synthesis by multiple agents.

The *Multicast Contract Net* policy is a simplification of the well-known Contract Net protocol (Smith 1980) where the Manager is the agent sending a request to a role, and the award is determined by the bidder themselves, since everybody knows everybody else's bid. Thus, effectively this policy contemplates coordination only in the prework phase, while neither ongoing nor postwork are required. This policy has three parameters: the winning criteria (lowest or highest bid), a currency for the bid (which can be any string), and a timeout within which bids must be sent.

Multicast Contract Net works as follows. As soon as a request arrives at the role, all participating agents send their bid to the role. Since everybody receives everybody else's offer, each agent can easily compute which one is the winner. At the expiration of the timeout for the bid, the winning agent declares its victory to the role, repeating its successful bid, and starts working.

Some degraded cases must be handled. The first happens when two or more agents send the same winning bid; to solve this issue, as in the policy negotiation protocol, we arbitrarily chose a heuristic, which consists in taking as winner the agent with the lowest communication identifier. The second case happens because of a race condition when the timeout for the bid expires, or because of the loss of messages; as a consequence, it may happen that two or more agents believe they are winners. This is solved by an additional, very short wait after declaring victory, during which each agent believing to be the winner listens for contradictory declarations from others.

In spite of these precautions, it may happen that two or more agents believe themselves to be the winners and attempt to achieve the goal independently. The winner declaration mechanism, however, reduces its probability to the square of the probability of losing a single message, since at least two consecutive messages (the bid from the real winner and its victory declaration) must be lost by the others.

The *Master–Slave* policy has many similarities with the Multicast Contract Net. The essential difference is that, in place of a bidding phase, a master decides which agent is delegated to achieve a goal. The master is elected by the policy negotiation protocol by being handled as one of the policy parameters. Typically, agents that support this policy either propose themselves as masters, or accept any other agent, but refuse to be master themselves; this is because the master must react to all requests in order to select a slave delegated to achieve a goal, and must have an appropriate selection logic.

Master–Slave works as follows. When a request arrives, all agents willing to work send a message to the role declaring their availability. The master (which may or may not be among those available to work) collects all declarations, and issues a message to the role nominating the slave, which acknowledges by repeating the same message. Message loss is recovered by the master, handling a simple timeout between its nomination and the reply, and repeating the nomination if necessary. Thus, it is not possible for two agents to believe they are slaves for the same request.

5.6 Designing and Developing Implicit Organizations

The management protocols for the implicit organizations described above were packaged as a layer on top of our communication infrastructure, LoudVoice; a Java API and its computational model were made available to software developers. From the perspective of an application developer, using implicit organizations then becomes a matter of adding a few steps to a standard software engineering process:

1. Designing (or redefining) the system architecture in terms of roles providing services to each other and channels on which they interact.
2. Defining the interaction scenarios among these roles, in terms of use cases and protocols.

3. Defining which agents may fulfill a certain role in each scenario, and what is the best coordination policy to be applied by the corresponding implicit organization, i.e., how the agents cooperate or compete to provide the service.
4. Identifying how the agents keep their context updated by overhearing certain interactions on certain channels.
5. Writing the application logic within the agent so that the organization management layer knows which policy instances are supported, automatically deals with negotiations and coordination, and calls the application code when appropriate to perform the service.

In the following, we provide a *design pattern* for implicit organizations, introduce a graphical notation for representing interaction scenarios, discuss a simple (but not straightforward) example of implicit organizations, present a few more examples, and briefly introduce a use case for the Buonconsiglio Castle visitor guide.

5.6.1   Microlevel Architectural Design for Service-Providing Teams

A common software engineering technique for handling the design of complex systems is to reuse development experience and know-how expressed as *architectural styles* and *design patterns* (Gamma et al. 1995; Shaw and Garlan 1996) during the so-called "macro" and "microlevel" architectural design phases, respectively (Tahara et al. 1999). In particular, design patterns describe problems commonly found in software designs and prescribe adaptable solutions for them—at the architectural as well as at the detailed design and implementation levels—easing the reuse of these solutions. In our design patterns for multiagent systems, we adopt a metaphor inspired by research on cooperative and distributed real-world social structures, the so-called *social patterns*, exploited by the *Tropos* methodology and its graphical notation (Castro et al. 2002; Bresciani et al. 2004b; Kolp et al. 2001).

This section briefly sketches a novel microlevel architecture—elaborated on the PEACH experience—that allows for dynamic and collective schemata (Bresciani et al. 2004a; Penserini et al. 2005), as well as collaborative reconfiguration of service provisioning. This pattern should be applied whenever a service should be provided by multiple, co-located agents with different characteristics but aware of the context of the requests they receive.

To describe our approach, we need to introduce the notion of *service-oriented organization* (SOO). We define an SOO as a set of autonomous software agents that—at a given location at a given time—coordinate in order to provide a service. In other words, an SOO is a team of agents whose goal is to deliver a service to its clients. Examples of SOOs are not restricted to Web services and ambient intelligence; for instance, they include *virtual enterprises* or *organizations* (Franke 2001; Penserini et al. 2004) in e-Business.

SOOs can be implemented in a variety of ways. Typical group collaboration patterns in agent systems are based on some of mediators (or "middleagents"). These patterns allow for intentional relationships and request/response communication protocols among individual agents only, and not among groups (Klusch and Sycara 2001; Kolp et al. 2001; Tahara et al. 1999). Moreover, they adopt a centralized or semicentralized approach; as discussed below, some of the dependencies of these patterns force the system actors to rely on the mediator (matchmaker or broker) to keep an up-to-date picture of the situation. This may be hard to manage in real time, introducing single points of failure, and anyhow it does not care for the evolution of the context once requests have been allocated to specific providers. Similar problems arise when trying to implement SOOs with direct agent-to-agent communication (e.g., peer-to-peer) and request/response-based communication styles such as those presented in Sycara et al. (2002). To overcome these issues, we foresee agents exploiting some forms of groupwide "implicit communication", which simplifies the maintenance of a shared view of the context and allows dynamic decisions on how to best satisfy a request even as a situation evolves.

For example, the figure below shows two important design patterns, which are described by means of Tropos actor diagrams. Both the patterns satisfy the need for mediation between a consumer and (one or more) providers. Figure 3a shows a *matchmaker* pattern. Here, the actor *Matchmaker* searches for *Providers* that can match the requested service (*provide service description*). This is done on the basis of the capabilities advertised by the providers themselves, e.g., by means of a subscription phase that carries out both the service description and the service provider information. Then *Consumer* itself will directly interact with *Provider*(s) to obtain the needed service. That is, in terms of Tropos dependencies (as shown in Fig. 3a, the *Consumer* depends on the *Matchmaker* to *locate good provider*, and on the *Provider* to *provide service*. The *Matchmaker* depends on the *Provider* to *advertise service*. Similarly, the *advertise service* dependency is present also in the *Broker* pattern (Fig. 3b). Here the dependency to *provide service* is on *Provider* from *Broker*, since *Consumer* depends on the latter to have the requested service delivered (*forward requested service*). That is, *Broker* plays an intermediary role between *Provider* and *Consumer*.

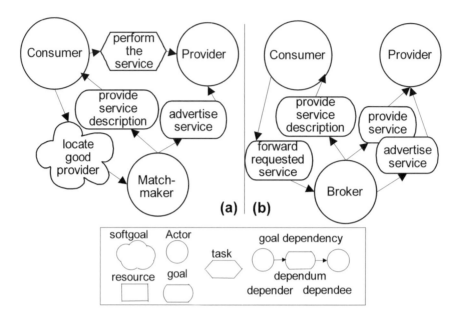

Fig. 3. Matchmaker *(a)* and broker *(b)* patterns (Tropos goal diagram)

Both of these well-known patterns can be adopted to accommodate architectural needs deriving from a service-oriented computing (SOC) application scenario since both allow for the discovery of service providers in a dynamically changing environment without requiring awareness of them to be defined at design time. However, they do not address some of our requirements for SOOs in active environments (like PEACH). In particular, they do not have:

1. *Group-based communication* to overcome rigid agent-to-agent interaction schemata, enabling overhearing and thus context awareness.
2. *Dynamic service reconfiguration* such as load balancing, fault tolerance, and support for user and device mobility.
3. *Reduction of system–consumer interactions* that avoid discovery and binding phases which could be replaced by context-awareness.
4. *Flexibility to cope with mediator role reassignment* which would enable dynamic readjustments as the context evolves.

Our solution is a social pattern that we call *implicit organization* (IO), of which the work presented in the previous sections is a possible implementation. An IO is a SOO where there is no predefined (or design-time defined) role in charge for organizing providers, such as brokers or match-makers. That is, each of the providers participating in the IO may, at run-time, assume the role of organizer, as a result of an *election* to select the organizer (here called the Winner). All the organization members play the same role, but they may do it in different ways. In particular, we may have redundancy (as required in fault-tolerant and load-balanced systems), where agents are perfectly interchangeable. Instead, in traditional agent patterns, each time a request (*provide service description*) is proposed, the mediator role (*Broker* or *Matchmaker*) plays a central role in interpreting and reformulating the request for the other providers. Then, it coordinates all the offers (from *Providers*), selecting the best ones to be forwarded (at the end) to the *Consumer*.

By contrast, inside the IO, no control role is required since each member receives (overhears) the initial request and immediately decides by itself whether to participate in achieving the organizational goal established by the request (Fig. 4). Thus, an IO is only composed of the *Providers* which autonomously and proactively agree to participate in that IO. Moreover, in the IO architecture, there is no call for service dependency. Instead, each IO member directly depends on the *Initiator* for the goal *formulate request*; this is highlighted in the figure by the dependency *formulate request* bet-ween the whole *Implicit Organization* and the *Initiator*. Among all the *Providers* of the *Implicit Organization,* a (see the "isa" link) run-time *Winner* is selected according to a policy. The *Winner* then plays the role of coordinator. Thus, the coordinator can be different each time an IO forms. A very simple coordination policy can be established by assuming the winner to be the first member to react to the service request. At this level of design, we are not interested in the details of the election process. However, we did see that several negotiating policies can be adopted, such as those described in a previous section.

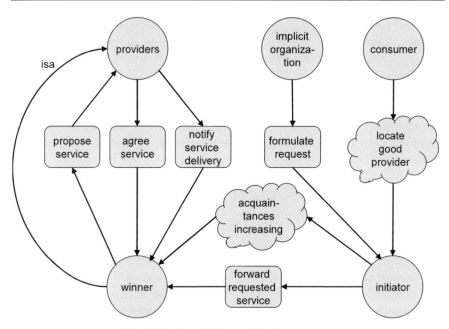

Fig. 4. The implicit organization pattern

5.6.2   Representing Interactions with Implicit Organizations

In order to represent interactions with and within implicit organizations, we needed a diagram that could show both roles and organizations; individual agents are represented only if necessary either for clarity or for representing different implementations of the same role. We decided to extend the standard UML sequence diagram, as shown in Fig. 5.

Vertical lines represent agents, rather than objects. A large rectangle above a few of them represents an organization; the dashed lines falling down from its left and right margins represent the entire organization, and may include one or more representative members. The gray areas are the organizational equivalent of the "focus of control" in reaction to a message. Requests to an organization are represented as arrows terminating in a dot at the border of an organization; conversely, organization replies are represented as arrows starting from a dot on the organization border.

The figure presents the case of agent A requesting a service from organization X. The request is addressed to the organization's role, not to a specific agent. Members within X communicate either to coordinate or to request services from others (as X.2 does to Y). When the request is serviced, a member replies on behalf of its organization (as done by Y.1 and X.1).

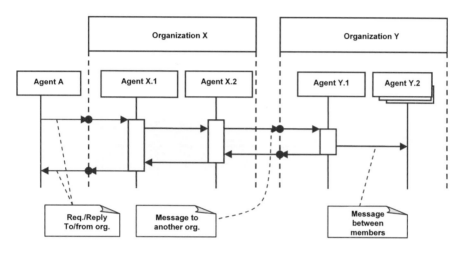

Fig. 5. Extended UML sequence diagram

5.6.3   A First Example

As an example of implicit organization, consider the so-called floor control functionality of a groupware application that allows multiple users distributed on a network to collaboratively work on a shared object (e.g., a visit book compiled by a classroom during a visit to a museum, a tutorial exercise controlled by a teacher, and so on). All users simultaneously see the effects of any editing operations, but only one user at the time (the one who has floor control, indeed) is authorized to use its keyboard to work on the shared object. A user's keyboard manager is part of a multiagent system whose agents play one of two roles, called *KeyboardManager* and *FloorControl*. There is one agent per user for each role. When a user joins a collaborative editing session, her agents tune on a LoudVoice channel for that purpose.

A *KeyboardManager*, in addition to other things, manages a "floor control" button on the user's graphical user interface. When pressed, i.e., when the user asks to manipulate the shared object, a "take_control" request is sent to the *FloorControl* role on the editing channel. Agents playing *FloorControl* form an implicit organization that decides who owns the floor control and answers "yes" or "no" to requests from *KeyboardManagers*. If the answer is no, a *KeyboardManager* has to reiterate its request until it is granted control or its user gives up.

Figure 6 represents a possible interaction between these two roles when two users ask to take control almost simultaneously; *KM - X* is the agent playing the role *KeyboardManager* for user *X*, *FC - X* is the *FloorControl* agent for *X*, and so on.

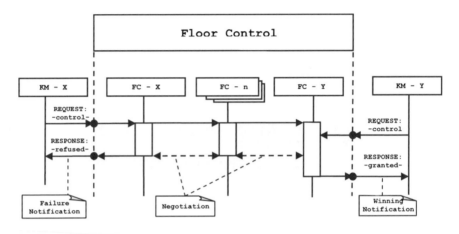

Fig. 6. Interacting with the Floor Control implicit organization

The default policy adopted by the *FloorControl* organization is Multicast Contract Net, i.e., an auction. Bids are a function of the time a user has been granted—or has been waiting for—control of the input devices. A user that presses the button for taking control of the input is allowed to use the shared application only after everybody else that asked for it earlier; once given control, the user keeps it as long as nobody else requires it and at least for a predefined minimum amount of time. A Master–Slave policy is better suited to situations such as classroom exercises, where one user (typically the teacher) has the authority to decide for everybody; her *FloorControl* agent has a GUI that shows the current users and allows the selection of one of them if it is the current Master.

It is worth stressing that *FloorControl* is commonly implemented in computer-supported collaborative work (CSCW) systems by a centralized controller that grants or revokes authorization to edit the shared object. By contrast, our *FloorControl* is distributed, and does not require any central point to work. Different types of *FloorControl* agents can be simultaneously present and adapt to the outcome of the policy negotiation.

5.6.4   Further Examples

To give the reader a feeling of how to use implicit organizations, we briefly introduce some more examples which may be useful even outside active museums. The first is a case of *collaboration among search engines.* A *CitationFinder* accepts requests to look for a text in its knowledge base and returns extracts as XML documents; in a typical situation, different CitationFinders work on different databases, but they may well be redundant. Any coordination policy of those presented above is acceptable for this simple role; the choice depends on the context, and more importantly on the objectives of the system architect for the role within an application. For instance, Plain Competition would be suitable in the case of duplicated knowledge bases. Simple Collaboration, where an agent done with searching accepts the role as merger of the results (indeed, in this case, synthesizing is just concatenating all results by all agents), is the choice in case of extensive searches on different information sources. Indeed, consider the situation where CitationFinders are on board PDAs or notebooks. A user entering a smart office causes its agent to tune into the local channel for its role; consequently, in typical peer-to-peer fashion, a new user adds her knowledge base to those of the others in the same room. This could be easily exploited to develop a CSCW system. In this case, collaboration may be enforced by a CSCW supervisor agent acting as the oracle during policy negotiation.

Our second example concerns *choosing among multiple screens.* Smart rooms (including active museums) may contain multiple places for showing things to users, including: large screens on different walls, the user's own PDA, and computers scattered about the room. Location, as well as quality and logical congruence with the tasks being performed by the user, are all important factors in choosing the "right" screen. Also, it is not necessarily the case that a single screen is a good choice. A presentation to a group of people may be best shown in multiple locations simultaneously. Let us call *SmartBrowser* an agent able to show a multimedia presentation and aware of its position (which may be static, if its display is a wall screen, or mobile, if on board of a PDA). An organization of SmartBrowsers should accept a policy that allows a clear selection of one, or (better) a fixed number of agents (that is, screens) when requested to allocate one to show a presentation. Thus, Plain Competition and Simple Collaboration are not suitable; Master–Slave works, but seems unduly restrictive in a situation where SmartBrowsers are context aware. The best choice is to adopt Multicast Contract Net and use bids as a function of screen resolution, distance from user, impact on other people in the same room (e.g. when audio is involved). Only SmartBrowsers visible to the user from her current position, having all required capabilities, and not busy showing something else, can participate in the subteam bidding for a multimedia presentation.

5.6.5   An Example from Buonconsiglio Castle

The visitor guide system at Buonconsiglio Castle (the case study for PEACH) contains various examples of use of LoudVoice and implicit organizations. The example we present here (extracted from Kuflik et al. 2004; Bresciani et al. 2004a) concerns presentation planning and delivery to a visitor.

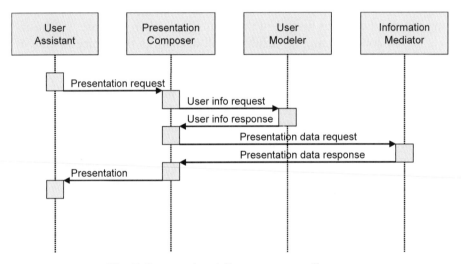

Fig. 7. Presentation delivery sequence diagram

Figure 7, a part of the high-level architectural description of the system, shows classical interaction among the main roles involved. A *User Assistant,* typically running on the visitor's PDA, makes a request for a presentation to be prepared (for instance, in reaction to a button being pressed, or when the visitor stops in front of an exhibition long enough to appear interested). The *Presentation Composer* asks the *User Modeler* for data about the user, and then combines multimedia fragments obtained from the *Information Mediator*, which looks for them in its knowledge base.

The architectural diagram above could be used for a traditional client–server implementation of the visitor guide. Instead, in the following diagram (Fig. 8), produced during detailed software design, the roles are replaced by implicit organizations; coordination within roles is left to the infrastructure (and represented as a shaded rectangle in the diagram).

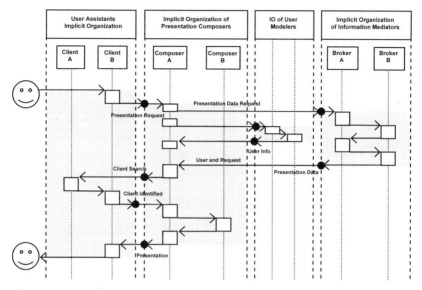

Fig. 8. Presentation delivery by implicit organizations (IO) sequence diagram

While the overall interaction is substantially unchanged, it now becomes clear that all roles are played by multiple agents with different capabilities, and the decision about which one is most suitable to deliver the required service at a particular time and for a particular visitor is deferred until run-time. The visitor (represented by the faces on the left) initially interacts with a specific user assistant, which may not necessarily be the one delivering the presentation (e.g., the first may be running on a PDA, the second may be on a wall screen). Within the Presentation Composers, some ask the implicit organization of User Modellers for information (since several user modellers can run in parallel, applying different techniques and using different information sources), others ask the Information Mediators (for additional information required for generating presentations). Once presentations are ready, requests are issued to the implicit organization of User Assistants to find out the most appropriate clients for displaying the presentations. Once the process is completed, the best presentation (in terms of information, presentation quality and display device) is presented to the visitor. Observe that, via overhearing, all agents can benefit from answers to queries submitted by others. For instance, all presentation composers may benefit from visitor preferences requested by one agent.

5.7   Conclusions

This chapter presented the software infrastructure developed for the PEACH project, focusing on its most innovative aspects from a software engineering point of view. Its objective is to support context awareness and automatic coordination among components in a highly dynamic distributed system such as an active museum. To this end, we have exploited group communication (in a form that we call channelled multicast) and defined a form of teamwork that we call implicit organizations. In this chapter, we have introduced the basic concepts, proposed a design pattern, and shown a few examples of use of implicit organizations.

6 User Modelling and Adaptation for a Museum Visitors' Guide

T. Kuflik and C. Rocchi

6.1 Introduction

The learning experience that takes place in museums nowadays supports free choice. It tends to be personal; it is self-motivated, self-paced, and exploratory by nature. The visitor chooses what, where and when to learn (McLean 1996; Falk and Dierking 2000). Multimedia museum visitor guides can communicate large amounts of often complex information in a user-friendly and interesting way, whilst allowing visitors to access the information they require at their own pace (Alison and Gwaltney 1991). Museum curators always face the challenge of how to select information to present to museum visitors. The amount of information available is usually much greater than the time of the visit permits. Hence, personalization (providing information following personal preferences) could play a crucial role in enhancing the museum experience. New technologies, such as multimedia museum visitor guides, pose a new challenge: they can deliver more information in better ways (hence the amount of information available to the visitor increases) and at the same time can also support personalization (hence allow delivery of relevant information to visitors) (Alison and Gwaltney 1991). Supporting personalization and adaptation is a particularly challenging task in the museum environment, given the nature of the visit described above, where "nonintrusiveness" is fundamental. User modelling, a key factor in personalization, has to take advantage of the observation of events and visitor behaviour, and needs integration of various complementary techniques in order to provide an accurate representation of the visitor. In the framework of PEACH, user modelling was exploited for two services in particular: dynamic presentation (several museum visitor guide prototypes were developed using different user models and adaptation techniques, Chap. 1) and report generation (Chap. 3).

As mentioned earlier, the main challenge for user modelling and adaptation in PEACH was that it was required to be "nonintrusive"; hence visitors were not required to provide any personal information and user modelling was based solely on monitoring visitor behaviour. PEACH faced two more challenges: how to bootstrap a user model without initial knowledge about the visitor and the requirement for a "lean" user model—use only whatever is available as part of the system and not build a specific mechanism and knowledge base for user modelling.

Unlike other personalized museum visitor guide publications, this chapter focuses on the details of the different approaches taken for user modelling and adaptation in the museum environment, trying to address their specific challenges. The use of these approaches will be detailed in later applicative sections. The chapter starts with a general survey of the state of the art in user modelling in the museum environment, presents PEACH challenges, and then details the approaches taken for user modelling. The chapter concludes with a look to the future of user modelling for individuals and groups in the museum environment.

6.2   User Modelling and Adaptation in Museum Visitors' Guides

Adaptive hypermedia systems build a model of the goals, preferences and knowledge of each individual user, and use this model throughout the interaction with the user, in order to adapt to the needs of that user (Brusilovsky 2001). As such, systems providing personalized services will provide different services to different users, based of their user models. User modelling is an area of growing interest since the appearance of computerized systems. Initial work started about 30 years ago, and a good example of this early effort is the work of Rich (1979, 1983), which looks at generating an individual user model by integrating several stereotypes, forming a personal user model. The interest in user modelling has grown constantly since as part of the constant growth in human–computer interaction and intelligent user interfaces. A good example of that growth is the book *User Modelling in Dialog Systems* that appeared in 1989 (Wahlster and Kobsa 1989).

A series of user modelling (UM) conferences started in 1986, later on came a journal dedicated to UM: *User Modelling And User-Adapted Interaction. The Journal of Personalization Research* was founded in 1991 (http://www.umuai.org/), and a user modelling organization was also founded in 1994 (http://www.usermodeling.org/). In parallel, commercial personalization applications evolved, like the personalized mall (www.personalizationmall.com) and more.

Given the growing interest in UM, it is quite surprising that there is little information published about user modelling and adaptation techniques in museum visitors guides. One of the most recent surveys, by Raptis et al. (2005), surveys 12 context-based mobile museum visitor guide applications, but hardly says anything about their adaptability to the individual user. Following Dix et al. (2000), they too define "domain context", as related to the adaptability of system to specific users. Like Dix et al. (2000), who state that museum visitor guides should be considered as a general-purpose device due to the lack of user information, they too state that adaptivity is not of prime importance in museum applications due to the lack of information about the users. However, they briefly discuss personalization attempts in museum visitor guide systems, stating that systems meant to provide personalization require the visitors to answer a set of questions in order to bootstrap a user model that is limited to language, level of expertise, and physical needs.

Raptis et al. (2005) presented several personalization aspects including proactiveness vs. reactiveness of the system, the possibility to learn and adapt to user feedback, and to offer flexible alternative ways of presentation. They present several systems that do adapt to their users, based on their behaviour; examples are Imogi (Luyten and Coninx 2005), Points of Departure (Samis 2001) and Antwerp (van Gool et al. 1999). Imogi does not address any personal aspect of the user, only location and time. In Points of Departure, again, there is no information about user modelling/personalization.

Specht and Opperman (1999) and Opperman and Specht (1999), in their description of the HIPPIE system, published one of the few works explicitly addressing user modelling for museum visitor guides. They suggest that user modelling in "Nomadic Information Systems", as they called it, would be based on monitoring user activities in the information space and would take into account localization information. Their system, developed within the Hyper-Interaction within Physical Space (HIPS, Benelli et al. 1999) project, takes into account user preferences, knowledge, interests, and movement in the physical space. User preferences are acquired by explicit interaction (filling a questionnaire), and a knowledge model is built by monitoring user interaction. The interests, according to the aut-hors, are more dynamic and as a result difficult to model. Again, even in their work there are few details about the actual mechanisms applied, but the details provided are enough to understand that for user modelling the system has to build and maintain a complicated user model combined with a detailed domain knowledge base. Another work describing user modelling in the museum environment is the work of Kay et al. (2005), which describes an application of user modelling in a museum, where visitor "interest level" in the content of the exhibits is inferred, recorded and used to customize presentations to visitors. Unlike HIPPIE, the description is quite brief and refers the reader to a general user modelling application, server for user models (Kay et al. 2002, 2003), but the specific details of the application user modelling are not presented.

Hatala et al. (2004) and Stock et al. (1993) were the only examples we found for a personalized museum visitor guide application where the user modelling component was detailed. Stock et al. (1993) in the ALFRESCO multimodal dialogue project (which is a predecessor of the HIPS system described above) developed a user model that consisted of an activation/inhibition network whose nodes were associated with ordered sets of individual domain concepts, drawn from a domain knowledge base. The grouping of the individuals was performed according to a measure of domain dependent pragmatic closeness; whenever a set is activated; all the entities composing it are considered to be somehow relevant to the visitor. This in turn supported the generation of personalized hypertextual presentation.

Hatala et al. (2004) developed ec(h)o, an "augmented reality interface" for a natural history and science museum. They tracked the visitors in the museum and modeled visitor interaction behaviour. They used a domain ontology for inferred interests representation that later on guided the selection of audio objects that were suggested to the visitors following a set of inference rules.

As can be seen, there is a wide variety of context-aware museum visitors guide systems, but not many apply user modelling, mainly due to the limited availability of information about the visitors. For those that were developed, very few details are published about the specific mechanisms applied.

6.3   PEACH Challenges

The nature of the museum visit and the richness of the multimedia pose some challenges for the museum visitor guide in general: the system should not take the place of the "real thing" (e.g., the exhibit itself); it should also support the visit by providing complementary information that enriches the visit experience. Moreover, due to the nature of the museum visit, being self-motivated and self-paced, it seems that the best option of supporting it is to provide personalized information. The PEACH project required the system to: (1) work in a nonintrusive mode, mainly so as not to distract visitors (Another reason is that users simply do not tend to provide personal information while filling in questionnaires, or even provide feedback to information presented to them). As a result, it has to (2) start from "scratch" with no information about the user. (3) It should have a "lean" user model (exploiting already existing domain knowledge base used for natural language generation), and (4) it should support several distinct applications. While the first two challenges are common to museums in general and are well understood, the remaining ones complicated the user modelling task.

6.3.1 Nonintrusiveness

The information that was available for user modelling was based on monitoring user behaviour, or "implicit visitor feedback". That means that the system has to "speculate" about the visitor's level of interest in the information presented to him or her from his or her behaviour. In addition, the visitors could provide some explicit feedback regarding presentations by interacting with the graphical interface of a PDA (Chap. 1).

To be nonintrusive, the system had to closely track visitor behaviour. This included movement in space, events that occur, and actions taken. Each event is regarded as a source of information about the visitor's current preferences. An inference mechanism was needed to transfer the available information to user models, while compensating for the uncertainty that is an inherent part in such scenario.

6.3.2 Bootstrapping

Initial activation of a user model in a museum is one of the most challenging UM tasks. Usually, there is no a-priori knowledge about the visitor, but in order to be effective, a system must quickly generate a user model to guide the personalization of information presentation. The easiest way of doing so is to ask the visitor to answer questions about his or her knowledge, preferences, etc., to generate an initial user model. However, this activity is something users do not like in general. They do not like to spend precious time filling questionnaires and they refrain from disclosing personal information. One possible way to overcome the lack of initial information problem is to bootstrap the user model with some initial information. This may be available in a form of a stereotype the visitor is assigned to (Rocchi et al. 2004), or a user model for that specific user imported from external sources (assuming that such information exists and the user agrees) (Berkovsky 2005).

6.3.3 "Lean" User Modelling

Another specific challenge of PEACH was the decision (unlike previous projects like HIPS) not to develop an extensive knowledge base for user representation (due to the vast amount of effort required), but to use an existing one, originally used for natural language generation of text for multimedia presentations and visit reports summaries (Chap. 4). The decision was to exploit existing sources of information and since no explicit information is provided, the main source for information was the behaviour of the visitor in the "information space", as represented by the system's knowledge base. This is somewhat similar to the ideas suggested by Carr and Goldstein (1977) and Hatala et al. (2004), where a user model is overlaid on domain knowledge. However, unlike Hatala et al., who generated a specific domain ontology for that purpose, we used an existing one.

6.3.4 Supporting Several Distinct Applications

The PEACH project involved two distinct applications that required user modelling: dynamic presentation generation—during the visit, and report generation—post visit summary report. The two applications had different requirements for the modelling component.

Dynamic presentation generation is an application that generates and delivers information to the visitor during the visit by building individual adaptive presentations tailored from available pieces of information (for more details see Chap. 1). It requires a lot of personal and contextual information: for example, spatial information (current visitor position and whether the visitor has already been there: Is his or her in front of an artwork, or just near it?), visitor interest with respect to the current exhibits and discourse history (what particular presentations were delivered to the visitor).

In addition to specific details regarding the current visit—which consist of the visitor's path through the museum, presentations delivered, and visitor feedback—there is a need for a more abstract representation of user interests to guide future generations of presentations. Several works have dealt with adaptable guides. For instance, in HIPS (Proctor and Tellis 2003), work on adaptation included the classification of user movement patterns in the course of a visit. Here the situation is different: our UM must support dynamic multimedia, including video generation and seamless presentations on mobile and stationary devices (Rocchi et al. 2004; Chap. 7).

Visit Summary Report Generation is an application that summarizes the whole visit for the individual visitor and generates a summary with major exhibits of interest and suggestions for future visits (for more details see Chap. 4). It requires consideration of many aspects:

- Factual aspects of the visit (such as exhibits visited, the visit sequence, the time spent at different locations, the presentations delivered to the visitor, and visitor actions).
- Cognitive aspects related to the exhibitions (such as interest for themes, pleasure, boredom, etc.).
- Extra subject-centered aspects (such as persons met, discussions held, and additional events that occurred).
- Attention-grabbing elements as well as hints for subsequent reading and visiting.
- The appearance of the report (combining text, images, and possibly additional forms of media, in a personalized manner either on paper or in an electronic form).

Unlike the abstraction required for dynamic presentation generation, a user model that supports report generation should provide detailed descriptions of information presented to visitors who seem to have specific interest in a subject, in addition to the abstract representation of interests (for more details see Chap. 4).

6.4 PEACH User Models and Adaptation: Approaches and Techniques

Within PEACH several approaches for user modelling were tried, all trying to exploit the available information—for bootstrapping and non intrusive user modelling, without building complicated user modelling knowledge base, but by using what was already available—"lean" user modelling.

6.4.1 User Data Available for User Modelling

While visiting an "active museum" (a museum that interacts with its visitors), visitors move in the museum space and interact with the environment.

Visitor behaviour can be recorded and used to infer their state, including, among many other things, what interests them and what does not. In PEACH, the information stored in the user modelling component includes the history of the visit. (Due to the requirement for "nonintrusive" user modelling, this is the only information that was available for the task.) The visit history is information recorded about all the events that occur during the visit; such events include positions visited (based on positioning technology like IR, WiFi, or RFID), presentations delivered at every position (exhibit), and implicit and explicit visitor feedback for every presentation. This information is continuously reported by various system components during the visit as information is delivered to the visitor. This information is continuously and dynamically used by the presentation composer component to support online presentation generation, while the accumulated data is used at the end of the visit for visit summary generation.

An example for such reports can be seen in Fig. 1: a visitor moves in the museum and stops at the January fresco. The visitor's new position is recognized and reported by the system, as seen in the <userPosition> message, at line 1 of Fig. 1. When the visitor's position is recognized, a presentation about that fresco is starting and this event is reported by the <startPresentation> message at line 3. The presentations are composed of individual shots.[1]

The first shot presents a snowball fight scene of that fresco, and the event is reported by the <startMediaItem> at line 6. During that shot, the visitor expresses positive feedback by pressing a WOW button on the PDA, expressing a positive response to the presentation. This event is reported by the <wow> message at line 10. The shot normal termination is reported by the <endMediaItem> message (line 11). Then, a second shot about a hunter scene is presented, and during the second shot, the visitor is not happy for some reason and the shot and the whole presentation are stopped (<stopMediaItem> message, line 19 and <stopPresentation>, line 22). Then, after a new presentation is started, the process continues.

Visit history is composed of such events reported in XML format by the various system components and recorded by the user modelling component. This information is continuously used for inferring user interests during the visit to help prepare personalized presentations for the visitor (as detailed in Chap. 1).

---

[1] Shot—one picture with associated text and possibly animation or cinematic technique (Chap. 2).

```
                                                                     ...
<userPosition   userId="p02av"   device="d004"   position="january"
                    orientation="facing" timeStamp="1094473884472" />
<startPresentation    id="p02av-1"    userId="p02av"    device="d004"
type="movie"          length="125790"            location="january"
                                  timeStamp="1094473889519" />
<startMediaItem     id="shot01"     userId="p02av"     device="d004"
type="shot"          length="36045"            position="january"
timeStamp="1094473889740"><concept    topic="SNOWBALL-FIGHT-SCENE001"
                  /><perspective type="generic" /></startMediaItem>
<wow  userId="p02av"  userDevice="d004"  timeStamp="1094473916666"
                                                                    />
<endMediaItem      id="shot01"     userId="p02av"     device="d004"
type="shot"          length="36045"            position="january"
timeStamp="1094473926222"><concept   topic=" SNOWBALL-FIGHT-SCENE001"
                  /><perspective type="generic" /></endMediaItem>
<startMediaItem     id="shot04"     userId="p02av"     device="d004"
type="shot"          length="42000"            position="january"
timeStamp="1094473926843"><concept     topic="HUNTER-SCENE001"
                  /><perspective type="generic" /></startMediaItem>
<stopMediaItem      userId="p02av"     type="shot"     id="shot04"
device="d004"  position="january"  timeStamp="1094473969354"><concept
topic="HUNTER-SCENE001"          /><perspective      type="generic"
                                        /></stopMediaItem>
<stopPresentation    id="p02av-1"    userId="p02av"    device="d004"
type="movie"          length="125790"            location="january"
                                  timeStamp="1094473970696" />
<startPresentation    id="p02av-2"    userId="p02av"    device="d004"
type="movie"          length="43745"             location="january"
                                  timeStamp="1094473975863" />
<startMediaItem    id="castle-deep"    userId="p02av"    device="d004"
type="shot"             length="21000"             position="january"
timeStamp="1094473976204"><concept     topic="CASTLE-SCENE001"
              /><perspective type="historical" /></startMediaItem>
<endMediaItem     id="castle-deep"     userId="p02av"     device="d004"
type="shot"            length="21000"            position="january"
timeStamp="1094473997304"><concept     topic="CASTLE-SCENE001"
              /><perspective type="historical" /></endMediaItem>
                                                                     ...
<endPresentation     id="p02av-2"     userId="p02av"     device="d004"
type="movie"          length="43745"             location="january"
                                  timeStamp="1094474002061" />
<userPosition   userId="p02av"   device="d004"   position="february"
```

Fig. 1. Example of visitor log

At the end of the visit, the user modelling component computes the total time spent at every location, and the overall user modelling information is used to drive the generation of a visit summary report, done by the report generation component. This report includes details about the visit, and suggestions for future activities, for future visits to this and other museums, as described in the report generation section (see a detailed description in the report generation section).

Several different user modelling approaches were considered and tried as part of the PEACH project. The following sections describe the details of the various approaches taken.

6.4.2   Content-Based User Modelling

The content-based user model draws some ideas from prior work in projects such as Al Fresco (Stock et al. 1993), HyperAudio (Sarini and Strapparava 1998) and HIPS (Benelli et al. 1999), regarding user interest representation and visitor level of interest inference. The basis for user modelling is a set of concepts associated with the individual presentations that are prepared and delivered to visitors. These concepts are terms which give a "title" and "keywords" for the presentation and describe its content.

In one case in PEACH, the user modelling mechanism used concepts drawn from an existing knowledge base (planned and used primarily for natural language generation) as a source of information for user modelling. In another case, a simple taxonomy was defined where the concepts associated with the presentations were leaves of a tree and a few layers of abstraction were defined, allowing the aggregation of specific concepts under more abstract and generic terms, thus representing relations between domain-related concepts. The representation and inference mechanism are similar, so only the former will be discussed further since it includes the later.

6.4.2.1   Visitor Interest Representation

As mentioned earlier, the visitor interests are defined in terms of domain concepts, which are associated with individual presentations given to the visitor (Fig. 2). These concepts provide a short description of the content of the presentations, thus representing their themes.

The concepts are drawn from a domain knowledge-base that was primarily designed for natural language generation (Chap. 4). Semantic links with concepts in the domain knowledge base allow the user modelling component to infer and maintain a comprehensive domain-related user model. It is composed of terms directly associated with presentation delivered to the visitor, as well as terms related to them in other ways. Actual visitor interests are represented by a set of domain concepts associated with a level of interest inferred by the user model.

Figure 2 presents part of the user interests represented by the user model. It contains a list of domain concepts with the associated level interest (five different levels of interest were used: not interested, not so interested, interested a little, interested and very interested). Figures 3 and 4 show a few examples of the domain concepts and their interrelations. The concepts appearing in the system's knowledge base are the source for user modelling concepts.

```
<userTopInterests userId="p02av" >

<interest topic="LEISURE-ACTIVITIES" level="very interested" />
<interest topic="SNOWBALL-FIGHT-SCENE001" level="very interested" />
...
<interest topic="PLEBEIAN-CHARACTERS" level="very interested" />
...
<interest topic="ARISTOCRATIC-CHARACTERS" level="interested" />
...
<interest topic="CASTLE-SCENE001" level="interested a little" />
<interest topic="JANUARY-FRESCO001" level="interested a little" />
<interest topic="SOCIAL-CLASS" level="interested a little" />
<interest topic="HUNTER-SCENE001" level="interested a little" />
<interest topic="PICNIC-SCENE005" level="interested a little" />
<interest topic="PLEBEIAN-VILLAGES-AND-FARMS" level="interested a
little" />
...
<interest topic="BLACKSMITH-SCENE002" level="not interested" />
<interest topic="july-boat" level="not interested" />
...
</userTopInterests>
```

Fig. 2. Visitor interest representation

The approach taken in this case is somewhat similar to the approach taken in prior work at Al Fresco (Stock et al. 1993), HyperAudio (Sarini and Strapparava 1998) and HIPS (Benelli et al. 1999). However, unlike prior work, only visitor interests are modelled and there is no modelling of user characteristics or level of knowledge, which would require prior knowledge based on an explicit interaction with the visitor and a more complicated user modelling mechanism.

6.4.2.2   The Inference Mechanism of the User Modelling Component

As mentioned earlier, the museum visitor guide system does not have any initial user model since there is no prior knowledge about the visitor. Hence, user modelling is based solely on the system's knowledge base and the concepts associated with the individual presentations delivered to the visitor during the visit. Implicit and explicit visitor feedback is used to trigger user modelling inference and adapt the user model during the visit. Figures. 5, 6, 7, and 8 illustrate this process.

```
;; January
(JANUARY-FRESCO001 :NO-VALUE
 (INSTANCE-OF (FRESCO-ART))
(HAS-SCENES (SNOWBALL-FIGHT-SCENE001 CASTLE-SCENE001 HUNTING-SCENE001))
 (META-ELEMENTS (BEING0011 DOMINATING001))
 (HAS-THEMES (REPRESENTATION001))
 (HAS-REPRESENTATION (REPRESENTING001))
 (HAS-MAIN-THEME (SNOWBALL-FIGHT001))
 (HAS-MAIN-EVENT (HAVING001))
 (HAS-IMAGES (JANUARY-IMAGE001))
 (HAS-SUBIMAGES (HUNTER-IMAGE001 CASTLE-IMAGE001))
 (HAS-SUBAREAS ())
 (SPECIALTY-OF (JANUARY-MONTH001)))
(SNOWBALL-FIGHT-SCENE001 :NO-VALUE
 (INSTANCE-OF (SCENE))
 (SCENE-OF (JANUARY-FRESCO001))
(CONTAINS-ELEMENTS (GROUP001 SNOWBALL-FIGHT001 SNOWBALL001 SNOW001))
 (CONTAINS-EVENTS (HAVING001 THROWING001))
 (PERSPECTIVE (ARISTOCRACY LEISURE NATURE PRESERVATION))
 (META-ELEMENTS ()))
(SNOWBALL-FIGHT001 :NO-VALUE
 (INSTANCE-OF (SNOWBALL-FIGHT))
 (PARTICIPANTS (ARISTOCRACY))
 (MAIN-THEME-OF (JANUARY-FRESCO001))
 (ELEMENT-OF (SNOWBALL-FIGHT-SCENE001))
 (ACTIVITY-IN (SNOWBALL-FIGHT-SCENE001))
 (HAS-IMAGES (SNOWBALL-FIGHT-IMAGE001)))
(GROUP001 :NO-VALUE
 (INSTANCE-OF (GROUP))
 (NUMBER-OF-UNITS (2) (2 :A-NOVALUE))
 (GROUP-MEMBERS (NOBLEMAN001))
 (ELEMENT-OF (SNOWBALL-FIGHT-SCENE001))
 (CHARACTERISTICS (ARISTOCRATIC)))
(NOBLEMAN001 :NO-VALUE
 (INSTANCE-OF (NOBLEMAN)))
```

Fig. 3. Torre Aquila-specific concepts examples drawn from the system's KB

This mechanism resembles the activation network implemented by prior work in Al Fresco (Stock et al. 1993), HyperAudio (Sarini and Strapparava 1998) and HIPS (Benelli et al. 1999; Opperman and Specht 2000). User models in these systems included visitor preferences acquired from a questionnaire filled out by the visitor, visitor knowledge acquired through tracking of presentations delivered to the visitor in the course of the visit, and visitor interests acquired by monitoring visitor behaviour during the visit. The interest model in HIPS associated sets of concepts, in the form of taxonomies with classes of objects. These classes were sets of topically related concepts and they were "activated" or "deactivated" (i.e., enabled to be used as visitor representatives or not), based on the inferred level of interest in the class. In addition, there was an option to assign keywords to classes of objects not defined in the taxonomy.

In PEACH, individual concepts (and not complete sets) taken from a domain knowledge base are used to model visitor interests. These are augmented by additional concepts by following ontological links in the domain knowledge base. There was no attempt to model visitor interaction preferences (presentation and interaction style) or knowledge.

```
(ARISTOCRACY :NO-VALUE
  (GENERALIZATIONS (SOCIAL-CLASS))
  (MEMBERS (KNIGHT NOBLEMAN LORD LADY-NOBLE NOBLEWOMAN GENTLEMAN PRIEST))
  (HABITATION (CASTLE MANOR-HOUSE))
  (LEXICAL-INFO …)

(LORD :NO-VALUE
  (GENERALIZATIONS (PERSON PROFESSION))
  (MEMBER-OF (ARISTOCRACY))
  (INSTANCES (LORD001 LORD009)))

(NOBLEWOMAN :NO-VALUE
  (GENERALIZATIONS (PERSON PROFESSION))
  (MEMBER-OF (ARISTOCRACY))
  (INSTANCES (NOBLEWOMAN001)))

(KNIGHT :NO-VALUE
  (GENERALIZATIONS (PERSON PROFESSION))
  (INSTANCES (KNIGHT002 KNIGHT0022 KNIGHT009))
  (MEMBER-OF (ARISTOCRACY))
  (PRONOMINAL-FORM (SINGLE-MASCULINE-REFERENT))
  (LEXICAL-INFO …)
```

Fig. 4. General domain concepts (Middle Ages) and their interrelationships

The visitor's level of interest in the various concepts is defined in a five-level scale: "Very Interested", "Interested", "Interested a Little", "Not so Interested" and "Not Interested". In addition, due to the inherent uncertainty of relying on implicit feedback, concepts do not immediately become part of the user model. There is a definition of uncertainty factor which reflects the fact that for implicit feedback or inferred interests (concepts linked to the concepts associated with presentations) there is a need to accumulate evidence about user preferences before actually using these concepts as part of the user model or changing the inferred level of interest the visitor has in them.

The process of inferring visitor interest is continuous and takes place whenever an event where the visitor is involved is reported. The inference mechanism starts from concepts associated with the current presentation delivered to the visitor and updates the level of interest the visitor has in them on the basis of visitor feedback. Then it follows ontological links in a domain knowledge base from the concepts associated to the presentations to other concepts and adds additional concepts to the model (or updates their values if they already exist in the user model). The certainty level of the inferred interest in the specific concepts associated with the presentations delivered to the visitor is relatively high. However, it decreases when semantic links to related concepts are followed (while augmenting the user model with additional, more abstract concepts). This is reflected by an uncertainty factor (a numerical value between 0 and 1) associated with the concepts. This inference enables the extension of the user model to concepts beyond those that are directly associated with the presentation seen by the visitor. Before changing the inferred level of interest, when dealing with implicit feedback and/or following ontological links to related concepts, there is a need to accumulate evidence or gain confidence in the interest of the visitor. Hence, only when the level of certainty reaches a predefined threshold (again a numerical value) is a specific concept updated with the inferred level of interest for the user.

Explicit and implicit visitor feedback is used to trigger the inference mechanism, determining visitor interest level in the various concepts associated with the presentations delivered. Explicit user feedback can be provided by pressing a WOW button (for positive reaction) or a STOP button (for negative reaction) on the PDA. (In later versions of the system, this mechanism was replaced by a five-scale *like-o-meter*. For more details see Chap. 1.) Implicit positive feedback is activated by the completion of a presentation delivery to the user, without interruption (e.g., no STOP button pressed or position changed). Explicit feedback has a higher priority than implicit feedback in the sense that explicit feedback is more reliable, so it drives an immediate change in inferred level of interest the user has in the concepts associated with the delivered presentation. Since implicit feedback is less reliable, it requires accumulation of evidence for every concept (several implicit responses, where the exact number is a parameter) before visitor interest level in that given concept is changed.

When a presentation is delivered to the user, the user modelling component updates the level of interest associated with the concepts representing that presentation. When a new concept is encountered, it is added to the list of interests, and it gets a neutral value—"interested a little".

For example (as illustrated by Fig. 1), let us assume that the visitor seems interested in the snowball fight scene depicted by the January fresco, as determined by the WOW event reported during the presentation about the snowball fight scene. In particular, that visitor was interested in the group of noblemen taking part in it. These noblemen belong to the aristocracy, hence the user modelling component records the specific interest the user had in the snowball fight scene and its participants, and infers that the visitor is interested in aristocratic characters and activities (and additional, related concepts like the nobleman actions, clothes and more details related to aristocracy in general), as reflected by the user model presented in Fig. 2. As a result, when the user arrives at the February fresco, this knowledge may lead to the presentation of information about the jousting scene, which is another aristocratic activity. See Figs. 3 and 4 for ontological details illustrating the inference process. In the figures, **bold** words illustrate terms used for inference while following the ontological links of the above example. As a result of this process, the concept "snowball" fight is added to the user model with the level of interest set to "Interested", while the aristocratic characters and activities may be added as candidate concepts, to be added to the User model when additional evidence is accumulated. Figure 2 represents the user model after additional evidence is accumulated regarding the level of interest hence, the Snowball fight level of interest is "very interested" and the aristocratic characters and events is assumed to be a valid concept with interest level of "interested".

Figures 5, 6, 7 and 8 illustrate the process of inferring the level of interests. Figure 5 illustrates the general process—whenever an event that may impact the user model is reported (implicit or explicit feedback to presentation) knowledge base concepts are associated with presentations and are reported as part of user interaction events. If these concepts are part of the user model (appear in the list of interests), so are their neighbours (related concepts) and the inferred level of interest the visitor has in them is updated ("Update Interest Level"). If they are not part of the user model, they may be part of the candidates list. In this case, the inferred level of certainty in the relevance of these concepts for modelling the user is updated ("Update Confidence Level"). If a concept is not yet known, it becomes a candidate, as well as its neighbouring concepts ("Updates Neighbours").

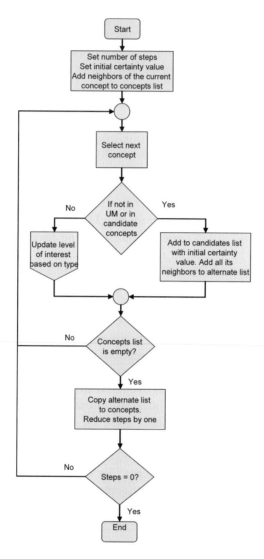

Fig. 5. User interest inference process

Figure 6 illustrates the propagation of the levels of interests to neighbouring concepts, while the level of certainty decays as we get further away from the original concept, until a predefined limit of steps is reached.

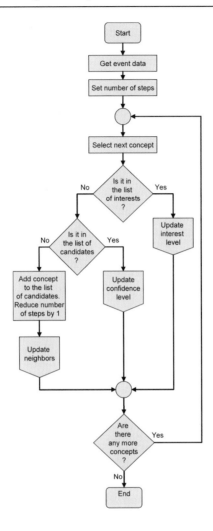

Fig. 6. Updating concept neighbour interests

Figures 7 and 8 illustrate the process of updating the level of inter-est/level of certainty, based on explicit or implicit feedback. If explicit feedback is provided, the interest level is updated because the visitor exp-ressed interest in the presentation. When implicit feedback is inferred, there is a level of uncertainty inherent in the process. This is represented by an uncertainty value that requires an accumulation of evidence before the level of interest is updated. The same rationale applies to the process of adding concepts to the representation of user interests. The concepts start as "candidates". When enough evidence is accumulated, as presented in Fig. 6, the concepts become part of the user model.

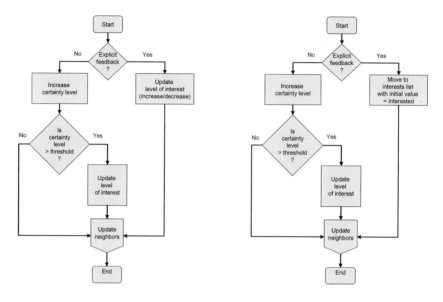

Fig. 7. Updating level of interest for UM concepts

Fig. 8. Updating candidate's level of interest

6.4.3   Stereotypic User Model

The stereotypic user model was intended to bootstrap an initial user model due to the lack of user information. Having no information at all about the user is quite problematic; hence the idea was to initiate a user model based on initial information implicitly provided by the user. This in turn can help in bootstrapping a personal user model or serve as a model throughout the visit. One option for stereotype definition was to attach an initial definition of levels of interest to stereotypic user models associated with virtual characters the visitor selects to accompany him or her during the visit (Rocchi et al. 2004; Chap. 7). These virtual characters represent points of view (or perspectives) from which exhibits are described. Thus, the selection of a specific virtual character as a companion for the visit allows the system to bootstrap a user model with initial information associated with that character, rather than starting from scratch. In practice, the stereotypic user model is a limited version of the content-based user model described earlier, with some level of interest already preset. The virtual character selection event reported to the user model triggered an initialization process that loaded the user model with an initial set of concepts and interest level. The initialization allowed the system to provide personalized service that is adopted later on during the visit, based on visitor feedback, as the regular content-based model. In some versions of the PEACH museum visitor guide system, the stereotypic approach was tried with no further updates (adaptation). Figure 9 illustrates a stereotypic user model as used in one of the Torre Aquila prototypes.

```
<profile>
 <loadUserInterests>
   <interest topic="WINTER" level="interested"/>
   <interest topic="SPRING" level="interested"/>
   <interest topic="SUMMER" level="interested"/>
   <interest topic="FALL" level="interested"/>
   <interest topic="LEISURE-ACTIVITIES" level="interested"/>
   <interest topic="HANDICRAFT-ACTIVITIES" level="very interested"/>
   <interest topic="ARISTOCRATIC-CHARACTERS" level="interested"/>
   <interest topic="PLEBEIAN-CHARACTERS" level="very interested"/>
   <interest topic="ARISTOCRATIC-BUILDINGS-AND-CITIES" level = "in-
terested a little"/>
   <interest topic="PLEBEIAN-VILLAGES-AND-FARMS" level="interested a
little"/>
   <interest topic="NATURE" level="interested a little"/>
   <interest topic="ANIMALS" level="interested a little"/>s
   <interest topic="UTENSILS-AND-PRODUCTS" level="interested a lit-
tle"/>
   <interest topic="PAINTING-TECHNIQUES" level="interested"/>
 </loadUserInterests>
</profile>
```

Fig. 9. Stereotypic user model example

6.4.4   Propagation of Interests

As an alternative to the knowledge-based UM approach presented above, we implemented a prototype based on propagation of interests into a network of content (Rocchi and Zancanaro 2003). The nodes in the network are templates that encode a set of possible sequences of video clips which describe the same topic. Relations among templates encode the semantic closeness of the material contained.

Interest shown towards a template may be propagated to its neighbours. For instance, if a template describes the overall fresco and the visitor expresses interest (for example, using the *like-o-meter*, as explained in Chap. 1), the system then propagates interest to templates which are connected to the current one. In interactions that follow, this information is more likely to be selected for presentation.

The interest value assigned to each template ranges from –2, meaning current lack of interest, to +2, meaning strong interest. As feedback is received through the interface, the system updates the interest value of the current template and also propagates such information to its connected templates.

There are several types of presentations and the type of presentation is relevant when inferring the interest of the visitor and the resulting action to be taken. The presentation types are:

- *Introduction*: a general introduction to an exhibit.
- *Abstract:* describes generally a part of the exhibit (e.g., the snowball fight scene).
- *Content:* provides more details about a part of the exhibit.
- *Follow-up:* additional information about general theme of the exhibit that may be presented to the visitor (e.g., hunting in the Middle Ages).
- *Conclusion:* concludes the sequence of presentations about a given exhibit.

The choice of follow-up is determined by the level of interest the visitor has in the contents that relate to the topic presented. Propagation is based on the following dependency relations:

1. *Introduction affects abstract*: a positive or negative degree of interest, expressed when the system presents the general introduction to an exhibit, is propagated to all the abstracts pertaining to the same exhibit (the abstract is the basic information on an exhibit with respect to a certain topic).

2. *Abstract affects content*: the degree of interest towards the abstract updates the value of its related content, (i.e., a more detailed description of the exhibit with respect to the abstract). When a content template has an interest value greater than zero, it is selected and presented to the visitor right after the abstract.

3. *Content affects follow-up*: the degree of interest towards contents affects its connected follow-ups (if any). Follow-ups are selected and proposed to the visitor when they have an interest value of +2. A follow-up contains general information about a topic shared by two or more exhibits.

4. *Follow-up affects content*: the degree of interest towards follow-up is propagated to all of the connected contents. Follow-ups act as bridges by propagating the interest values on one exhibit to other similar exhibits.

The selection mechanism creates the presentation as a sequence of templates. The introduction is always present as well as all the abstracts (sorted according to their interest values); contents and follow-up may also be selected.

This realization, instead of referring to a knowledge base, simply stores information related to each single user's interaction with the system, e.g., exhibits visited, presentations watched, and visitor explicit feedback. The template engine merges such information with the templates, to create the final presentations. The advantage of using the content network rather than a knowledge base is that the latter is difficult to build and to update. The disadvantage of this variant is that it allows less flexibility than the system based on explicit user modelling. In addition, the representation cannot be used easily for unconnected contents (e.g., a temporary exhibition on a similar theme).

6.4.5   Using the User Model Component

A personal user model component is created for every visitor who starts a visit at the museum (in fact, more than one can be created, based on the UM approaches taken). The component "accompanies" the visitor while in the museum. It tracks and collects information about the visitor in the form of events reported by other system components (the presentation composer when presentation is delivered to the visitor, the visitor's mobile client, reporting start/end of presentations, as well as position change and explicit feedback, etc.).

```
<hasUserExperienced  userId='p01av'  topic='JANUARY-FRESCO001'  per-
spective='generic'/>
<hasUserInterest userId='p01av' topic='LEISURE-ACTIVITIES'/>
<hasUserSeen  userId='p01av'  type='shot'  id='jan-hunting-deep-art'
/>
```

Fig. 10. XML query examples

The information collected is stored, providing a visit history. It is used for inferring visitor interest in the domain concepts. The stored and inferred information is available for use by other components as needed. The presentation composer, while preparing a presentation to be delivered for the user, needs to know about prior presentations delivered, exhibits already visited, and the level of interest the visitor has in concepts that are candidates to be included in the next presentation. The report generator needs to know the visit history, details about feedback to specific presentations, their details, etc.

An XML-based reporting and querying language was developed for this purpose. XML messages are sent by the system components reporting events, and queries are posed by these components and answered by the user model as needed. (Some query examples are presented in Fig. 10.)

The queries may address facts such whether the visitor has seen a specific shot or been at a specific position. They also may inquire about the level of interest the visitor has in a specific concept and even request a summary of the whole visit up to the point of time when the report is requested. The user model searches the events log and responds to these queries regarding specific events, or it reports about the level of interest the visitor has in specific concept. This information is used by the various components to build personalized presentations, taking into account the context and preferences of the visitor.

6.5   Discussion and Future Work

6.5.1   User Modelling in a Multiagent Active Museum

The multiagent architecture (Chap. 5) opens new opportunities for user modelling (as well as for additional services in active museums). There is no longer a need to rely on a single user model: several user models can work (and develop) in parallel: a stereotypic user model, a content-based, adaptive user model, a collaborative one, and more. All of them play the same "role" of user model, and they form an implicit organization of user modellers for any given individual visitor. Whenever there is a need for information for a specific user, a query can be posed to the implicit organization of user modellers. In LoudVoice terminology, the query is distributed on a channel to which all agents playing the role of user modelers are tuned. Each and every user modeller can reason about the request and suggest a reply, if available. The user modellers can negotiate among themselves in order to determine which reply is the most accurate at a given moment, and the winning agent provides the reply to the requester as a reply of the implicit organization. The user modellers can compete (bid) for winning the opportunity to reply, or collaborate in order to generate a mutual response, applying the negotiation policy selected by the organization (as presented in the multiagents architecture section). This may be a better and more flexible solution than relying on a single user model. A simple example can illustrate the benefits of this architecture: at the beginning of a visit, there may be no information about a user, so a stereotypic user model may be the only source of user modelling information. Such a model can be invoked following the visitor's selection of a virtual character that can accompany him or her. During the visit, information accumulates, and when an assessment of the user state is requested, each and every model can suggest one, together with a certainty factor, based on the confidence the agent has in it. The individual model assessments may be combined, taking into consideration the individual certainty factors. At a certain point the personal user models may provide better predictions than the stereotypic one and take over completely, and this moment can be determined dynamically, based on performance of the models. Moreover, this situation may be changed dynamically and they may switch back whenever a visitor arrives at a new exhibition/section where the content-based and/or collaborative model may have limited or no relevant knowledge; hence the stereotypic may again provide a better prediction.

This dynamic behaviour is a fundamental characteristic of the Loud-Voice multiagent infrastructure that can be easily applied in any active environment and in particular in the active museum. This type of capability enriches the possibilities for user modelling with very little additional effort, allowing for the application of several different techniques in parallel and for use of the best possible composition of services at any given moment.

6.5.2   User Modelling Based on Visiting Style Analysis

To further exploit the potential of the architecture, other user models are currently being revisited, for example, museum visiting style, a research issue dealt with in the past. Here, Veron and Levasseur (1983) conducted a field study on people's behaviour in artistic exhibitions. Their study identified four categories of visitors based on paths and movements in physical spaces and the time people spend in front of a single artwork and within the entire exhibition space. This work inspired parts of the user modelling work (Marti et al. 1999) done in the HIPS project. In order to verify if the Veron and Levasseur classification could be adapted to the HIPS context, observations and video-recording analysis were carried out in two museums in Siena. The results confirmed Veron and Levasseur's findings and their visiting style became part of the user modelling in HIPS: an Artificial Neural Network was trained with visitors' paths representing the different visiting styles in order to predict visitors' behaviour and plan presentations accordingly.

6.5.3   Ubiquitous User Modelling

The need to provide personalized information combined with the wish not to interfere and distract the visitor from the exhibits poses strict constraints on user modelling in such environment. Having some initial information about the visitor is crucial for good personalization. Hence, the emerging research in the area of "Ubiquitous User Modelling" becomes an interesting solution, where few recent research examples can be found in (Potonniee 2002; Kay et al. 2003; Niederee et al. 2004; Mehta et al. 2005; Heckmann et al. 2005). The possibility to use partial user models, already available elsewhere, in order to bootstrap the ad hoc user model needed for the museum visit, will greatly enhance the ability of the museum visitors guide system to provide personalized presentation to the visitor and solve the "cold start" problem, which is one of the major challenges in such a system. Moreover, with the progress of technology, more and more solutions will be available for tracking the visitor in space. Not only visitor position (and possibly speed of movement) will be tracked, but also the visitor orientation and focus of attention can be tracked and provide better understanding of his or her specific interests at a given moment which can lead to better personalization.

The individual user modelling tried in PEACH can be taken a step further in order to support group visits. Since museum visits are conducted in many cases in small groups (with family, friends), the individual user models can be combined for group modelling. They can support each other in mutual recommendation; the overall information space can be covered in a way that will encourage interaction among the group members during and after the visit, thus enriching the mutual museum visit experience.

6.6   Summary

The museum environment is indeed challenging, especially when the system has to adapt to its users in a nonintrusive manner, with no initial information about them. The PEACH project tried to address the challenges of user modelling in the museum environment by applying and combining various techniques. The idea of "Active Museum" using the multiagents infrastructure developed within the PEACH framework allows for the dynamic combination of a variety of technologies in order to cope with user modelling in the museum environment. The combination of technologies, together with the extension of user modelling beyond the borders of the museum by applying Ubiquitous User modelling, opens new opportunities for personalized information delivery in active museums and in active environments in general.

Part III
Stationary Devices

7 Integration of Mobile and Stationary Presentation Devices

A. Krüger, M. Kruppa and C. Rocchi

7.1 Introduction

In this chapter, we address the issue of the seamless interleaving of interaction between a mobile device and stationary devices in the context of the PEACH project. There is a great need for intelligent information presentation in the cultural heritage and tourism domains. Cultural experience has been taking place for centuries with little change. However, young people seem to require novel modes of exposure to cultural material in order to engage them and to provide an entertaining experience. Thus, there is a natural demand for a quality shift from the presentation of "mass produced" cultural heritage offerings (comparable to supermarket goods) to an individualized approach where each person acquires information and understanding about the things that interests him or her the most. This implies not just rethinking the content of the presentations, but also reconsidering how content is delivered. We find this to be true especially in the museum setting. This led us study the use of multiple presentation devices with seamless transition between presentations on stationary and mobile devices.

Mobile guides are often available in today's museums. However, they mostly provide just auditory information. One of the goals of PEACH was to design mobile museum guides that combine dynamically adapted language-based output with dynamically produced visual documentaries. While the first part is an improvement of well-established techniques, the second is based on cinematic techniques (Chap. 2).

To this end, we developed a system that relies on input to from visitor location and from observations the system itself makes about the visitor's behaviour, presumed interests and previous exposure. All the material is presented coherently throughout the visit. Personalized information (such as dynamically generated video-clips) is presented on a mobile device, while background material and additional information is provided on larger stationary screens distributed throughout the museum (so-called *Virtual Windows*). A virtual presenter follows visitors in their experience and provides advice on both the types of devices available and on the museum itself. In the following sections, we explain the interaction concepts that arise in such a setting (Sect. 3), the way we used virtual, life-like characters to present information seamlessly on both device types (Sect. 4) and the architecture needed to realize and implement these ideas (Sect. 5). Section 6 presents our conclusions. Before going into the details of the concepts, Sect. 2 gives an overview of related work.

7.2   Related Work

Sumi and Mase's AgentSalon (2001) was designed with a metaphor of a salon in mind, where characters that represent different users can meet and exchange ideas. Mase developed the idea of migrating agents that are able to move from the user's personal device to a large screen, where the user's character could meet with characters of other users and start a discussion on various topics. The focus in AgentSalon was on stimulating discussions between participants of an exhibition or conference. For this purpose, it was sufficient to use the migrating agents in a rather narrow way (i.e., moving from a personal digital assistant (PDA) to a large screen). Our work differs and extends these concepts in two ways. First, we generalize the concept of migrating characters to make use of any possible projection and display capability in the environment to allow the character to move freely around. Second, we use the migrating characters mainly as a reference mechanism to physical objects in the user's environment and not just as a representation of the user's interest as originally intended in AgentSalon.

Virtual characters are not the only way to provide references to physical objects in instrumented spaces. Pinhanez' original work on the Everywhere Display (Pinhanez 2001) also includes several ideas on how to reference physical objects in the environment, mainly by annotating them with arrows and labels. SearchLight (Butz et al. 2004) is a system that uses a steerable projector-camera unit to return search.

The Sotto Voce prototype (Aoki et al. 2002) consists of several guidebook devices. These devices combine a handheld computer with a high resolution colour touchscreen and wireless local-area network (WLAN) card. It uses headsets that do not fully occlude the ears, allowings users to communicate verbally with each other. Finally, two guidebook devices can be paired over the WLAN for audio sharing.

The HIPPIE system (Oppermann et al. 1999) is an Internet-based museum guide for use in a stationary context at home as well as in a mobile scenario. The selection of content presented to users is influenced by a number of factors such as physical location and personal interests of users, as well as user knowledge and preferences. While the stationary version of the Hippie systems runs on any computer connected to the Internet, the mobile version is especially designed for use on a handheld computer. The user's physical location within the museum is determined by a combination of infrared beacons and an electronic compass. The electronic compass is used to determine the user's orientation, while the infrared beacons are employed to determine the user physical location. The different configurations of mobile and stationary hardware demand different application layouts and content presentation on the different devices. The content is automatically adapted according to the capabilities and limitations of each device. Sometimes information presented using a specific presentation modality has to be converted to another presentation modality. An example is written text, which may be presented in an appropriate fashion on the large screen of the stationary device but which is inconvenient for the small display of the mobile device. In such a case, the written text would be substituted by prerecorded spoken utterances, which would then be rendered on the mobile device. Another adaptation strategy is the alternation of quality. For example, a large-scale image may be shown on the stationary device, but may have to be reduced in resolution prior to its presentation on the screen of a mobile device.

Other projects have aimed at developing concepts for combined interaction of large and small screen devices. One examples is the PEBBLE project (Myers 2001) that focuses on Computer Supported Collaborated Work with handhelds and a framework described in (Pham et al. 2000) for the distribution of media on different devices, however without focusing on adaptive presentations with virtual characters.

Overall, none of the projects described has made use of virtual characters in the museum context. In the next section, we describe how we adopted the idea of migrating characters to a museum guide application.

7.3 Migrating Virtual Museum Guides

The main objective behind the lifelike characters developed within the scope of the PEACH project was to realize so called "virtual museum guides". A virtual guide should imitate the behaviour of real museum guides by taking users on a museum tour and, furthermore, show a certain degree of social competence by automatically adapting to user interests and attitudes.

To realize the vision of such a virtual museum guide, several preconditions had to be met. First, the virtual guide has to be able to move throughout the museum along with the user. Second, much like a human museum guide, the virtual guide must know its position as it moves from exhibit to exhibit so that it can present localized information. However, knowing its own location is only a first necessary step. Beyond knowing information about specific exhibits, the virtual guide also needs to know the physical layout of the museum, including the location of each relevant physical object. Finally, a virtual museum guide should imitate the way in which human museum guides adapt to audience needs. While some information may be available to the guide beforehand (e.g., the visitor group is a school class which is taking a history course focusing on ancient Greece), additional information is gathered by both observation and interaction with the audience. In the following subsections, we will take a more detailed look at each of the aforementioned preconditions.

7.3.1   Virtual Guide Locomotion—Mobility

Locomotion is the key element for developing a virtual museum guide. It allows virtual guides not only to accompany users while exploring the physical world, but also to assist users by means of deictic gestures.

We distinguish between active and passive guide locomotion. In the active locomotion category, we find all the methods that allow the guide to relocate itself, regardless of user movement: for example, when the guide "jumps" from one device to another (similar to Kruppa et al. 2003 and Sumi and Mase 2004) or moves along a projection surface. Whenever the guide depends on the user to relocate itself, we refer to this movement as passive locomotion: for example, when the guide is located on a mobile device carried around by the user. Both categories yield different advantages and implications:

- Using active locomotion, the guide can position itself freely in the environment. Active locomotion could be the result of an explicit user request or an action performed by the guide itself.
- Using passive locomotion, the guide stays close to the user. But this system depends on the user moving to a defined position.
- Depending on the locomotion method chosen, the guide uses either the same (passive locomotion) or a different (active locomotion) frame of

reference with respect to the user, and must change its gestures/utterances accordingly.

These conditions demand different guide behaviour depending on the locomotion method. We assume that the guide is always driven by a certain objective. When it is necessary to move to another location to fulfil a specific goal, the guide can either move to the new location—an active move for the guide—or convince the user to move to the new location—a passive move for the guide. Either way, the guide needs to be aware of the users movements/actions in order to react appropriately.

7.3.2   Physical Context—Sensitivity

In order to determine the optimal solution to a given task in the physical world, a virtual guide needs to be aware of the physical objects around it (i.e., the objects around the user) as well as of the physical context of the user (i.e., position and orientation. These are detected by means of various sensors, some of which we mention in Sect. 4 of this chapter). Furthermore, the guide needs detailed knowledge of the object of interest and its location (e.g.: *What is it? How big is it? Which other objects are close to it?*). While user position and orientation may limit the choice of appropriate devices to be used by the character due to physical restrictions like visibility, it may also indicate that a the user must be in a certain position before performing a task related to a particular physical object.

7.3.3   Personal Context—Adaptivity

To maximize user satisfaction with the virtual guide, it is necessary to adapt to the user's specific preferences. Preferences may be related to specific devices. (For example, a user may prefer to limit the use of the screen of a mobile device to a minimum, even though he might have to move to another room in order to do so.) In addition, users should be given the opportunity to prevent the use of certain devices or reference strategies in specific situations. For example, a user might not want the guide to use a spatial audio system in a public situation, while the user might have a different preference in a private situation. Furthermore, in order to generate a personal tour for the user, specific interests stated by the user beforehand should be taken into account when selecting a subset of the information available in a museum. Based on these initial data, a museum tour can be planned and initiated. However, similar to a human guide who observes the moods of its audience and changes his or her plans accordingly, the virtual guide should try to evaluate user satisfaction with the chosen tour and the information subsets presented. If the user guide detects that the user is not satisfied with a chosen tour, it should be flexible enough to change the tour accordingly.

7.3.4   Remote Control Mechanism and Voting

As explained earlier, an important concept of our the system is the combination of a mobile personal tour guide that provides information of individual interest to the users and a large stationary display, located at various key positions in the museum. These displays act as Virtual Windows to the information space providing in-depth and detailed information on selected topics of major user interest. To support multiuser interactions, we adopt the metaphor of a remote control. Users interact with the Virtual Window by pressing on buttons displayed on their mobile device. Using LAN technology, this interaction is communicated via a server to the Virtual Window. The server selects the content to be presented on the Virtual Window on the basis of the user interaction history. If the preselected topic does not interest the user, the user may choose a different presentation from a list arranged in order of highest interest. When another user approaches the Virtual Window, the presentation lists of all users in front of the Virtual Window are combined to form a new list, which only holds items which are of interest to all users. If the list is empty, very general presentations of interest to most visitors of the museum are included. When the current presentation finishes, a newly generated list is shown on each mobile device and on the Virtual Window (see Fig. 1).

Fig. 1. Multiuser interaction using a voting mechanism

At this point, each user chooses a presentation on the mobile device. After the first user has chosen a topic, a countdown is started on the Virtual Window. Each user can make a decision by pressing a corresponding button on the mobile device, until the countdown is finished, or each user has made his or her choice. In order to avoid situations in which there is no definite voting result, each user is assigned a different weight in the voting process. These weights are given according to the order in which the users appear in front of the Virtual Window. In doing so, the voting results become unambiguous and early arriving users are given the most controlling power regarding presentation selection. In each constellation, all users voting weights sum up to 1. Even though the user who arrives first at the Virtual Window has the most power, it is still possible to outvote her when several other users agree on a different topic.

7.4   Using Virtual Characters to Present Adapted Information in Museum Settings

The museum guide was adapted for two different museums, namely the Buonconsiglio Castle in Trento and the Völklingen Old Ironworks. Since these two museums have different settings (i.e., a medieval castle with frescoes in Trento, Italy, and an industrial plant in Völklingen, Germany, which was recently transformed into a cultural heritage site), the application and character layout were modified accordingly. Figure 2 gives an impression of the two sites and the corresponding layouts.

Fig. 2. Cooperating museums and corresponding application and character layouts

The PEACH museum guide prototype combines a number of different system components. In the following sections, we explain each of the components as well as the underlying communication structure.

7.4.1   Different Characters for Different Stereotypes

Four different Migrating Characters were developed for the PEACH project, two for the Völklingen Old Ironworks and two for the Buonconsiglio Castle (see Figure 3).

Fig. 3. Characters designed for the PEACH museum guide

While the characters for the Völklingen Old Ironworks have a rather modern design that fits the scenario of an industrial plant, the characters for the

Buonconsiglio Castle have a medieval appearance that fits into the scenario of a medieval castle.

Each character represents a different view of the content of the specific museum. Users are free to switch between two characters at any time. Depending on the chosen character, the focus of the information presented while exploring the museum is modified accordingly. For example, one character in the Buonconsiglio Castle setup has the appearance of an artist, and hence the information presented by this character has a strong focus on artistic aspects of the exhibits. The design of the second character was derived from a figure in one of the frescoes at the museum. Information presented by this second character is focused on social and historical backgrounds because the character was designed as a contemporary witness. Both characters have easily understandable visual features that indicate their roles within the context of the museum. For the Old Völklingen Iron Works one character was in the role of the engineer, who explains technical details and another character informed on the social circumstances of the workers.

7.4.2   Device-Independent Migrating Characters

The Migrating Characters developed for PEACH were designed to work on both mobile and stationary systems. Due to the different screen sizes of these devices, each character features two different layouts. While the layout for mobile devices shows only head, shoulders and arms (see Fig. 4), the layout for stationary systems shows the whole body of the character (see Fig. 3).

Fig. 4. Example of character layout for mobile devices

Hence, the character is more flexible on the stationary device (That is, it may move across the screen towards a specific object.) while it occupies less screen space on the mobile device.

The characters were created as stand-alone movies in Macromedia Flash MX and are loaded and runtime executed in a surrounding player environment. These animations may hence be transferred from one device to another independent of the visitor controlling the characters.

7.4.2.1   Two Different Character Roles: Anchorman and Presenter

Following the television metaphor, two main roles were realized within each character: the *presenter* and the *anchorman*. When playing the role of the presenter, the character introduces new media assets and uses pointing gestures. When playing the role of the anchorman, the character just introduces complex presentations without interfering with them any further. Although simpler than the presenter, the role of an anchorman can help the visitor understand many different presentations. In its role of an anchorman, the character also supports the seamless integration of the mobile devices' small screen and the large screen of the stationary system. Similar to a TV-presenter who walks around in the studio to present different content, the character is able to move between the mobile device and the stationary device.

Mobile device   Stationary device

Fig. 5. Keyframes of the transition between a mobile and a stationary device. As the character disappears on the mobile device (*left*), it starts to reappear on the stationary device in full size (*right*)

7.4.2.2   Character Migration Between Devices

In order to guide the user's attention focus while the Migrating Character is moving from one device to another, a combination of a character animation and a spatial audio clue is used. While the character disappears from the initial device, a sound is played back on that device. As soon as the character has completely disappeared, it starts to reappear on the target device. While reappearing, the target device plays another sound. In this way, users are presented with both visual and aural clues which help them to direct their attention focus towards the correct device. Figure 5 illustrates the character transition between different devices.

7.4.2.3   Consistent Speech Generation for Mobile and Stationary Devices

In order to make consistent, high-quality speech synthesis available to both mobile and stationary devices, we invented a technology that allows speech synthesis to be run on a stationary server. The result is then converted into an MP3[1] encoded audio file and shared among all the clients connected to the network. The resulting speech synthesis produces the same high quality sound on mobile- and stationary devices.

We made use of AT&T's Natural Voices.[2] To generate MP3 files from text, we used TextAloud[3] by NextUp. Whenever a new text file is available, TextAloud generates a new MP3 file. By generating speech instead of using prerecorded speech, the system can generate personalized presentations (e.g., use the name of the user, or the time of day). It is also possible to generate presentations according to the special interests of the user, by combining text-parts into new text blocks. Another advantage is the easy support for different languages. Instead of translating the texts and having them spoken in a professional studio, one may simply translate them, and the system may do the rest. AT&T Natural Voices supports many languages (e.g., English, German, Italian, French) and different speakers. In the demo setup at the Völklingen Old Ironworks, we have a complete support for both German and English (i.e., layout and spoken text) while in the Buonconsiglio Castle, we support English and Italian.

---

[1] The MPEG audio layer 3 coding scheme for the compression of audio signals.
[2] AT&T Natural Voices homepage: http://www.naturalvoices.att.com/.
[3] The TextAloud homepage: http://www.nextup.com/.

7.4.3   Localized Information Presentation

While exploring the museum site, users are presented with localized information on their PDA. This information is directly related to the physical location of the user and the surrounding objects. In order to determine the user position, we use infrared beacons (see Fig. 6) mounted on walls and ceilings. The beacons emit a unique number, and have a signal range of 8 to 20 meters and a variable transmission angle between 10 and 25 degrees. The resulting area in which the signal of an infrared beacon may be received is a cone. In addition, we also make use of active RFID tags (see Fig. 6). Since these tags do not need a direct line of sight between sender and receiver, they serve as a backup mechanism to guarantee a positional signal even in situations, where the infrared signal fails. An exemplary setup of infrared beacons and RFID tags is shown in Fig. 6.

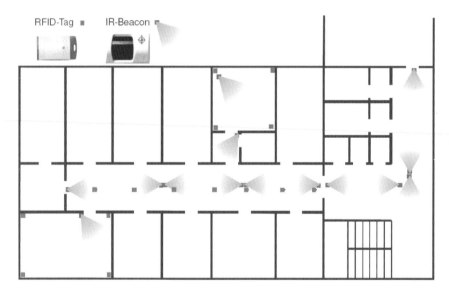

Fig. 6. Example of infrared beacon and RFID tag positioning system setup

Because a direct line of sight between the infrared beacon and the receiving PDA is necessary, the system also provides information about the orientation of the user (i.e., information on the orientation of the PDA in the user's hands). To further improve the precision of the positional information, it is possible to mount several infrared beacons so that their emitting ranges overlap. Since the PDA can receive signals from several infrared beacons at the same time, we narrow down the user's position by calculating the overlapping infrared beacon signal regions.

7.4.4   Stationary Information Systems

The stationary information systems within the PEACH scenario were based on the metaphor of a "window into the outside world". The stationary system was therefore called "Virtual Windows". While the localized information on the PDAs is directly related to a physical object, the information presented on the stationary information system offers additional information on exhibits visited while exploring the physical site of the museum. The additional material is automatically selected on the basis of the specific user model built as the user explores the museum.

Fig. 7. Screenshots of the stationary presentation system at Museo Castello del Buonconsiglio. Two characters were designed for this purpose: a noblewoman and an artist

In addition, the stationary systems provide options to change the character accompanying the user on the mobile device. In the Buonconsiglio Castle installation, both characters present information on the stationary system. Figure 7 shows two screen shots of a presentation running on the stationary system. However, when leaving the stationary system, the user has to decide which of these characters to take with him on the mobile device. If the user wants to switch to the other character later on, he can choose a different character at the next available stationary system.

7.4.5   Automatic Adaptation to User Interests by Observation

The user's behaviour while exploring an exhibition is constantly monitored (time spent in front of certain kinds of exhibits, the additional information requested, presentations skipped, etc.) and analyzed by the system. Based on this data, the system selects an appropriate user group. The system monitors the user until he reaches the end of the museum tour.

The statistic analyzer module categorizes users into different groups according to the interests they show while exploring the museum. While the presentations on the mobile devices are not influenced by this categorization, the content presented at the stationary system is preselected by the system based on these calculated user interests.

7.4.6   The Long-Term User Model

In addition to the internal user model built up by the server during a user's museum visit, there is a second, long-term user model (Kruppa et al. 2005). This user model serves as an initial preference setup, whenever a user visits a museum. The actual user model is stored on an Internet server[4]. In this way, information gathered during previous museum visits may be used to preclassify a user in a new museum. However, since the data collected may be sensitive, users are always free to turn of the long-term user model feature. In this case, when starting a museum visit, the museum guide system handles the user with a default preference setup. In case, the user agrees to share the information on the Internet, the initial setup sequence works as illustrated in Fig. 8.

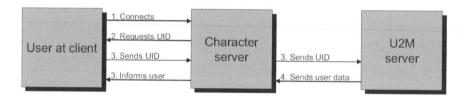

Fig. 8. Initial user model setup sequence

Users who participate in this service are identified by a unique ID, the User ID (UID). When the visitor uses his own mobile device, the UID is stored on it and gets automatically transmitted to the museum guide server. If the visitor uses a rented mobile device, he is asked to enter the UID. After receiving the UID, the museum guide server requests available information about user preferences from the user model server. The information acquired is then integrated with the internal user model. Once this setup process is complete, the user is informed about the initial setup chosen by the server. At this point, the user is free to change this setup or to completely disable the whole user adaptation process.

---

[4] The server is available online at: http://www.u2m.org.

7.4.7   Presenting Video Content with Virtual Characters

In order to adapt the video generator system to work within the PEACH prototype, the layout of the player component had to be changed in order to fit the small screen area available on the mobile device. Since the video playback had to be integrated seamlessly into the whole presentation performed by the Virtual Characters, the communication mechanism between video player and video composer was also changed. Instead of a direct communication via the graphical user interface (GUI), the PEACH server requests specific videos from the video generator. The generated video script is send back to the PEACH server. The server then incorporates the script into a larger presentation script for the mobile device (including instructions for the Migrating Characters and slide show instructions). In this way, a coherent presentation is generated, allowing the Migrating Character to announce a video clip, to watch the clip together with the user, and to summarize the content as soon as the clip is finished (the integration of the video generator and player component in the PEACH prototype is described in detail in Rocchi et al. (2004).

Fig. 9. A migrating character announcing and watching a video clip

Figure 9 shows a sequence of screenshots of a character announcing a video clip and watching the clip together with the user. By automatically showing relevant details of large-scale images while playing back audio commentary, the system generates and integrates video clips in a way that maximizes use of the small screen of a mobile device.

7.5   Information Presentation for Mobile and Stationary Devices

One goal that we had in mind when designing the concepts for PEACH was to transparently combine mobile and stationary output devices. In the previous section, we described the role of the presentation agent which can travel from one device to another and thus guide the focus of attention from the mobile device to the Virtual Window, and vice versa. At the same time, the presentation agent is a metaphor for a special perspective on the cultural heritage explored; it represents the stereotype that is actually used to classify the visitors. In the Buonconsiglio Castle, two stereotypes were implemented: an artist character representing the interest of the visitor in artistic techniques and a noble dame character representing the user's interest in social aspects of the period (see also Fig. 9). In addition, it is necessary to adapt the style and content of the presentation to the situative context of the users in order to provide a coherent presentation throughout the visit. This helps the underlying technology remain as unnoticed as possible, thus emphasizing the content of the presentation. Figure 10 shows the system architecture that supports this adaptation process. It is designed as a client–server architecture, where all mobile devices and Virtual Windows have to register with a central presentation server.

A salient feature is its ability to simultaneously generate presentations both for mobile devices and Virtual Windows. Given a visitor-specific situative context, the presentation server first selects the appropriate content and the degree of adaptation that is necessary. For this purpose, we make use of different strategies that adapt the presentation not only to the location and the interest of the visitor, but also to the available modalities. Since we can distinguish between users who are only listening to the presentation and visitors who are looking, the system can decide when to provide video-clip or audio-only presentations. The strategies also take into account technical resources of the output media, i.e., the screen resolution and display size. The content for presentations in a Virtual Window is selected according to visitor interest as displayed during the visit. Rather than just providing additional material according to the stereotype (e.g., general vs. artistic view), the system provides further details on the exhibits that were of specific interest to the visitor (according to the *visiting history*). Metastrategies allow us to provide the visitors with information that helps to change their situative context if necessary. For example, the system can advise the visitors to look at an image that is displayed on the mobile device. One specific strategy even allows the system to guide the visitor to the next Virtual Window where the content can be better presented.

After determining the content and structure of the presentation, the server starts to plan the behaviour and role of the virtual character and, where appropriate, also plans the structure of a video clip. For this purpose, the server relies on the cinematographic strategies described in Chap. 2. The behaviour of the life-like character is captured in its own set of strategies, helping the system to decide, for example, which of the two roles (presentation agent or anchorman) the character should play during a part of a presentation. Finally, the server renders the overall presentation with material retrieved from a multimedia database that contains graphics and text. At this point, the video-clips are generated from static graphics and the text for the character is transformed into spoken language. The final presentations are then delivered either to the mobile devices or to the Virtual Windows.

7.6   Summary and Outlook

In this chapter, we described our concept for making museum visits more engaging through the delivery of seamlessly integrated presentations with migrating virtual characters on mobile and stationary devices. We introduced the notion of character locomotion and presented experiences from two case studies located at different museums in Germany and Italy. We believe this may lead to further developments in the area of educational entertainment. There are many themes that remain completely open. Perhaps the biggest challenge concerns keeping the attention of the users high and achieving a long-term memory effect. We need to be able to design presentation techniques that "hook" visitors and which continuously build anticipation and release tension.

Another interesting question is how groups of visitors can be better supported by the described infrastructure of mobile and stationary devices. Some interesting, open challenges are tailoring presentations to the needs of groups and individuals and defining the role that life-characters can play in such settings. There is much to be done also in the way of visit modalities, which is particularly important for children.

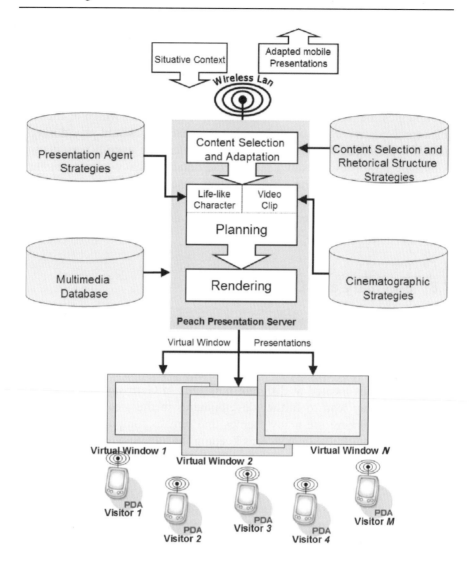

Fig. 10. The architecture used to combine presentations on virtual windows and mobile devices for multiple visitors

8 Children in the Museum: an Environment for Collaborative Storytelling

M. Zancanaro, F. Pianesi, O. Stock, P. Venuti, A. Cappelletti,
G. Iandolo, M. Prete and F. Rossi

8.1 Introduction

In the field of education, the issue of technology to support learning has long been debated because of concerns about young children's physical and cognitive readiness to use computers (Bailey and Weippert 1991). One of the concerns about the impact of computers on children's social development is that traditional computer interfaces do not enable collaboration while it has been shown that working in small groups benefits learning and development.

Recently, there has been growing interest in the use of novel technologies that support collaborative interaction among children. Among many, KidPad and the Klump (Benford et al. 2000) and the Magic Carpet (Stanton et al. 2001) were developed as collaborative storytelling technologies for young children, subtly encouraging collaboration so that children can discover the added benefits of working together (as an example, children were able to combine digital crayons to produce new colours).

Also, there has been some exploration of technologies that allow children to reflect after performing activities outside the classroom: for example, Ambient Wood (Price et al. 2003), where children first explored a digitally augmented woodland to find out about plant life in the different habitats, and then, back at the classroom, used an interactive screen display to show their information to one another and start forming predictions. Similarly, the Savannah project is a collaborative, location-based game in which groups of children role-play being lions on a hunt in a virtual savannah; an interface for replaying a system-recording of each completed level is then provided in the classroom so children can reflect on how they performed (Benford et al. 2005).

The use of physical tools has also been explored to support storytelling in systems such as MIT's KidsRoom (Bobick et al. 2000), StoryRooms (Alborzi et al. 2000) and StoryMat (Ryokai and Cassell 1999). Storytent, a system developed at Nottigham University, is a projected display shaped like a tent which allows children to immerse themselves in a virtual world (Green et al. 2002). The TellTale interface (Ananny 2002) explores the idea of providing ways of making the pieces of a story "tangible". TellTale is a caterpillar-like toy with five modular, coloured body pieces on which children can record their own voices; once linked together, the audio is played back in sequence.

Some research has been focused in having the system working as a companion of a child. Sam, a tool developed at Media Lab (Ryokai et al. 2003), consists of a 3D, animated virtual child that can pass physical toys back and forth to real children and can cooperate with children in constructing stories

All these research projects recognize storytelling as a learning activity that allows children to develop skills such as creative problem-solving, collaborative learning, expressive design, the development of multiple forms of literacy, and the exploration of knowledge (Peterson and McCabe 1983).

The Story Table system described in this chapter differs from the works mentioned above in many respects. First of all, it does not feature any kind of virtual companion, but directly targets (small) groups of children. Secondly, it aims at supporting them by actively enforcing cooperation while planning and building the story. In particular, key activities are explicitly synchronized; to this end, we relied on the notion of muiltiuser actions.

A particular aspect of Story Table is that it has been designed for and it is meant to be used in the context of a museum visit as a tool that helps children reflect on their experience and that also stimulates meaningful shared "cultural" activity. The overall idea is that children learn and get involved in the cultural domain if they can play an active role in re-elaborating the material and in creating new material (see, for example, Tunnicliffe and Beer 2002), especially if they can do so by working together collaboratively. By adopting technology that fosters collaborative storytelling, several aspects of user experience are enhanced at the same time: children's motivation and interest in the museum, their appreciation of different contributions and points of view, their capability of negotiating an integrated, balanced and coherent result, and the linguistic form of their account, especially as far as the exploitation of cohesion tools is concerned. The main tenet for our work is to provide the children with a tool for working together and discovering the benefits of collaboration.

In cooperative learning theory, we recognized a valid method for driving the design of a tool that would fit this goal. Cooperative learning is an instructional method that involves students working in teams to achieve a common goal. The emphasis is on the cooperation between children that must be established and appropriately maintained in order for the methodology to display its benefits. To do so, means for group reflection and individual self-assessment are needed.

Many studies have shown that when correctly implemented, cooperative learning improves information acquisition and retention, higher-level thinking skills, interpersonal and communication skills, and self-confidence (Johnson and Johnson 1999).

In order for group work to be effective, five criteria need to be met:

- First of all, positive interdependence must be established among children so that they feel linked with group mates such that they cannot succeed unless their group mates do, and they feel that they must coordinate their efforts with the efforts of their group mates to accomplish the task. Positive interdependence has different facets. The first is positive goal interdependence, which is established when individual goals equal those of the group. Another one is positive resource interdependence, which holds when the resources needed to solve the problem have to be shared by the group members.
- Second, the group must be accountable for achieving its goals, and each member must be accountable for contributing his or her share of the work. The team has to be clear about its goals and be able to measure both its progress in achieving them and the individual efforts of each member. When it is difficult to identify the contributions of members, or when members are not responsible for the final group outcome, they may be seeking a "free ride".
- Furthermore, teammates need to do real work together in which they promote each other's successes by sharing resources and helping, supporting, encouraging, and praising each other's efforts to learn. This criterion is called "face-to-face promotive action".
- Next, group members must know how to provide effective leadership, decision making, trust building, communication and conflict management, and be motivated to use the prerequisite skills.
- Finally, regular self-assessment of team functioning is required. Teachers and students should periodically analyze and reflect on the dynamics of group sessions to determine what actions were helpful and whether changes should be made.

8.2   Story Table Design and Implementation

The Story Table interface was designed by a muiltidisciplinary team encompassing psychologists, graphic designers and computer scientists. Their aim was to support pairs of children in the activity of storytelling in the context of a reflective re-elaboration of a museum experience

The system is based on DiamondTouch Dietz (2001), a muiltiuser, touch-and-gesture-activated screen designed to support small-group collaboration. It has a 32-inch diagonal surface (a 42-inch diagonal display is also available) that can be placed flat on a standard table. The graphical user interface (GUI) is projected onto this surface. It contains an array of antennas embedded in the touch surface. Each antenna transmits a unique signal. Each user has a separate receiver, connected to the user, typically through the user's chair. When a user touches the surface, antennas near the touch point couple an extremely small amount of signal through the user's body and to the receiver. This technology supports multiple touches by a single user and distinguishes between simultaneous inputs from multiple users.

Figure 1 illustrates the system architecture of StoryTable, which is implemented in Macromedia Flash using Macromedia CommServer to manage audio recordings. The connection with the DiamondTouch API is established through a C# layer that embeds the Flash interface. The event system was extended—as explained below—and the extension is imp-lemented in ActionScript.

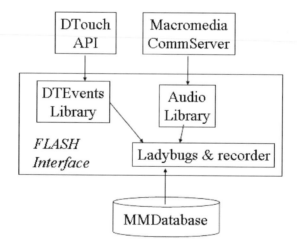

Fig. 1. Story Table system architecture

8.2.1   Multiple-User Gestures

Exploiting DiamondTouch's capability to distinguish between simul-taneous input from multiple users, we extended the event system of standard touchable interfaces (that is, the touch, the double touch and the drag-and-drop events), allowing multiple-user events such as the multiple-user touch, the multiple-user double touch and the multiple-user drag-and-drop.

A multiple-user touch is an event that is triggered when two or more users click together on a button (Fig. 2). Indeed, since we wanted the new events extend the standard event system, we have a chain of events generated by the user actions. In the case of two users touching a button, the system first triggers a standard touch event when the first user touches the button. When a second user touches the same button, a new multiple-user touch event is triggered. When one of the two users releases the touch, a multiple-user release event is triggered. Finally, when the other user releases the button the standard release event is triggered.

 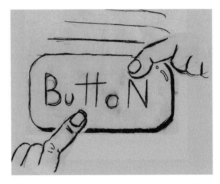

Fig. 2. Sketch of a preliminary design phase and conceptualization of a muiltiuser touch gesture

The multiple-user drag-and-drop event is a little bit more complicated because it requires that users not only touch the objects together (and, therefore, trigger the chain of events described above for the multiple-user touch), but also that they move their fingers on the surface in a synchronized way. Since this can be difficult to achieve, a threshold for avoiding an unexpected closing of the event was determined empirically.

8.2.2   Design Rationale

The design rationale is based on a methodology known as Family Bears (Bornstein 1985; Cesari and Venuti 1999), where a child is invited to play with puppets representing a family of bears and their living environments (the house, the school, and so on) and then to invent stories about what happens to the family. This approach is used in both educational and therapeutic settings to measure the linguistic capabilities of the children and their relations with the world.

Story Table provides many different scenarios (i.e., backgrounds) in addition to the Family Bears; each one has different characters for which children can invent stories. The interface was designed according to the concept of ladybugs wandering around the table surface (Fig. 3). A mixture of standard touch events and the new multiple-user events described above were used as a means to control the objects.

In particular, the multiple-user events were used to "force" children to work together at a very basic level. The hypothesis is that these constraints instantiate the criterium of face-to-face promotive action and they foster the children to acknowledge the presence of the partner, encouraging additional collaborative behaviour.

 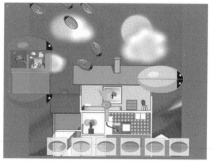

Fig. 3. The interface of the Story Table on the MERL's DiamondTouch

One ladybug carries the backgrounds, the stages on which the story will be set—e.g., a wood, a medieval castle, and so on. This ladybug can be opened to access the stages by double touching on it (see Fig. 3, right). Since the selection of the background is crucial for determining the story, the system forces agreement by requiring that background setting be done jointly by the children—that is, through a multiple-user touch event.

Another ladybug—the Character Ladybug—carries the various elements (for example, the Princess, the Knight, and so on) that can be dragged onto the current background. Again, the ladybug can be opened by a single-user double touch event. However, in this case, the elements can be dragged autonomously by each child.

A third type of ladybug of a different in shape (the smaller ones in Fig. 3) contains the audio snippets that will form the story. In order to load an audio snippet into one of these ladybugs, a child has to drag it into the recorder and then keep the button pressed while speaking. The audio snippets are recorded independently by the two children and—according to the criterion of *individual accountability*—once loaded with audio the ladybug displays a coloured shape meant to represent the child who recorded it. Once loaded, an audio ladybug can be modified by the child who recorded it, but the system refuses modifications attempted by the other child. Therefore, a ladybug is "owned" by the child who records it. Yet, the two children may agree to free a ladybug by a multiple-user drag-and-drop action. That is, if they drag the ladybug together onto the recording tool, the system removes the content and the highlighting. The ladybug is now free to be used by anyone. Again, this design choice is meant to foster face-to-face promotive actions.

Following the principle of *limited resources,* just six Audio Ladybugs are available following the criterion of positive resources interdependences and no more than 30 seconds of voice can be recorded on each ladybug. The system does not force the children to share the ladybugs, but we expect that the indication of the child who recorded each one—by means of the coloured shape—is enough to foster an appropriate use of collaborative skills and group processing.

To summarize, the main objectives pursued with the design of the interface are related to the basic principles of cooperative learning. The story is composed collaboratively by both children (positive goal inter-dependence) using a limited number of Audio Ladybugs (positive resources interdependence); each contribution is clearly attributable to the child who recorded it (individual accountability). Each child is allowed to work on an individual level, but crucial operations have to be performed by both children simultaneously (appropriate use of collaborative skills and group processing).

From the point of view of improving storytelling capabilities, we claim that the limited portion of audio that each Ladybug may hold encourages children to reflect on the surface structure and the words they use to form their stories. Moreover, the possibility of reorganizing Audio Ladybugs will promote the reflection on the coherence among story segments. Finally, given that each Audio Ladybug can be rerecorded, children are encouraged to consider the role of each story unit in their narrative.

8.3   Pilot Studies

We conducted two user trials to assess design choices. The studies suggest that, according to the claim of cooperative learning, cooperative storytelling can increase the level of engagement of less motivated children without affecting the involvement of the more active ones.

8.3.1 First Trial

The purpose of the first trial was to assess the capability of children of different ages in recognizing and using the basic elements of the Story Table interface. Ten children were invited to play, in groups of two, with the Story Table. As a control situation we set up a "low-tech" table with the same backgrounds used in the Story Table but drawn on sheets of paper; puppets replaced the Story Table characters, and a standard tape recorder was proposed as a device to record the story.

The children were grouped according to age into five groups: (i) two 4-year-old girls; (ii) two 5-year-old boys; (iii) two girls, 5 and 6 years old; (iv) two 6-year-old girls; (v) one boy (7 years) and one girl (8 years).

Each pair of children was first introduced to each other and then spent 10 to 15 minutes playing with one experimenter to get to know each other. During this initial phase, they were asked about stories and storytelling. Then, they were given a short "hands-on" tutorial on the Story Table that lasted a few minutes. The tutorial was organized as a quick and interactive introduction to the available operations. Each operation was first introduced by the experimenter, and then the children were asked to repeat it. The children were taught that the Story Table had two magic carpets, each in a different colour. Each child owned one of them and was given a sticker of the same colour to put on her finger. The colour corresponded to that of the shadow that would appear on each Audio Ladybug after the child had recorded it.

The children were then invited to play with the Story Table for up to half an hour. In this phase, the experimenter intervened to help the children only when they had failed at three attempts to perform an action. Finally, the children were asked to play with the low-tech storytelling table and debriefed with a short interview.

There was a great amount of variation in the duration of the sessions, due to the fact that we did not force the children to play with the Story Table for longer than they wanted. The durations were respectively: 11 minutes with 44 actions for the first group; 11 minutes with 233 actions for the second one; 5 minutes with 81 actions for the third; 35 minutes with 63 actions for the fourth; and 24 minutes with 162 actions for the fifth. As can be seen, it was not possible to reveal clear age-related patterns for duration and number of actions performed.

Fig. 4. Children interacting with the Story Table and with the paper-based control version during the first trial

For the purpose of analysis, we collected the actions performed by the children in three groups. *Muiltiuser actions* were needed to select backgrounds (double-touch), listen to the story (double-touch the first Audio Ladybug in the holes sequence) and change the ownership of an Audio Ladybug (muiltiuser drag-and-drop). *Actions related to the management* of the world comprised opening the Background Ladybug or the Characters Ladybug to choose a background and drag-and-drop a character, respectively. The third group encompassed *actions related to the storytelling*, namely positioning the snippets on the microphone (single user drag-and-drop), recording and listening to an Audio Ladybug (single-user touches), and listening to the story (muiltiuser touch). The last and the first group partially overlap. The older children had a greater success rate in performing muiltiuser actions. While younger children clearly understood the operations, the number of errors in performing them was very high. The most frequent causes of error were double touches that were too fast or too slow, and faltering movements during drag-and-drop. Interestingly, the children were almost always able to self-diagnose the problem and to correct it in their next attempts.

The children did mind the constraints imposed by DiamondTouch. In particular, they easily managed to remain on the carpet while operating the StoryTable and to use their forefinger to touch the device. The only exception was noticed with the 4-year-old children, who were too small to reach the upper part of the table and in their attempts sometimes needed to lean on one hand, thus touching the table. Interestingly, they usually recognized their mistake and promptly recovered.

They always listened to an Audio Ladybug after having recorded it, and they usually respected their partners' ladybugs. For example, they asked to listen to the content rather than just double-clicking it. The 5-year-old girl of the third group fiercely claimed the last empty Audio Ladybug since her partner had already recorded three while she had only two. Finally, we noticed the unanticipated phenomenon of the affective relationship with the Audio

Ladybugs. They always referred to them as "mine" and "yours" and they did not like to give their ladybugs to the partner (even if, when asked, they demonstrated they understood the procedure to do this, namely drag together the ladybug on the recorder). On the one hand, this hampered the children from freely using the Audio Ladybugs to build the story, while on the other, this stimulated the shier children to take an active role.

The control sessions with the "low-tech" table were usually quite short. The children usually complained about the difficulty of audio recording. In most cases, one child in the group did most of the activities while the other barely participated.

8.3.2   Second Trial

The objectives of the second trial were first, to understand whether the Story Table may be effectively used as a tool to support children in telling stories; and second, to assess to what extent the interface can foster a collaborative behaviour by forcing joint actions.

The same two 7- and 8-year-old children from the first trial, a male and a female, were invited to participate in four further sessions with the Story Table. The experimenters played a more active role that was aimed at favoring a real storytelling activity. They strongly suggested to the children roles for characters, events of the story, and sometimes even which sentences to record. The involvement of the experiments was then progressively decreased from the first to the last session; more precisely, the time taken by the experimenter for this kind of intervention was 70% of the total time in the first session, 44% in the second, 26% in the third, and 5% in the last. To control the effect of the Story Table, at the beginning of the first session we asked the children to tell an individual story each. We also asked the children to invent a joint story using puppets instead of the Story Table at the beginning of the last session.

Fig. 5. The children of the second trial interacting with the Story Table

All the stories were evaluated using the NICHD Coding Scheme, a methodology specifically devised to measure the level of complexity in stories invented by children (see below for details). Since the NICHD methodology was not designed to measure cooperation between the children, we decided to deal with this aspect by taking the different types of contributions made by the children during the entire interaction as a measure of their cooperation. To this end, we used the classification of language functions introduced by Halliday (1973). According to Halliday, the way language is used in communication can be analyzed according to the different functions the speaker wants to perform while speaking. The most relevant functions for our purpose is the *regulatory* function, which is used to regulate the behavior of others (e.g. "Get me water because I'm thirsty"). It can be *positive* when it is used to suggest, or *negative* when used to blame. In addition, the *imaginative* function enables children to relate to their environment using language to create a fantasy environment.

In the individual stories created without the Story Table, the girl was very verbose, telling a story of 12 episodes in 41 sentences, which scored 9/11 on the cohesion scale and 4/5 on the structure scale. The boy told a very simple story of 5 episodes in 7 sentences, which scored 3/11 in cohesion and 4/5 in structure. The story told jointly without the Story Table was invented almost exclusively by the girl; it comprised 12 episodes in 123 sentences and scored 10/11 in cohesion and 5/5 in structure. Regarding the Story Table, we only considered the stories produced in the last two sessions since the role of the experimenters in the first two sessions was too strong. The story invented in the third session comprised 5 episodes (3 invented by the girl and 2 by the boy) in 12 sentences (10 recorded by the girl and 2 by the boy). The scores were 4/11 for cohesion and 4/5 for structure. After the session, the experimenters used the story recorded in the ladybugs to help the children point out problems in cohesion. The children then autonomously decided to re-record some parts of the story. The final version comprised 4 episodes (3 by the girl and 1 by the boy) in 8 sentences (5 by the girl and 3 by the boy). After the elaboration, the story scored 5/11 for cohesion.

The story told in the last session with the Story Table comprised 6 episodes (3 invented by the girl and 3 by the boy) in 13 sentences (10 recorded by the girl and 3 by the boy). The story scored 6/11 in cohesion and 5/5 in structure. After the discussion with the experimenters and the elaboration performed autonomously by the children, the final version comprised 6 episodes (3 for each child) in 10 sentences (7 by the girl and 3 by the boy); the score for cohesion grew to 7/11.

Regarding their cooperation, the girl always led the interaction, offering 25 contributions of the imaginative type for the collaborative story with puppets, and respectively 22, 27, 22, and 21 contributions of this type in the sessions with the Story Table. She performed very few heuristic and regulatory types of contributions, and these were always positive. The boy did not perform any contribution of the imaginative type for the collaborative story with the puppets, while he performed 2 contributions of the heuristic type and 4 of negative regulatory type. During the Story Table sessions, his contributions of the imaginative type grew respectively to 9, 15, 16 and 11. His preference for heuristic and negative regulatory contributions was still high.

The first important result is that working with the Story Table helped the boy to be more involved (more contributions with respect to both his individual story and the puppet-based jointl story). On the other hand, the girl did not diminish her own level of engagement. The increased involvement of the boy is probably partly due to the novelty effect of the Story Table and the attractiveness of the technology. Though he was often distracted, the boy was always kept involved by the girl, who needed him to listen to the story (by muiltiuser actions) and was, therefore, motivated to have him involved. Furthermore, as already emerged from the first trial, both children developed a strong affective relation with their Audio Ladybugs; none of them ever lent their own Audio Ladybugs to the other, even when they were criticized for the contents and were explicitly requested to rerecord it. It can be conjectured that this strong affective relationship also favoured the boy's involvement.

The stories invented with the Story Table were significantly shorter than the stories told with the puppets. This is most probably related to the limited number of ladybugs available. The paucity of resources, together with the affective relationship that the children showed with respect to these, apparently improved the level of cooperation in the interaction. At the same time, being able to listen to the content of their recordings made the children more critical towards the form (i.e., false start, repetition, and pronunciation errors were always pointed out by the children themselves without the intervention of the experimenters).

The stories invented with the Story Table scored relatively lower than both the individual stories and the cooperative story with the puppets. This might be at least in part due to the cooperation itself, since inventing a story together is a significantly more complex activity than telling a story alone. Indeed, the cooperative story with the puppets was actually invented by the girl alone with very few contributions by the boy.

8.4   The Experimental Study

The aim of this study was to compare the impact of the Story Table in children's narration in shared play compared to a "low-tech" control condition.

From the results of the second pilot study, we expected that the following would hold true:

- Hypothesis 1: Story Table induces more complex and mature language because the children have the possibility to listen the content recorded in the audio ladybugs and critically reason about it.
- Hypothesis 2: there is a tendency towards less structured and less cohesive stories using the Story Table, but it is not very strong.
- Hypothesis 3: the contribution to the story and the interaction between the children will be more balanced in the Story Table than in the control condition.

8.4.1   Method

Seventy children from two local primary schools were invited to play a collaborative narration game based on the Family Bear methodology. Taking into consideration the results of a sociometric test, the children were paired so as to have a neutral pair (i.e., children that have neither strong positive nor strong negative attitude toward their partner). The experiment was a between-subject study with two conditions: ST for the narration using Story Table and BT for the Family Bears low-tech condition. The two conditions were randomized.

8.4.2   Measures

The WISC-R tests for vocabulary comprehension (Wechsler 1986) and the "energy" scale of the Big Five-Q questionnaire for children (Barbaranelli et al. 1998) were used to assess the individual characteristics of the children.

The quality of the stories was assessed by the NICHD method. The variables considered are the number of words (*WORDS*), prepositions (*PREPS*), and episodes (*EPISODS*) used in the story as well as the number of problematic elements introduced in the story (*PROBS*) being either positive solutions, negative solutions, or without solution. Finally, there are variables for the narrative structure (*STRUCT*) and the cohesion (*COHES*) of the story; the former measuring whether the story has a well-formed structure containing an introduction, a problem, a resolution, and a conclusion, while the latter measures how much a story possesses internal cohesion, that is, whether the episodes are connected and the problematic elements are solved. For the cooperative narrations, we also counted the number of words that the children used other than in the stories (*INT*).

8.4.3   Procedure

The children were invited to the ITC-irst premises for two sessions on two different days.

Fig. 6. The three phases of the experiment: an individual child narration (*left*), a pair of children using Story Table (*centre*) and the control condition using puppets (*right*)

At the beginning of the first session, the children were separated in two rooms and invited to tell a story individually about the Bear Family using puppets. This initial phase was meant to assess the literacy ability of the children. The story produced was analysed using the NICHD coding scheme. In this phase, the pretest questionnaires were also administered. Then, the two children were invited to tell a story together using Story Table. This phase was meant as a training session for the system and the stories produces were not analyzed.

During the second session, the children were invited to tell a story using Story Table (ST condition) and then, after a short break, to tell another story using the puppets (BT condition). The two tasks were randomized. The two stories produced were then analyzed using the NICHD coding scheme.

8.4.4   Results

The children's ages ranged from 102 months (8.5 years) to 129 months (10.5 years) with a mean of 114.40 and a standard deviation of 7.93. There were 28 males and 42 females. Statistics for WISC and Energy are reported in Table 1.

Table 1. Descriptive statistics for WISC and Energy

	N	Minimum	Maximum	Mean	Std. Deviation
Energy	70	22	38	29.81	3.209
WISC	70	9	19	17.70	2.656
Valid N (listwise)	70				

WISC scores do not differ for sex, while Energy scores are significantly larger for females than for males even if the difference is small (respectively, 30.57 and 28.69; t=-2.419, df=50,7, p<0.05, equal variances not assumed). A multivariate analysis using Energy and age as covariate shows that none of the independent variables is affected by sex.

Table 2. Descriptive statistics for the independent variables in the two conditions (BT=1 and ST=2)

	N	Minimum	Maximum	Mean	Std. Deviation
# words BT	35	102	536	311.49	102.747
# words ST	35	67	480	276.06	124.931
# propositions BT	35	11	120	58.34	23.147
# propositions ST	35	6	85	44.91	22.099
# episodes BT	35	6	77	34.17	12.963
# episodes ST	35	7	56	23.03	12.104
structure BT	35	1	6	4.11	1.388
structure ST	35	1	6	3.91	1.522
cohesion BT	35	4	10	7.77	1.610
cohesion ST	35	4	10	7.40	1.459
# words interaction BT	35	0	299	73.06	79.800
# words interaction ST	35	94	647	257.74	139.675
valid N (listwise)	35				

Regarding differences in the two conditions, a multivariate analysis with repeated measures (BT vs. ST conditions) showed an overall significant within-subject effect (Wilk's lambda=0.19, F=203.792, Hypothesis-df=7, error-df=28, p<0.01, partial eta squared=0.981, observed power=1).

Univariate tests showed significant differences between the number of propositions (Type III sum of squares=3155,7144, df=1, F=7.615, p<0.01, partial eta squared=0.183), the number of episodes (Type III sum of squares=2172,86, df=1, F=15.772, p<0.01, partial eta squared=0.317), and the number of words produced during the interaction (Type III sum of squares=596904,23, df=1, F=88.392, p<0.01, partial eta squared=0.722) produced in the two conditions.

Comparing these results with the figures in Table 3 above, it can be seen that our children's story had significantly more propositions and episodes in BT (58.34 and 34.17) than in ST (44.91 and 23.03). At the same time, the two conditions did not significantly affect either the quality of the stories produced, which were substantially identical both in terms of narrative structure and cohesion, or the number of words that make up the stories (even if there is a tendency for lower scores in ST). This confirms Hypothesis 1 above.

The verbal interaction was richer in ST than in BT (257.74 vs. 73.06). Qualitative analysis of the interactions suggests that ST prompted more negotiation and mutual agreement effort, which may have led to the more complex, articulated language just mentioned. This result confirmed Hypothesis 2 above.

Regarding Hypothesis 3, Table 3 plots the differences in contributions (as a percentage of the total) between the two children with respect to the relevant variables.

A multivariate analysis with repeated measures (Wilk's lambda=0.664, F=3.914, Hypothesis-df=4, error-df=31, p<0.05, observed power=0.851) confirms that there is an effect due to the condition. The univariate tests, however, show that the only significative difference that can be found is for the INTER variable, that is, the number of words not belonging to the narration (Type III sum of squares= 1732.103, df=1, F= 8.716, p<0.01).

The lack of differences in the other variables may be due to the weakness of the index used: the test might not be sensitive enough given the small sample.

Table 3. Descriptive statistics for the distances between the pairs in the two conditions

	Mean	Std. Deviation	N
Distance words BT	36.0419	26.32739	35
Distance words ST	26.1910	22.14513	35
Distance props BT	34.2889	25.53821	35
Distance props ST	29.2032	20.27624	35
Distance episodes BT	37.1977	24.84807	35
Distance episodes ST	29.6119	19.92581	35
Distance interaction BT	36.6934	28.48535	35
Distance interaction ST	26.7447	23.12788	35

In order to gain qualitative evidence towards Hypothesis 3, we can take into consideration the direction of change of the difference of BT with respect to ST (see Table 4): the average of the decrements from BT to ST is consistently greater that the average of those pair whose difference increases in ST with respect to BT. This effect leads us to think that Story Table has a positive effect on fostering a more balanced division of labour within the pair.

Table 4. Average of decrements and increments from BT to ST

	Decrement (BT->ST		Decrement (BT->ST	
	Avg.	StdDev.	Avg.	StdDev.
WORDS	0.18	0.20	0.09	0.14
PROPS	0.16	0.20	0.11	0.15
EPIS	0.19	0.24	0.11	0.20
INTER	0.13	0.04	0.16	0.07

Similarly, by ranking the percentage contributions of the children in 10 levels (representing 10% of the contributions, 20%, and so on), we note that in the ST condition, the distributions are more concentrated around 50%. On the other hand, the BT conditions present greater variability. Figure 7 shows the chart for the WORDS variable. Similar charts result for the other variables.

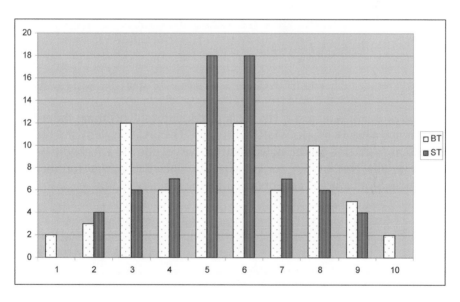

Fig. 7. Rankings for the WORDS variable for the BT condition (*left*) and the ST condition (*right*)

Finally, taking inspiration from the field of econometrics, we can examine the plots of the Lorenz curves obtained, considering each pair as a population and the story as an income measure shared between the two children. In case of perfect equality in the contribution, the graphical representation is a straight line of 45 degrees.

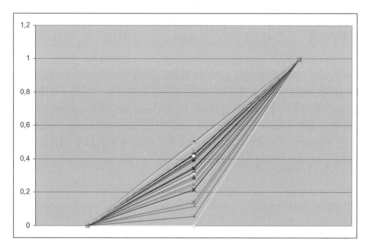

Fig. 8. Lorenz curve for the BT condition for the number of words composing the story

Figures 8 and 9 represent the plots of the curves concerning the words used in the story (variable WORDS) for the BT condition (left) and the ST condition (right). It can be noted that the curves for the ST condition are closer to the line of the perfect equality than the curves for the BT condition. Similar graphs are obtained for the other variables.

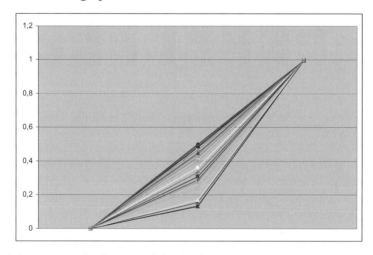

Fig. 9. Lorenz curve for the ST condition for the number of words composing the story

8.5 Conclusion

In this paper, we presented the design and the evaluation of a tool for reflective learning based on the notion of collaborative storytelling. This tool is meant to represent a first step for children to have an active role in a museum environment. The overall idea is that children learn and get involved in a cultural domain if they can play an active role in re-elaborating the material and in creating new material, in particular if they can do so by working together collaboratively. By adopting technology that fosters collaborative storytelling, several aspects of user experience are enhanced at the same time: children's motivation and interest in the museum, their appreciation of different contributions and points of view, their capability of negotiating an integrated, balanced and coherent result, and the linguistic form of their account, especially as far as the exploitation of cohesion tools is concerned. The main tenet for our work is to provide the children with a tool for working together and discovering the benefits of collaboration.

The design of Story Table was informed by the theory of collaborative learning. The hypothesis that the use of the system makes a difference in the way children interact and in the quality of the stories produced were discussed and tested.

The system is based on DiamondTouch, a muiltiuser, touch-and-gesture-activated screen designed to support small-group collaboration. Exploiting the capability of this device to distinguish between simultaneous inputs from multiple users, we extended the event system of standard touchable interfaces allowing multiple-user events such as the multiple-user touch, the multiple-user double touch and the multiple-user drag-and-drop. In particular, the multiple-user events were used to "force" children to work together at a very basic level. The hypothesis was that these constraints foster the children to acknowledge the presence of the partner and therefore encourage collaborative behavior.

The pilot studies suggest that, according to the claim of cooperative learning and the design hypothesis, Story Table may increase the level of engagement of less motivated children without affecting the involvement of the more active ones. This result was then further consolidated by an experimental study with 70 children from a local primary school that proved that (i) Story Table induces more complex and mature language because the children have the possibility to listen the content recorded in the audio ladybugs and critically reason about it; and (ii) there is a tendency toward less structured and less cohesive stories using the Story Table, but it is not very strong. Moreover, qualitative analysis provides initial evidence that contributions to the story and the interaction between the children is more balanced in the Story Table than in the control condition.

The experiments reported here help us consolidate our view that collaboration-enforcing technology can offer an important prospect for children in a museum. It is only a beginning for collaborative storytelling technology: the integration of mobile and "reflective" environments is a novel aspects to study and technology appropriate for more complex situations, involving grown ups rather than children, are themes to be studied further. Some of these prospects will be discussed in the final chapter of this collection.

8.6   Acknowledgments

The authors wish to thank Franco Dossena and Adriano Freri for their contribution to the graphical and conceptual design of Story Table.

Part IV
Virtual Reconstructions and Simulations

9 Photorealistic 3D Modelling Applied to Cultural Heritage

F. Voltolini, A. Beraldin, S. El-Hakim and L. Gonzo

9.1 Introduction

For applications such as cultural heritage, achieving real-time visualization and interactive manipulation of highly textured surfaces will give a vista to scientists, conservationists, historians, and visitors for looking at and studying important frescoed surfaces in virtual reality.

As a case study, we present the results from modelling and visualisation of the "Cycle of the Months", a major masterpiece of international Gothic art which is located in the Aquila tower in Buonconsiglio castle, Trento, Italy. The main room in the tower is completely frescoed with the "Cycle of the Months", a rare example of medieval painting on a nonreligious subject. The frescos depict the medieval period month-by-month with stunning landscape details. Texture is the most important part of the model and any reduction in quality can affect scene comprehension.

The first step is to create a geometrically correct 3D model of the room. We considered three alternatives for 3D scene reconstruction:

1. Image-based rendering (IBR): Although this does not include creating a 3D geometric model (Kang 1999), it may be considered to be like a model since the room is simple and has no other objects but the walls and the ceiling. This requires taking overlapping images from the middle of the room. IBR is basically restricted to static scenes with static illumination, though some papers make suggestions on how to work around this problem. A second problem associated with certain techniques is that the movement of the viewpoint is confined to particular locations. In addition, without a geometric model there is the possibility of perspective distortion.
2. Image-based modelling: These techniques are suitable for regular geometric surfaces like architectures and monuments (Debevec et al.

1996, El-Hakim 2002). Photogrammetric methods can achieve high geometric accuracy, albeit without capturing all fine geometric details. The geometry of the room is a typical candidate for this approach. The same images used to construct the geometry are also used for the texture.

3. Range-based modelling: These techniques—mainly laser scanning—are capable of capturing most geometric details, but the accuracy varies notably from one scanner to another. Having a scanner that can achieve reasonable accuracy for our room size is difficult since most commercial scanners are either designed for long range (over 10 m) or close range (less than 3 m). Besides, the walls are mostly flat, thus there are no fine details to capture by scanner. Regardless of which scanner is used, it is necessary to acquire geometry and texture separately. Scanners with integrated texture or colour acquisition cannot provide the quality required for the detailed frescos in a room of this size. Separate high-resolution digital images should be taken and properly calibrated and registered with the geometric data (Beraldin et al. 2002).

We collected the data with digital cameras and a laser scanner, but we focus on the image-based modelling approach as the most appropriate technique.

9.2   Image Based Modelling

In this section, we provide an overview of the main issues associated with the modelling and real-time rendering of highly textured real environments, and the main techniques currently used to address these challenges. We then present details on the approach we employed to achieve photorealism and interactive visualisation.

As mentioned before, the objective of our work in the PEACH project was to acquire the most suitable data and generate a textured 3D model for interactive manipulation and creation of a photorealistic walk-through movie of the "Cycle of the Months".

Since photorealism of the frescos is of utmost importance, it became apparent that many issues related to geometric and radiometric distortions had to be addressed. For example, texture data is typically collected as images containing with real lighting conditions. When these images are stitched together, discontinuities are usually visible. Another predicament is the real-time requirement of visualization and manipulation of 3D models. Since it is important to maintain the best texture quality to visualize the details of the frescos and at the same time have smooth interactive visualization, memory problems had to be addressed. We built upon existing techniques developed for texture acquisition and reconstruction to generate efficient maps of high visual quality.

9.2.1   Modelling Issues

We divided the problems into those affecting visual quality or photorealism (photorealism means there is no difference between the rendered model and a photograph taken from the same viewpoint), and those affecting manipulation or interactive visualization (visualization here will always mean interactive visualization). Obviously the purpose of visualization is to provide smooth navigation through the model. This should be at a rate of at least 20 frames-per-second, otherwise the human brain can detect latency or jitter, with the likely consequence of loss of interactivity. For most cases developed with current hardware, it is usually impossible to achieve both photorealism and smooth navigation without some compromise. In fact, the state of technology is such that, for most detailed models, neither is fully achievable yet.

9.2.1.1   Photorealism

The issue of acquiring and constructing high-quality texture maps has received less attention than the issue of capturing high-quality geometry (Bernardini et al. 2001). Traditional texture mapping techniques, which are simply draping static imagery over geometry, are not sufficient to represent reality.

Geometric distortions can affect photorealism. Due to the highly detailed contents of the frescos, it is crucial to preserve every line or edge and all minute painting details. Such textures on the models can be visibly affected by any small geometric errors. Sources of these geometric distortions can be divided into three categories:

- Mapping between triangle plane and image plane.
- Camera calibration and image registration.
- The assumptions made in surface reconstruction and the simplification of shapes into triangles.

The correct mapping between the triangle plane and the image plane is given by a projective transform. Since most viewers do not use this transform, distortion arises, especially for large triangles. For example, the projection of a straight line inside the triangle may become crooked. In addition, after the correct mapping is computed and the texture is warped, the image must be resampled or filtered. The easiest texture filtering method is point sampling, wherein the texture value nearest the desired sample point is used. But in general, this results in strong aliasing artefacts. To get rid of those artefacts, sophisticated filtering methods are needed such as space variant filters whose shape varies as they move across the image.

When cameras with standard lenses are used, lens distortion corrections must be applied. Otherwise, geometric distortions such as line discontinuity will be visible at common edges of adjacent triangles mapped from different images. It is therefore important that full camera calibration be applied, and that it remain valid for all images by keeping camera settings constant or applying self-calibration. Accurate image registration, mainly photogrammetric bundle adjustment, must also be implemented to minimise geometric distortions.

Too large a deviation of the triangle mesh from the underlying true object surface gives rise to geometric errors. Since a triangle represents a plane, applying triangles that are too large on even slightly curved surfaces will result in projections of features near the edges onto the wrong surface or the total disappearance of these features. This has occurred frequently with the frescos, which meant that we had to add more 3D points to the surfaces at appropriately selected locations.

Another factor affecting photorealism is the presence of *radiometric distortions* that usually result along common edges of adjacent triangles mapped from different images. The main reasons for this kind of distortions are:

- Differences in sensed brightness due to different camera position and/or change in illumination.
- Nonlinearity of the image response function.

A typical system captures a collection of images containing particular invariant lighting conditions at the time of imaging. Variation in the sensed brightness between images will result when taking images from different locations and at varying ambient lighting. When these images are stitched together, discontinuity artefacts are usually visible.

The digitised brightness value for a pixel is not a measure of scene radiance (radiance is the amount of light energy reflected from a surface in all directions). There is an unknown nonlinear mapping between the pixel value and the scene radiance. This nonlinearity is largest near the saturated part of the response curve. Knowing the response function allows images to be merged even if they are taken at different exposure settings, at different angles, or with different imaging devices. The inverse of the response function is used to recover the scene radiance (Debevec and Malik 1997). The response function can be applied to any image taken by the imaging system. Therefore, we can use a calibration process to determine the function for a given camera in a controlled environment, then apply it to the project images.

Blending methods for the creation of seamless texture maps have been developed (Bernardini et al. 2001; Pulli et al. 1998; Rocchini et al. 2002, Wang et al. 2001). These techniques use the weighted average of pixel values of triangles in the overlapping sections between two adjacent textures. For example, (Pulli et al. 1998) used the best three views to calculate a new texture image. The colours of the compatible rays are averaged together via a weighting scheme that uses three different weights: directional, sampling quality, and feathering. The task of the directional weight is to favour rays originating from views whose viewing direction is close to that of the virtual camera. Not only should the weight increase as the current viewing direction moves closer, but the weights of the other views should decrease. Sampling quality weight directly reflects how well a ray samples a surface. The algorithm assigns each ray/pixel of each input image a weight that is defined as the cosine of the angle between the local surface normal and the direction from the surface point to the sensor. Feathering weight is used mostly to hide artefacts due to differences in lighting among the input images. Guidon (1997) achieved seamless radiometric continuity by radiometric normalization. He combines scene-wide statistical normalization (matching scene grey-level means and variances) with local operations such as feathering or blending in overlapped regions. Blending techniques do not always work in our application since some triangles can be too large to have textures from several images.

When the lighting in the virtual environment where the texture map is used differs from the lighting under which the texture map was captured, the resulting rendering will appear unrealistic without light-dependent texture mapping (Gelb et al. 2001). However, this method adds considerably to rendering processing time since the system repeatedly computes light directions using triangles normal.

In the planner walls, the rendering may look too smooth and unrealistically flat even when proper lighting is used. An improvement can be achieved by applying bump mapping. This is done by introducing small variations in surface normals, thus adding roughness to create a more realistic look to the lighted surface (Rushmeier 1997) without the need to model each wrinkle as a separate element.

When textured models are viewed from a long distance, aliasing, moiré effect, jagged lines, and other visible abnormalities may result. This is because when the surface is far away, a pixel on that surface may be associated with several texels from the original texture map. MIP-maps (MIP stands for "multum in parvo"), a sequence of textures each of which has progressively lower resolution (by a factor of 2) with respect to the original image, are commonly used to solve this problem (Williams 1983). The most appropriate texture is selected depending on the polygon size or distance. Bilinear or trilinear filtering (to remove aliasing) and texture memory caching are also needed. Since real-time resampling and filtering can be computationally expensive, the required filtered representations of the original texture may be precomputed and stored. This increases the total size of texture by a maximum of one third. Although most recent hardware supports MIP-mapping operations, the actual management and set up of the caching scheme is up to the application.

The *dynamic range* of a scene (the ratio between its brightest and darkest parts) is usually much higher than the inherited limit in the digital image dynamic range (8-bits per colour channel). This results in the flattening of the response curve (saturation) at the bright areas and the inability to resolve details in the dark areas. A high dynamic range (HDR) image can be assembled from multiple low dynamic range images on the scene taken at different exposure settings (Debevec and Malik 1997).

9.2.1.2   *Interactive Visualization*

Because this project focuses on high-quality textures, the texture size could end up being quite large. The rendering algorithm should be capable of delivering images at interactive frame rates, even for very large textures.

Specifications affecting performance of a rendering system are: the number of geometric transformations that can be performed per second, the number of triangles that can be rendered with texture per second, the available main and texture memory and the disk and network access speed (bandwidth). Memory limitations become the main issue for large textures. Some of these hardware specifications will only affect start up time. For example, significant computations are initially needed for the rendering software to build an internal representation of the scene graph. Also, high bandwidth is crucial to load the model and texture in memory in a reasonable amount of time at start up.

Most existing techniques for real-time rendering (Baxter et al. 2002; Cohen-Or et al. 2003) focus on the geometry (reducing the number of triangles) rather than the texture. For example, hierarchical levels of detail (LOD), where objects far away from the viewpoint are rendered with presampled lower resolution representations, is a standard technique that is supported by most scene graph libraries. No further details will be given here since, in image-based modelling, it is typically texture size rather than geometry that affects real-time rendering when high-resolution images are used.

In fact, for a project like this, the total texture size is likely to be several hundred megabytes. If the on-board texture memory is less than the active texture (the texture that must be in texture memory), swapping will occur, resulting in noticeable performance degradation. Fortunately, it is rare for all the textures to be needed for one frame. To take advantage of this, two techniques are suitable in our case: view frustum culling, which skips rendering and loading into memory parts of the model that are outside the view frustum, and MIP-mapping, which was originally developed to reduce aliasing. If all the texture fits into texture memory, then there is usually no problem. If it does not fit, the viewing application must work out a texture caching routine that to decide which texture to keep and which to move to RAM, or even to the system virtual memory (Cline and Egbert 1998 and Dumont et al. 2001). To make texture caching more efficient, it is recommended to divide the scene into smaller uniform groups, each with a small texture with width and height at a power of two. This makes it possible to more precisely control file size and rendering speed.

Another effective performance enhancement technique for both geometry and texture is occlusion culling, which skips objects that are occluded by other objects. This is not needed in our room model since there are no occluding objects.

9.2.2 Modelling and Rendering Procedure

The image-based modelling approach used for this project is the semi-automatic technique described in (El-Hakim 2002) and partially implemented in the ShapeCapture commercial software (www.shapecapture.com). This software has all the tools we needed and was used to create each individual model. The bundle adjustment in the software was done by free network, and model scales were determined from a small number of linear measurements (such as window dimensions) collected while taking the images.

The steps performed in our approach are:

- Create geometrically accurate models with photogrammetric modelling.
- Divide the model into optimum—efficiently sized—groups of triangles.
- Select the best image for each group.
- Compute texture coordinates of vertices using internal and external camera parameters.
- Compute radiance images of all images from the calibrated response curve.
- Resample and filter pixels within each triangle based on projective transformation between the triangle plane and the image plane.
- Apply radiometric corrections to the textures.
- Create MIP maps.
- Create bump maps.
- Render with efficient rendering software.

Since the room shape is rather simple, and all the geometry is properly modelled, there is no need for view-dependent texture mapping. Also, since the room lighting dynamic range is not high (except for the scene in the windows that does not interest us), we decided to use standard images digitised at 10-bits per colour with the digital camera, or 14-bits with a scanner, rather than high dynamic range images. In the future, the effect of using HDR images will be studied.

With sufficient image overlap, the texture of a triangle can be obtained from a number of different images. A reasonable choice is to select the image in which the triangle appears largest and taken along the normal. However, this may result in having too many different images assigned to adjacent triangles. One method to repair this is to locally reassign triangle patches to images. In this step, the initial assignment is changed based on the image assignment of the adjacent triangles and the image area covered by the triangle in alternative images. In effect, local reassignment generates larger groups of triangles mapped from the same image and eliminates isolated triangle texture mappings. Thus, the number of triangle edges where adjacent triangles are mapped from different images is reduced (Fig. 1).

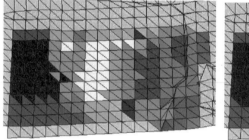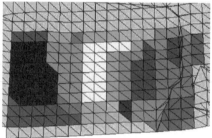

Fig. 1. Triangle shades in the mesh correspond to images from which the texture is obtained. *Left*: before local reassignment. *Right*: after local reassignment

Another method of texture selection for reducing texture discontinuities is that of texture blending. In blending, the mapping algorithm does not try to find the best image for each triangle, but rather computes the texture from all images the triangle appears in by forming a weighted average. While blending is an algorithmically simple approach that diminishes geometric and radiometric discontinuities, it must be noted that it usually introduces a detectable blurring effect. It has to be decided case by case whether global and local grey-value adaptation is a better choice. This option produces sharper texture maps, but might show geometric artefacts at adjacent triangles, or may present texture blending, which reduces artifacts at adjacent triangles, but tends to blur the textures.

The employed method defines a local texel coordinate system for each 3D triangle. The texel size, in object coordinates, can be set to the desired resolution. Projective transformation between the plane of the triangle and image plane is determined and used to resample the texture within each triangle. This is followed by low pass filter to remove high frequency noise introduced by this resampling. Full lens distortion (three radial and two decentric parameters, Faig 1975) is used for all texture mapping transformations.

Our approach for radiometric texture corrections was originally developed in El-Hakim et al. (1998). We address this problem by a correction method termed "global grey-value adaptation" and another correction on a per-triangle basis, termed "local grey-value adaptation". Here, grey value means colour channel value (red, green, or blue). The global grey-value adaptation estimates grey-value offsets between images. The grey-value differences along the border of adjacent regions of triangle sets are minimized by least-squares adjustment. This adjustment is very similar to using a geodetic height network. Here the observed height differences are replaced with grey-value differences along region borders. Additional weighted observations of type $h_i = 0$ ensure nonsingularity and prevent the offset from drifting across larger scenes. The local grey-value adaptation modifies the grey-values of each triangle to ensure smooth transitions to all adjacent triangles. However, this is not straightforward: If we observe offset o_1 along triangle edge e_1 and o_2 along e_2, it is unclear how the grey-values in the vicinity of the triangle vertex—where e_1 and e_2 intersect—should be corrected. Thus, we adopted a technique based on an iterative procedure. In order to force a gradual change to grey-values within a triangle, we fit a plane to the grey-value offsets observed at the triangle borders. The plane parameters are determined by a least-squares adjustment that minimizes these differences. After correcting the grey-values according to the plane parameters, this process is iterated several times. Usually, there are no discernible changes after a few iterations.

Finally, in order to achieve the desired performance, a special software for interactive visualisation—"Il Teatro Virtuale"—was developed at VIT (Paquet and Peters 2002) using scene graph tools. Those tools are data structures used to hierarchically organize and manage the contents of spatially oriented scene data. They offer a high-level alternative to low-level graphics rendering APIs such as OpenGL. Examples of scene-graph supported languages are VRML, Java 3D, MPEG-4, and, of course, SGI Open Inventor, the earliest of these. Our PC-based loader was developed with Java 3D, which gives complete control over the rendering process (unlike other languages).

9.3   Results Achieved

One of the objectives of the project was to create a photorealistic walkthrough movie of the "Cycle of the Months" frescos. In order to portray the room in the proper context, the movie also includes the outside view of the Torre Aquila and the entrance to the room. Therefore, we created the following 3D models:

- The outside walls of the tower including part of the long walkway leading to the room.
- The entrance to the room from the walkway.
- The walls of the room.
- The ceiling of the room.

The images were acquired with a 5 Megapixel (1920 x 2560 pixels) digital camera.

Fig. 2. Room *top view* with camera locations

One of the restrictions was the size of the room (7.75 m x 5.95 m x 5.35 m (H)), which resulted in a small coverage per image. This required taking 16 images to cover the walls and 8 for the ceiling. This took a rather long time, during which lighting conditions changed: The result was in inconsistent illumination. For the outer tower model and the entrance to the room through the walkway, five and two images were taken, respectively. This resulted in a total image size of 472 Megabytes. After cropping the images to the size of the triangle groups, this was reduced to about one third. The average texture resolution was 2 mm x 2 mm area of the wall per pixel. Figure 2 shows a top view of the room with camera locations for wall images (white solid circles) and ceiling images (grey solid squares).

Results of the geometric modelling are shown in Fig. 3 in wireframe. Mesh size was small (10,000 triangles), but texture size was about 160 Megabytes.

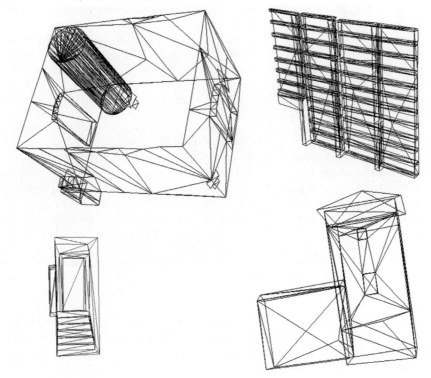

Fig. 3. Wireframe models of the different parts (*clockwise*: walls, ceiling, tower, and entrance)

After texture mapping, sometimes we needed to reconstruct the model with extra points to account for small deviations from plane for some walls. For example, in the corner shown in Fig. 4, we had to increase the number of points near the intersection between the two walls. When only using a small number of points and assuming planes in areas without points, the lines along the corner did not project on the correct wall and lines that span the two walls had visible discontinuity. This shows that any small geometrical error is visible in this class of models with frescoed walls. In most other types of architecture, where walls have uniform colours, such errors may be tolerated.

Fig. 4. Corner where geometric accuracy is critical

Without applying any texture correction, we notice in the corner where one wall texture was taken from the first image and the other wall texture was taken from the last image (the 16th) that there is a visible illumination difference (Fig. 5). This is because the difference in time between the two images was about 30 minutes, which was enough for the lighting conditions to change even though we used a flash. Correction to this problem was done with the technique presented before.

Fig. 5. Lighting variations, first and last image

The three interior models (the walls, the ceiling, and the entrance) were registered in the same coordinate system using common points. The outside model of the tower did not need to be registered with the others because the movie does not present a direct continuation between them. (The movie fades from the outside scenes into the inside scenes.) Images of the tower showing the surroundings were also used. Everything was put together using 3ds Max© and Adobe Premier© software. A few trials were necessary in order to get the proper viewing angle of the virtual camera, the path of the camera, and the rendering speed. Figure 6 shows a snapshot from the movie.

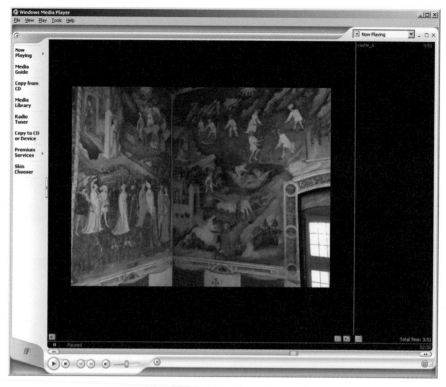

Fig. 6. Snapshot from the movie

9.4   Laser Scanning

9.4.1   Description of the Technique

Many applications require fast, dense and accurate noncontact 3D point acquisition for object shape recovery. Optical triangulation is a typical technique which achieves high range accuracy with simple calculations, provided the objects are located within a range of up to a couple of meters from the measuring setup. Depending on the particular application, however, a trade-off between acquisition speed and the density of acquired 3D points (voxels) must be found. In general, when high-speed range maps are required, triangulation-based light sheet systems are the choice. Here, a 2D position detector array is used to recover the profile of the intersection between the light sheet and the object being imaged. Full range maps are obtained by scanning the light sheet over the entire object. In this case, angular resolution is limited by the sensor size, while depth accuracy is limited mainly by the algorithm for centroid calculation, and, to some extent, by pixel pitch and fill factor. Examples of real-time range map capabilities of light sheet ranging systems for robotic guidance applications have been reported in the literature (Brajovic et al. 2001; Yoshimura et al. 2001; Oike et al. 2003; Massari et al. 2004).

On the other hand, when high density range maps are required, optical triangulation systems based on flying spot perform better than their light sheet counterparts. In this case, a collimated laser spot and a linear position detector are used to reconstruct, point-by-point, the range map of the object. The laser spot is scanned over the object by a 2D scanning system. In this case, the angular resolution is limited only by the properties of the laser spot (Rioux 1984), while the depth accuracy depends on the centroid calculation algorithms, not on photodetector geometry. In a system like this, the main acquisition speed is mostly limited by the fact that, as the spot position is not known a priori, the entire linear array must be read out before calculating the centroid. As for sheet of light based systems, in this case, too, VLSI photodetector integration may help to accelerate their deployment in many fields, including cultural heritage, reverse engineering and industrial process automation.

The block diagram of an integrated position sensing device is shown in Fig. 7. The photodetector, as well as analogue signal conditioning, timing control, analogue to digital conversion, and digital processing can be integrated on the same silicon substrate using standard microelectronic technologies.

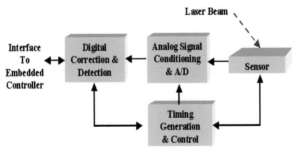

Fig. 7. Block diagram of an integrated position sensor

Two different types of photodetectors can be considered for integration: lateral effect photodiodes (LEP) and discrete response position detectors (DRPS), i.e., a linear array of photodetectors. The former are basically analogue detectors working as photoresistors and have been extensively studied (Laegsgaard 1979; Beraldin et al. 1992). Although they can be very fast and precise (Beraldin et al. 1992), they are limited by the fact that the shape of the light distribution on the sensor surface is never known. This limitation influences accuracy in measuring light distribution when operated in the presence of strong ambient illumination. From the VLSI point of view, one has to stress the fact that standard microelectronic fabrication processes are optimized for electronic circuitry, but not for optical sensors. Therefore, the designer has at her disposal only a few fabrication layers suitable for LEPs, and even those are not optimized. This allows for LEPs with higher noise figures.

Linear arrays of photodetectors, or DRPS, are a valid alternative to LEPs. These sensors are currently used in state-of-the-art flying-spot 3D camera rangers (Beraldin et al. 2000). They allow recovery of the full shape of the light distribution on the photosensitive area, making them very accurate. However, they suffer from speckle-limited spot position detection (Baribeau and Rioux 1991) and readout speed. The former is basically due to the continuous decrease in size of single photodetectors. Commercial devices, in fact, are thought to be for spectroscopic applications (Lee et al. 1994) where only the number of photodetectors within the array is important. This leads to a minimum size of photodiode in the order of a few microns. Speed is the second issue of DRPS. They, in fact, are slower than LEPs because all pixels have to be read out sequentially prior to the measurement of the location of the spot position.

A typical measuring geometry is depicted in Fig. 8. A collimated laser beam is scanned over the object of interest by means of precise scanning mirrors. A portion of the back-reflected light is collected by some optics and focused onto a linear sensor placed off axis with respect to the laser source. Changes in z coordinate of the object profile reflects a change in spot position on a position sensor.

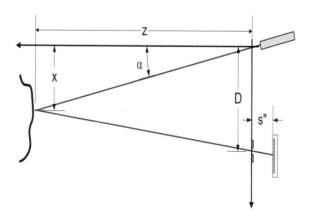

Fig. 8. Typical measuring geometry of a flying spot 3D range camera

The sensors used for position detection in most modern flying spot scanners are linear arrays of photodiodes (DRPS) either fabricated in CCD or CMOS technologies. They are mainly used for 2D imaging or spectroscopic instruments and, therefore, are not optimized for 3D imaging. For example, speckle noise found in flying spot 3D scanners dictates a large pixel (Laegsgaard 1979) which cannot be found in commercial DRPS. Readout speed of the DRPS is also a big issue in these types of scanners. Considering a 256-pixel DRPS and assuming a readout frequency of 5MHz, it results in a 3D data throughput of 20kHz which is quite low for applications like 3D tracking or human body scanning, for example. Finally, signal dynamic range issues might also be of concern since, in some conditions, the dynamic range involved is larger than the 8 to 10 bits offered by commercial DRPS.

9.4.2 Proposed Sensor and Results

In our work, a novel architecture for a DRPS optimized for flying spot 3D ranging camera is presented. The sensor, fully integrated in CMOS 0.6-μm standard technology, features random pixel access and, in a particular topology, colour detection, as well.

To get around of all drawbacks of commercial DRPS, the custom design of an optimized DRPS was considered. To take full advantage of VLSI integration processes, the new sensor as well as the driving and processing electronics has been fully integrated in standard CMOS technology. Issues like spot position measurement uncertainty, data throughput, and dynamic range have been addressed. Two eletro-optical constraints were used as the basis for starting the design of the sensor: the first regards the total back-reflected light collected by the optics covering two orders of magnitude, with minimum values in the range of 10 nW; the second is relative to the spot diameter on the sensor which may range from 200 μm up to 600 μm.

The basic idea underlying the design of the sensor has already been considered by Beraldin et al. (2001). The novelty of the sensor is that of defining, for read out, only a region of interest (ROI) around the real position of the spot, according to the estimate provided by a low resolution, but fast position detector. Therefore, only that window, of fixed width, is read-out leading to an increase of readout speed by a factor of 3 to 5. In practice the best performance is achieved when LEPs and CRPSs are merged. In its simpler version, two position sensors, an LEP and a DRPS aligned along their major axes are integrated on the same silicon die or on the same package. While the LEP, being faster, is used to calculate both spot position and intensity with low accuracy, the DRPS is used to calculate the spot position with high accuracy. The lower speed of DRPS with respect to the LEP is compensated by reading out only the ROI form the DRPS.

The new device, named COLORSENS, uses the same measuring principle describe above. However, major changes were introduced by substituting the LEP with a second DRPS, reducing in this way overall device dimensions and increasing flexibility, especially with regard to the need for optics and colour detection. This makes COLORSENS more suitable for full integration on the same silicon die.

The sensor architecture was thought to divide the position detection in three principal steps: fast spot position calculation, ROI window identification and accurate spot position detection. These steps can in part be done in parallel. The goal of this architecture is to improve the sensor readout speed and its dynamic range.

COLORSENS was fully integrated in 0.6-μm mixed signal CMOS technology (http://www.austriamicrosystems.com). The die measures 8.17 x 5.67 mm². Layout of the analogue part has been carefully covered with a grounded metal layer working as light shield. Power supplies for the digital block are separated from those of the analogue block and careful isolation of the digital block has been implemented.

Colour detection is of paramount importance in heritage applications. Most triangulation based 3D range cameras with colour detection capabilities use a monochromatic laser beam for shape measurement and a digital 2D camera for recovering colours. This is an efficient and quick way to recover colour information. But it is not independent from ambient illumination. Reflectance data can be obtained by using an RGB laser as probe (Baribeau et al. 1991), and measuring one-by-one the R, G, and B back-reflected components striking the sensor. The COLORSENS device—whence its name—was also designed to provide colour detection capabilities based on absorbance measurements, provided a post processing filter deposition is carried out. The device's electrooptical functionalities were fully characterized on an optical bench with spectral and power response measurement capabilities.

A novel architecture for an optical sensor for flying spot 3D laser scanners was successfully integrated in a standard CMOS process. Experimental results showed that the architecture implemented can be used to improve the performance of state-of-the-art flying spot 3D laser scanners both in terms of speed and dynamic range. Moreover, the architecture allows for an increase in pixel number without a decrease in speed. The results obtained so far have shown that integrated optical sensors have reached such a high level of development and reliability that they are suited for high-accuracy 3D vision systems.

10 Tracking Visitors in a Museum

R. Brunelli, O. Lanz, A. Santuari and F. Tobia

10.1 Introduction

Ambient intelligence is an emerging field that deals with electronic environments which are sensitive and responsive to the presence of people (Haritaoglu et al. 2000). In this context, sensitive means understanding behaviour from observations obtained through sensor measurements, while *responsive* means reacting on the basis of an understanding of the environment. Whether or not people accept electronic monitoring devices greatly depends on how people interact with them. Computer vision offers a powerful framework for interfacing the computing world with its living environment in a nonintrusive way.

The most basic, low-level information about people is their location in the environment. This information is of the utmost importance in surveillance systems that, among other things, handle protected or dangerous zones since suspicious behaviour may often be detected from trajectory data. More complex *intelligence* tasks relate to the understanding of complex motion patterns (e.g., groups of visitors) as indicators of critical situations, or to the recognition of deictic gestures used by a visitor to interface with a *smart* museum.

In this chapter, we focus on problems related to vision-based people monitoring in ambient intelligence applications. This application field poses many research challenges which derive from:

- The need to monitor wide-area, complex, multiroom locations.
- The requirement of extensive evaluation of algorithms performance.
- The crowding level of the environments considered.

Sensor networks for tracking and surveillance applications have been the subject of extensive research in the last couple of years. Using a *best view* selection scheme based on an information-content criterion, (Iwasawa et al. 1999) approach the problem of single-body pose estimation with a static ortho-trinocular setup. A collection of algorithms for cooperative multisensor surveillance is presented by Collins et al. (2001) in their VSAM surveillance system. VSAM implements the typical analysis chain: change detection through background subtraction, heuristic blob classification, and data fusion using a *winner takes all* criterion based on location, class, and color match scores. (Karuppiah 2001) focuses on architectural issues, while Matsuyama and Ukita (2002) cluster active sensors into agencies that gaze at the same target. Dockstader and Tekalp (2001) succeed in occluded situations by exploiting feature-based tracking on points that are suitably selected at each frame. The next section presents the structure of Olympus, the ambient intelligence architecture developed within the PEACH Project (Bertamini et al. 2004). We then offer a detailed description of how Olympus successfully meets the challenges. First, we present its distributed processing architecture, which provides the computational power and flexibility required by the monitoring of large environments. Second, we discuss the tools for generating simulated environments and visitors for extensive algorithm evaluation. Finally, we present a probabilistic framework for effective tracking of people even in the presence of occlusions.

10.2 System Architecture Overview

The design of the system was driven by the need to cope with the challenges identified in the introductory remarks. The resulting architecture (Fig. 1) can be best understood in terms of three main entities: the input sensors, the active (i.e., processing capable) transmission channels, and the *brain*, the ambient intelligence:

- Zeus/Hera: the graphical rendering engines that can generate synthetic but realistic imagery of dynamic environments.
- Gaia: a physical sensor system based on active cameras.
- Cronos: a puppeteer that controls the motion of virtual visitors who move in the synthetic environments generated by Zeus/Hera.
- Hermes: the network structure that transports signals from the sensors to the processing core, Athena.
- Athena: the ambient intelligence that is capable of monitoring the movements of visitors and which adapts its sensing infrastructure to optimally sample the environment.

A distinguishing feature of the architecture is its double (synthetic/real) sensing system.

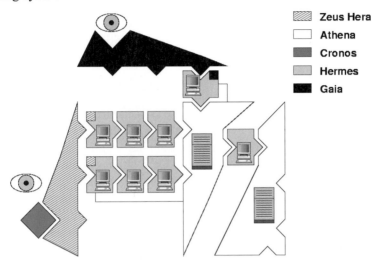

Fig. 1. The picture presents the modules of Olympus, a visual system for people tracking in large indoor environments. Gaia and Zeus/Hera provide, respectively, real and simulated sensor data which are then distributed (over Hermes) and processed (by Athena)

The system based on the synthetic worlds generated by Zeus/Hera is mainly useful in the first phase of algorithm development. Its ability to automatically generate ground truth information is extremely valuable for performance evaluation. Full control of the sensing infrastructure by means of active virtual cameras, supplemented by the ability to generate arbitrary motion patterns of the virtual visitors, allows generation of extensive synthetic footage. Studying various approaches to the development of ambient intelligence algorithms, in particular those based on the learning-by-example paradigm, becomes more affordable, as expensive acquisition sessions with human actors in difficult-to-access locations are no longer needed.

Effortless migration of the algorithms to the physical sensing system (Gaia) is granted by the availability of an abstraction layer which provides homogeneous data access to the signal processing modules. Because the layer fully supports local area networking, distributed processing can easily be set up, providing scalability and increased performance (Hermes). These advantages are not limited to the *low-level* processing of the sensory streams, but extend to the inner working of the higher level people tracking stage (Athena).

10.3 Simulated Environments and Visitors

Performance evaluation is a major difficulty in the development of ambient intelligence algorithms. The difficulty is both practical and conceptual. On the practical side, preparing a large environment, such as a museum, with cameras may be both expensive and difficult due to *environmental* constraints. Availability of the environment for training and testing sessions is also usually constrained in time. Oddly enough, the availability of visitors may also be a problem, due to privacy issues and to the difficulty of gathering enough actors. The conceptual difficulty is perhaps more interesting. Monitoring large environments requires flexible visual sensing strategies. The conflicting requirements of high resolution and large field of view may only be solved by using active cameras. Thus the control of camera parameters becomes an integral part of the algorithm, supporting active, foveated sampling of the environment. An immediate consequence is that no single sequence may provide support for training and testing algorithms based on active visual sampling. The problem is resolved by using simulated environments and visitors. Thus, the same scene can be repeatedly observed by active virtual cameras whose parameters are continuously changed by the algorithms to optimize tracking. Synthetic environments are always available and can be populated at will with virtual characters. Two *reality engines* were developed: Hera and Zeus. The former is an interface to Radiance, a physically accurate ray-tracing system.

Fig. 2. Zeus is able to generate photorealistic images (*left*) of indoor environments as well as special thematic images identifying each character with a unique label (*centre*) or providing the Z-buffer of the depicted scene (*right*)

The latter is a real-time rendering engine based on video game technologies which exploits the features of the latest graphic boards (Fig. 2). The advantage of real-time rendering made Zeus the engine of choice for the development of Athena. Zeus transforms the 3D data describing static geometry, i.e., the environment, and moving objects, i.e., people visiting museum exhibits, in realistic digital images that can be used to develop and test tracking algorithms.

Zeus is a portable renderer based on the widely adopted OpenGL standard and has the following features:

- Precomputed global illumination solution for the static environment.
- Moving-object shadow computation for coloured, static lights, with optional soft shadowing effects, based on a precomputed global illumination solution and subtractive rendering.
- Support for dynamic lighting of moving objects.
- Efficient rendering of complex indoor environments using Binary Space Partition trees and Potentially Visible Sets.
- High quality material rendering based on multitexturing.
- Articulated character rendering with the possibility of switching among different motion classes such as *walking* and *running* with automatic interpolation (Fig. 3).
- A client/server architecture, whereby distributed clients can request a view of the simulated world from any position, supported by *perceptual oracle* information such as an accurate depth map and a segmented image where every moving object is identified with a unique numeric label.

One of the most important features of the graphical simulator developed is its ability to provide convincing images of people moving in an indoor environment such as a museum.

Fig. 3. A flexible key-frame animation has been developed for Zeus: each character is composed of three different parts (legs, torso, and head) that can be controlled separately to synthesize novel motion patterns

While rendering the characters is, by itself, a challenging task (Fig. 3), creating suitable choreography of groups moving convincingly in the environment poses additional challenges. A crowd simulator, Cronos, was developed as a client application for Zeus (Santuari et al. 2003). It is based on a hybrid approach relying on flock simulation of internal group dynamics (Reynolds 1987) and on a specialized version of cofields (Mamei et al. 2002). Groups of characters move following their invisible *leaders* in environments with complex geometry and limited visibility. The implemented system permits simulation of groups with different interests in museum exhibits as well as different visiting strategies (detailed planning, casual, time limited, etc.).

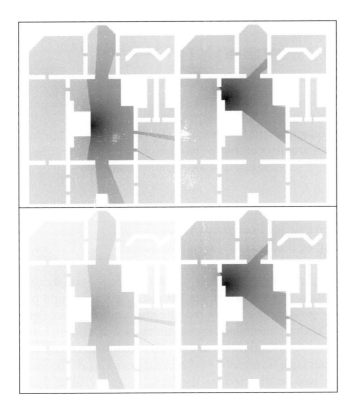

Fig. 4. The columns present a pictorial evolution of the co-fields associated with two different exhibits: the lighter the field the weaker the attractive power of the corresponding exhibit. Each group leader is captured by the strongest field. When the visitor is close enough to an exhibit, she starts experiencing it and the corresponding field decreases. The visitor is captured in turn by all the exhibits she is interested in, moving within the museum with purposeful behaviour

Each museum exhibits generates an attracting field whose strength decreases with distance (Fig. 4). Each visiting group is associated with a vector of *interest* factors that are used to scale the fields associated with available exhibits. These vectors represent, in a sense, the cultural preferences of each group. The motion of each group has two components: an invisible group leader moves according to the attraction fields of the exhibits and acts as a proxy attractor for the group characters whose trajectories are computed using a second-order differential equation:

$$F(x,\dot{x},t) = \nabla_x E(x,\dot{x},t), \tag{1}$$
$$x(t+\Delta t) = x(t)+\dot{x}(t)\,\Delta t + \frac{1}{2}F(x,\dot{x},t)\Delta t^2,$$
$$\dot{x}(t+\Delta t) = \dot{x}(t) + F(x,\dot{x},t)\Delta t,$$

where the potential field E depends on character position and velocity.

Varied, apparently purposive, motion of the groups can be obtained by defining E as a superposition of four components:

- E_C, to avoid collisions.
- E_L, responsible for group leader attraction.
- E_F, responsible for flock behaviour.
- E_V, enforcing local velocity matching.

Naïve implementation of follow-the-leader behaviour may result in unacceptable motion patterns whenever the characters lose sight of the leader. If geometry constraints are ignored, the character may accelerate towards obstacles. On the other hand, if constraints are considered, the character may have no leader in sight to follow. The solution adopted was to endow each character with a memory of the latest positions of the group guide so that motion can be directed by the most recent, visible, leader position (Fig. 5).

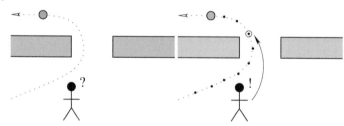

Fig. 5. Characters memorize the trajectory of their group leader thereby easing the implementation of realistic follow-the-leader strategies

As explained in Santuari et al. (2003), the idea of attracting fields is quite flexible. As an example, the strength of the field is modulated by the interest of the user in the given exhibit, which decreases while looking at the exhibit with a customizable decay which includes the spatial scale from which the exhibit becomes enjoyable. Cronos is able to manage several groups of different size at the same time, generating training sequences of graded complexity for algorithm testing.

10.4 Distributed Computing

The integration of multiple data streams gathered from a network of real or virtual sensors, the associated processing needs, and the long-term challenges posed by the cooperative surveillance of large and complex indoor environments by means of a population of cameras suggested the development of a flexible, distributed modular processing architecture for image processing and delivery. Hermes provides a multiplatform architecture for the acquisition of visual information from real and virtual sensors, its compression using the MPEG4 standard, and its transmission and processing using multiple distributed modules connected in a pipeline fashion via TCP/IP (Fig. 6). By supporting MPEG4 encoding of the video stream, the architecture enables efficient transmission of video data over low bandwidth channels, permitting the use of wireless infrastructure even for multiple input channels.

Different data streams may interact in the distributed system. The synchronization issue is handled by a timestamp technique, while global time knowledge relies upon the NTP time synchronization protocol of computer networks. Sensor calibration is also needed to integrate spatial information from different sources: novel algorithms tailored to active cameras were developed (Lanz 2004a; Chippendale and Tobia 2005).

Specialized modules can be used at the sensor interfaces to control real and virtual cameras, and to insert the corresponding data into the processing network which leads to the Athena core where the actual tracking of people takes place. The distributed processing architecture can also be used to increase the realism of the images produced by Zeus, by adding several kinds of noise or optical effects which characterize real cameras:

- Granular appearance induced by impulse/Gaussian noise.
- Motion blur realized by shutter time integration of temporally super sampled (synthetic) sequences.
- Depth of field implemented using depth information provided by Zeus
- Interlacing generating a single frame using two temporally close images.

In order to completely decouple data producers (sensor inputs) and data consumers (high-level processing agents), the software architecture was structured in multipurpose layers.

At the top level of abstraction, the architecture relies upon a *sensor layer*, which handles data acquisition and labelling, sharing this information with the world. This is split into other layers, each one dedicated to a specific job (e.g., interfacing with the hardware, low-level processing). The layer completely wraps the *real* sensors, hiding the implementation from the agents and showing instead a high-level interface for terminal nodes, i.e., *virtual* sensors.

A detailed schema of the first level of the distributed processing architecture, the one closest to the sensors, is reported in Fig. 6.

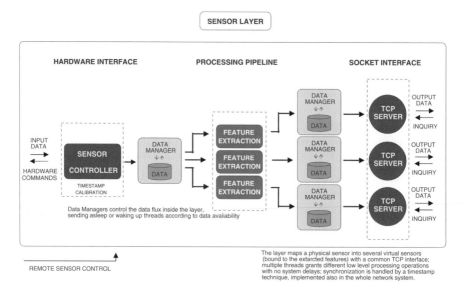

Fig. 6. The sensor layer provides the foundation on which the distributed processing architecture is built. The *hardware interface* interacts with the physical sensors, acquiring inputs and sending commands

The aim of the layer is to provide time-stamped and calibrated data (either raw data or low level features) coming from heterogeneous sources in a homogeneous way. High-level agents can gather input simply by connecting to specific sockets (virtual sensors), with real data sources completely transparent to them. Another goal of the architecture was to achieve coding flexibility. The software was organized in a streamlined hierarchy of C++ objects, in an easy-to-extend structure using derivation of abstract classes. This way, different kinds of sensors, feature extraction, and new functionality can be added and integrated with limited effort. The developed sensor layer relies on three base blocks: a hardware interface, a processing pipeline, and a socket interface.

To enhance system efficiency, each instance inside a block is implemented as a detached thread, and the processes communicate through shared memory. Parallel computation of data at different processing rates (i.e., multiple virtual sensors derived from the same physical one) is possible without adding delays to faster processes. Additionally, a multithread architecture makes optimal use of multiprocessor systems.

The *hardware interface* interacts with the physical sensors, acquiring inputs and sending commands. The (optional) *processing pipeline* is a collection of low-level feature-extraction segments. Colour quantization, compression, change detection, edge detection, and other instances of the processing pipeline are also obtained by deriving a base class that specifies only the data computing function. The goal of the *socket interface* is to share data with high-level agents distributed over an intranet; data is shared either by a streaming or an on-demand policy according to efficiency and bandwidth constraints.

In conclusion, a sensor-layer instance is composed of a specific hardware interface, an optional processing pipeline, and a socket interface. The combined action of the layers wraps the underlying physical sensors and maps them to virtual sensors with a neat socket interface. Extracted data are shared inside the Local Area Network (LAN) using the TCP/IP protocol and can be retrieved by the agents without any knowledge about the real source.

10.5 Probabilistic Tracking

The most fundamental information that an ambient intelligence system must provide is people location in the environment as a function of time. People *trajectories* can then be used for a variety of applications, from the monitoring of protected areas to the analysis of crowding or flow bottlenecks. Providing continuous location information in crowded environments is a very difficult task for vision based systems due to dynamic occlusions and people who appear to be similar. This section presents the framework developed within the PEACH project to deal with these issues (Lanz 2004b; Lanz and Manduchi 2005).

Target tracking is the problem of inferring target trajectory in space-time form a sequence of observations. Real-time applications require sequential methods that infer the current state from the incoming observation and past estimations. In the presence of background clutter and occlusions (even partial), classical methods based on segmentation and blob classifications have difficulties. A robust way to face such situations is to estimate the probability density function on the state space rather than the current configuration itself (a *fuzzy* decision rather than a *hard* one). This density is often called the *belief* distribution, and the tracking framework based on it is *Bayes filtering*. The current state of the system can then be estimated by analyzing the belief, e.g., by computing its mean or mode.

A Bayes filter recursively estimates the current belief distribution $p(x_t)$ for the object state x_t probabilistically conditioned on an incoming observation z_t using stochastic propagation and Bayes theorem. Under the assumption that the underlying process is Markov and that observations are conditionally independent (Isard and Blake 1998), the following holds:

$$p(x_t) \propto p(z_t|x_t) \int_{\mathbf{X}_{t-1}} p(x_t \mid x_{t-1}) p(x_{t-1}) \mathrm{d}x_{t-1}. \tag{2}$$

This update rule can be interpreted as follows. The current belief distribution $p(x_{t-1})$ first becomes propagated with a stochastic dynamic model $p(x_t|x_{t-1})$ describing how the system, assumed to be in state x_{t-1} at time $t-1$, is likely to evolve to time t. This operation shifts and blurs the belief according to prior knowledge acquired on the dynamics of the system. Once a new observation is available, this prediction is adjusted by applying Bayes rule with an observation model $p(z_t|x_t)$ that describes how well the observation matches with the prediction.

When the dynamic of the system is slow compared to the observation rate, the propagation model becomes less important. The key to a successful application of a Bayes filter relies, therefore, on reliable modelling of the observation likelihood function $p(z|x)$. This often presents a difficult problem because its underlying process is usually based on a high dimensional and highly nonlinear mapping from configuration into observation space where noise exhibits complex behaviour. Moreover, it depends on additional time-varying parameters such as lighting conditions, which may be too expensive or even impossible to model.

Several approximations to the general Bayes filter formulation have been proposed. In the extended Kalman filter, both the propagation model and the observation model are assumed to be linear and contaminated by white Gaussian noise. If the initial belief distribution is Gaussian, it will remain Gaussian, making the solution both computationally tractable and optimal. Unfortunately, in many real-world applications, the need to handle multiple hypotheses makes the Kalman approximation inapplicable.

Monte Carlo approximations of the Bayes filter can cope with multimodal densities thanks to their nonparametric nature (Isard and Blake1998;

Doucet et al. 2001). Such methods can, therefore, track successfully in situations much more hostile than those afforded by Gaussian Kalman filter approaches.

Multiple objects can be tracked with a single Bayes filter, the *joint filter*, by concatenating their configurations into a single super-state vector. By doing so, any kind of interaction at the process and observation levels can be incorporated in a straightforward way into $p(x_t|x_{t-1})$ and $p(z_t|x_t)$. Unfortunately, applying the joint filter soon becomes impractical as it suffers from exponential complexity in the dimension of the state space. However, if the domain permits any process independence assumptions between different object models, the joint filter can exploit this fact to greatly improve its performance.

While for the state space behaviour, the assumption of independence might be reasonable in many applications, this is often not the case for observations. They usually involve projection into a lower dimensional space where occlusions can occur. Tracking multiple objects with independent filters means ignoring interactions which have a significant impact on observations. It is well known that the Bayes filter can digest short occlusions even if not modelled. However, in the case of long-lasting occlusions, it is doomed to fail. We propose a method that includes these interactions through coupling of the independent filters at the observation level, while maintaining the same order of complexity of a set of independent trackers. This is reasonable from a computational point of view because belief propagation is more involved than the update step. The key idea is to introduce a *support pixel map* for each object of every incoming image. The map plays a weighting function role for the pixels of the observation and is used to calculate the likelihood.

Observations can be used in an optimal way in situations where tracked objects partially occlude each other for a significant amount of time. The underlying idea is to make use of the estimated belief distributions of other objects to mark each image pixel with a degree of reliability or, more precisely, of visibility. It is based on the probability that a pixel is occluded by other dynamic or static objects.

Let us suppose that a person's body becomes partially occluded by another one with a different appearance. When trying to match a reference full-body model against the corresponding image patch, we get a poor matching score even if the model is correctly located. If this occurs for several frames, any tracking algorithm will fail to track the person. However, even if the person is almost wholly occluded, there is still information in the observation that could be used to support tracking.

Let us first analyze how occlusions arise, borrowing from the field of *computer graphics*. The image formation process can be formalized by defining a rendering function $g(x)$ that maps a given configuration of objects into a picture of them. Function g is usually high dimensional and highly nonlinear. As a coarse approximation, this function can be factored into the composition of two functions. The first one involves a mapping from the object's configuration into its 3D shape and appearance model. The 3D object is projected onto the image plane by a perspective projection, generating the observation. This reduction in dimensionality is the origin of occlusions, where distant object patches are covered by near, opaque ones.

If the observed world is composed of several independently moving objects, its overall configuration can be split into several independent object states x^k, each one with an associated rendering function $g(x^k)$. Without accounting for shadowing and reflections, the resulting image is then obtained by merging all object renderings according to their depth order. If the tracked targets are opaque with respect to their rendering functions, the merging process reduces to looking for the object nearest to the sensor at each pixel and using its output $g(x^k)$. Therefore, interaction occurs at the merging level, while rendering can be regarded as a set of several independent processes.

The observation model proposed exploits this decomposition into independent rendering processes that can be directly incorporated in the split filter framework. In general, an observation model $p(z|x_k)$ can be defined by a distance $d(z_1, z_2)$ in observation space between the delivered observation and a rendered hypothesis x^k, generated by a simplified and smoothed version g' of g

$$p(z \mid x_k) = Ke^{-d^2(z, g'(x_k))}, \tag{3}$$

where g' plays the role of a synthesized model for the tracked object. Note that the observation model $p(z|x_k)$ can be specified up to the constant K if normalization of the belief is not required.

The key to a robust observation model is to take into account visibility in the definition of the distance d. This can be done by attributing to each observation pixel a weight that reflects our knowledge of the status of the remaining part of the system.

Let us see in more detail how to estimate the probability that a pixel has been occluded by one of the other objects. According to this probability, image pixels have more or less importance in the computation of the distance $d(z, g'(x_k))$. Given an object rendering function $g(x)$, let us define the *silhouette rendering function* $\Delta_g(x|s)$ as follows:

$$\Delta_g(x|s) = \begin{cases} 1, & \text{if } 0 < g_s(x) < s, \\ 0, & \text{elsewhere,} \end{cases} \qquad (4)$$

where g_s is the distance of the object surface points from the optical centre of the camera and s is the radius of a clipping sphere. The key question is now:

What is the probability that pixel u belongs to an object with esti-mated belief distribution p(x)?

To answer this question, we examine which of the object's configurations occupies pixel u. Let us introduce A_u, the set of object configurations that render on a selected pixel u:

$$\mathbf{A}_u = \{x \mid 0 < [g_s(x)]_u < s\}.$$

Therefore, Δ_g is the characteristic function of the set $\mathbf{A}_s$. From the relation between probability mass and probability density function

$$P(\mathbf{A}) = \int_{\mathbf{A}} p(x)\,dx,$$

we conclude that the support layer of an object with belief $p(x)$ at a given depth s is defined as

$$\mathbf{S}(s) = E_{p(x)}[\Delta_g(x \mid s)] = \int_{\mathbf{X}} \Delta_g(x \mid s)\, p(x)\,dx, \qquad (5)$$

which is the expected silhouette image (Fig. 7).

Fig. 7. The silhouette of a specific pose and its support layer computed from a bimodal belief. The silhouette becomes blurred due to estimation uncertainty

It should be mentioned that static obstacles can be straightforwardly incor-porated into this formulation. In this case, the belief $p(x)$ becomes a

Dirac impulse function, and the static probability map is given by its silhouette image. If one or more objects are potentially occluding the considered object k, we can define the probability of being occluded as the highest value among all other object maps. This corresponds to classifying the pixel to be owned by the most likely object. Another possibility is to use the sum of the values which belong to all other objects. The advantage of the first approach is that a value of $\mathbf{S}^l(s) = 1$, which means that the pixel is assumed to be occupied by object l, sets the weight to zero, which is not necessarily the case for the second possibility.

The pixel weight layer $\mathbf{W}^k(s)$ for an object k at depth s is then defined as the probability of not being occluded by other objects:

$$\mathbf{W}^k(s) = 1 - \max_{l \neq k}\{\mathbf{S}^l(s)\}.$$

Once these weights have been calculated, they can be used by the distance function of the observation model to give less importance to pixels that are likely to be occluded (Fig. 8). For example, the weights can define a kernel that can be used to calculate a weighted histogram that is then compared to a reference template.

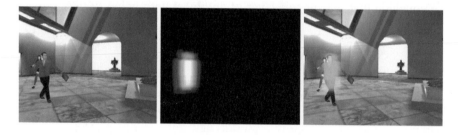

Fig. 8. The current image, the support pixel map of the head and upper body of the blue person obtained from his estimated belief, and the weighted image used for computing the likelihood for person at the back. (The highlighted area represents high occlusion probability, i.e., low weight)

Tracking can also be enhanced when objects are temporarily completely occluded. Such situations can be detected by considering low-weight regions of $\mathbf{W}$. In this case, the likelihood update is not performed because no measurement is available. In addition, the weights describe the coverage of the image by other objects and, therefore, contain a measure of information content within the image. It can be used as a cue to opportunistically control active cameras to gain as much information about the environment as possible. A simple indicator is given by the mean value of the weights calculated over the window. Optimal sensor cooperation in the proposed Bayesian estimation framework will be the subject of future research.

To make the computational problem tractable in a nonlinear, nonparametric setting, Monte Carlo approximations to Bayesian filtering must be introduced. The idea underlying particle filters is to maintain a compressed representation of the estimated belief distribution through a set of representative sample states, the *particles*. In perfect Monte Carlo sampling, these samples are chosen and independent and identically distributed according to the density $p(x)$ that they should represent. If the density is complex, such a representation can be used for a feasible, close *importance density* $g(x)$ and the introduced bias can be corrected by reweighting the samples.

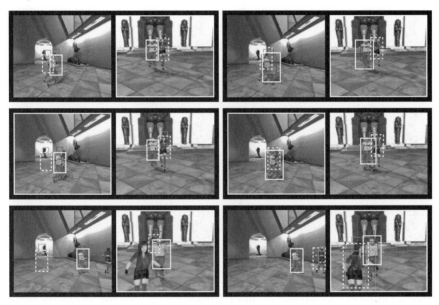

Fig. 9. The *left column* shows the behaviour of the standard particle filter. The dark lady is lost due to an occlusion. By considering the light-coloured man support layer, the same algorithm can track the woman without getting distracted (*right column*). Only the *framed image* is used as measurement

Formally, if d_A depicts the characteristic function of set **A** and x_i are the samples obtained through perfect sampling from $g(x)$, the importance sampling approximation of an arbitrary density function $p(x)$ can be rewritten as:

$$P(\mathbf{A}) = \int_{\mathbf{A}} p(x)\mathrm{d}x \approx \sum_i \pi_i d_{\mathbf{A}}(x_i), \quad \pi_i = \frac{p(x_i)}{g(x_i)}, \tag{5}$$

and is, therefore, fully described by the particle set $\{< x_i, \pi_i >\}_i$. The expectation over $p(x)$ of some function of interest $f(x)$ can be straightforwardly estimated by

$$E_{p(x)}[f(x)] = \int_{\mathbf{X}} f(x)p(x)\mathrm{d}x \approx \frac{1}{\pi}\sum_i f(x_i)\pi_i \tag{6}$$

with the normalization factor π given by the sum of weights π_i. The estimated state is often taken to be the mean, which is obtained setting $f(x) = x$ in the above relation. Given a weighted particle representation $\{x_{i,t-1}\}_i$ for the belief distribution at time $t-1$, the filter update equation becomes

$$p(x_t) = k_t p(z_t | x_t) \sum_i p(x_t | x_{i,t-1})\pi_{i,t-1}. \tag{7}$$

A common choice for the importance density is the mixture density derived from the transition model

$$g(x_t) = \sum_i p(x_t | x_{i,t-1})\pi_{i,t-1}. \tag{8}$$

In the propagation step, perfect sampling according to g is applied to obtain a new set of representative samples $\{x_{i,t}\}_i$. Then, observation z_t is used to compute the new importance weights $\pi_{i,t} = p(z_t | x_{i,t-1})\pi_{i,t-1}$. Due to the usually diffusive behaviour of the propagation model, the weight distribution becomes more and more skewed with each iteration. In order to avoid this degeneracy problem, particles are periodically resampled according to their weights. This is the basic version of the particle filter, also known as *condensation* algorithm (Isard and Blake 1998).

   We can now investigate the particle filter implementation of the ideas previously described. As already discussed, the key to a robust observation model is to take into account the occlusion probabilities $\mathbf{S}^l$ in the computation of the observation likelihood $p(z|x^k)$ as reported in Eq. (5). In the particle filter framework, the same map can be estimated by the sum of normalized weights of occluding particle configurations:

$$\mathbf{S}^l = E_{p(x)}[\Delta_g(x|s)] \approx \frac{1}{\pi} \sum_i \Delta_g(x|s)\pi_i. \tag{9}$$

The implementation of the algorithm is straightforward, and its computation precedes the update step in the basic particle filter algorithm. If the observation model permits a one-time ordering of the particles according to the distance of their renderings from the observation sensor for instances, the observation weight calculations can be speeded up. This is the case, for example, when tracking flat objects or convex 3D objects. In such situations, one can simply compute the occlusion probability maps incrementally, starting from the nearest configurations to the farthest one. In doing so, the complexity $O(N^2K^2)$ of the original algorithm that redraws the map for each configuration from scratch reduces to $O(NK)$ for K objects, with each one tracked with N particles. In fact, each configuration hypothesis is rendered just once per update cycle and, hence, the proposed algorithm is optimal. Experiments were performed on synthetic data delivered by the real-time graphical simulator Zeus. Each person is modeled by a coarse histogram in RGB color space. Its state is defined in terms of its 2D position and velocity on a horizontal reference plane. Two calibrated cameras capture images from two orthogonal viewing directions. During tracking, only one image per time step is analyzed, continuously alternating between the views.

Particle propagation is performed using a constant velocity model with additive Gaussian noise. After propagation particle positions are projected onto the image plane and ordered according to their camera distance. At each projected particle position, a coarse head-torso silhouette kernel is extracted from $\mathbf{W}$. The kernel is used to extract a rough 6×6×6 quantized RGB colour histogram. Its Bhattacharyya coefficient-based distance to the object's reference histogram defines the likelihood. Figure 9 shows the tracking of two people using 50 particles per target. The standard particle filter computes the likelihood of a particle by considering all pixels belonging to its silhouette. When a target is partially occluded, its histogram is contaminated by the other object's colour, which results in lower particle weights. This causes the belief mode to drift away from its true position, which can result in a lock on background clutter. This happens even if the target is occluded only in one camera and a bad likelihood is obtained only at each second time step. The proposed algorithm succeeds in tracking by ignoring likely occluded pixels. The histogram of a partially occluded configuration is extracted mainly from the visible part of its silhouette, resulting in robust tracking.

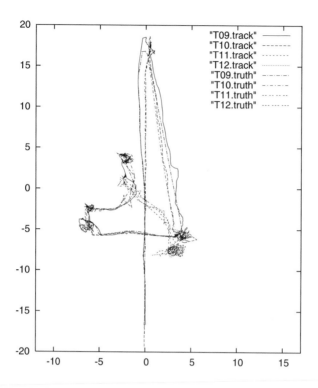

Fig. 10. Exploiting the oracle functionality of Zeus, extensive and accurate algorithm evaluation was obtained. The figure presents a plot of estimated target trajectories and computer-generated ground truth. Noisy regions identify exhibits where targets were standing still for a considerable amount of time

The advantage of the proposed algorithm over the traditional one is clearly demonstrated by the experiments performed on synthetic data. Examples of the trajectories computed for virtual characters are reported in Fig. 10 together with the corresponding ground truth. Assessing tracking performance on real data is currently addressed. The proposed framework is well matched to Olympus distributed architecture as the Bayes filter allows the distribution of computational load among several processing units. Likelihoods can be calculated on unsynchronized sensor nodes while a central unit maintains 3D target beliefs. The compressed particle belief representation reduces intercamera communication to a level such that even low-bandwidth connections could support it. From a theoretical perspective, it would be valuable to pursue the embedding of the proposed approach into the joint filter framework by deriving it as a belief marginalization approach.

10.6 Conclusions

We have described a flexible architecture for tracking of people in large indoor environments, of which museums are a relevant example. The proposed system successfully addresses several important aspects of ambient intelligence systems such as exploitation of a distributed processing environment, providing support for extensive algorithm evaluation, and delivering robust tracking in crowded situations characterized by dynamic occlusion patterns. Future research will focus on the difficult problem of optimally tracking many people in a multiroom environment when a limited number of cameras are available. It is expected that the probabilistic description upon which the current tracking algorithm is based will prove valuable in solving issues such as the selection of optimal parameters for active cameras and the choice of the most informative video streams.

Part V
Evaluation and Usability

11 Evaluation of Cinematic Techniques in a Mobile Multimedia Museum Guide Interface

F. Pianesi, M. Zancanaro, I. Alfaro and M. Nardon

11.1 Introduction

The use of portable multimedia devices for the exploration of cultural institutions has encountered much interest among researchers in the field. Hewlett-Packard (Semper and Spasojevic 2002) and Xerox PARC (Grinter et al. 2002) experimented with multimedia devices that can enhance a museum visit by providing users with information about what they are seeing in flexible and interactive ways. In some cases, such as the Egyptian Museum in Cairo and the National Museum of Cinema in Turin (Cigliano and Monaci 2003), these devices are already being provided as guide options for visitors. Usually these multimedia guides use static images, while others employ pre-recorded short video clips about museum exhibits. Some cultural institutions such as the Tate Modern Gallery in London (Proctor and Tellis 2003) recently conducted extensive user studies to assess visitor satisfaction with these mobile guides. Indications of the invasive nature of the PDA in the museum experience have been reported by Semper and Spasojevic (2002) and Woodruff et al. (2001). The former report that the handheld device tended to keep people from playing with the content of the exhibit and that this distractive effect can be only partially attributed to the "wow" factor induced by the technology itself. The latter further reports that some visitors complained about the attention overhead imposed by the device, yet, they recognize that allowing visitors to control the information received is one of the major ways to compensate for this problem.

In our work, we experimented with a multimedia museum guide on a PDA that uses cinematic techniques with the goal of enhancing the presentation of museum exhibits. Our hypothesis is that a user interface that employs cinematic techniques reduces the inherent invasiveness that the PDA brings to the museum experience by limiting attentional demands. To test this hypothesis, we implemented a simple audio guide similar to the one described in (Chap. 2), but without the personalization part; the presentations were manually prepared using the strategies based on the rhetorical structure of the texts as described in Sect. 11.3 below. The guide employs a localization system to detect the visitor's position and shares control with the visitor on when to start a presentation through the use of an intuitive spatial metaphor (below). Relying, however, only on the visitor's explicit control of the interface can be a dangerous solution, since more control usually means a more complex interface and a greater need to pay attention to the device. We thus also propose to rely on an implicit form of control.

In this chapter, we argue that one of the advantages of cinematic techniques is that these increase the predictability of the presentation (and thus of the system as a whole) by creating short-term expectations about changes on the PDA's display. The visitor experiences a diminished need to repeatedly look back at the display in order to check whether new information is being presented, in this way mitigating the distracting effect reported by Semper and Spasojevic (2002). In order to confirm our hypothesis on the effects of cinematic techniques in a multimedia presentation, a study was designed to compare our cinematic-based with standard[1] multimedia presentations by measuring the number of eye shifts caused by audio and visual stimuli.

The experimental results demonstrate that given an equal amount of time spent on the presentations, the group that experienced the cinematically enhanced version underwent lower attentional demands, as measured by a lower number of eye shifts between the fresco and the PDA in correspondence to an audio or video stimulus. We thus argue that (a) the cinematically enhanced presentation proved to be more effective in driving the attention of users and less demanding than the alternative presentation, and that (b) this makes for a less invasive and more efficient museum experience with the PDA.

11.2 The Prototype

As a test case, we chose Torre Aquila, a tower at the Buonconsiglio Castle in Trento, Italy, that houses a fresco called "The Cycle of the Months," a masterpiece of the Gothic period. The fresco was painted in the 15th century and illustrates the activities of aristocrats and peasants throughout the year. It consists of 11 panels, each one representing a month of the year (March was destroyed over time), and occupies the four walls of the tower (Fig. 1).

---

[1] While there is no established standard for a multimedia presentation, most systems currently use slide-show formats.

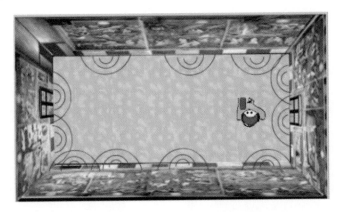

Fig. 1. Torre Aquila and the grid of infrared sensors

The multimedia guide was implemented with Macromedia Flash on an iPAQ PDA. In order to detect the visitor's position inside the tower, we employed a set of infrared emitters that were placed in front of each panel. Interaction is thus proposed by the system itself and accepted by the user, in a shared-responsibility paradigm of information access. When the system detects that the visitor is in front of one of the four walls, a picture of that wall is displayed on the PDA and, after a couple seconds, if the user has not changed his position, the panel he is facing is highlighted (Fig. 2). At this point, the visitor can click on the panel and receive a multimedia presentation of the selected panel.

Unlike other museum layouts, the environment at Torre Aquila presented particular constraints in terms of space and amount of details available. Each panel is immediately connected to the next one and each one is loaded with small details easily missed by a visitor. It was hence important for us to utilize a highly accurate localization system that would be able to quickly identify not only the visitor's location, but also his orientation within the tower. The use of infrared sensors allowed us to keep a good level of accuracy, as each panel was assigned its own sensor. In this manner, interaction between the user and the PDA was clear and effective, even when the user's position changed only by a meter or two.

Fig. 2. Snapshots of the multimedia guide

11.3 Cinematic Presentations

The multimedia presentation consists of an audio commentary accompanied by a sequence of images that appear on the PDA display, which help the visitor quickly identify and focus on the fresco details mentioned in the commentary. For instance, when a specific detail of the panel is explained by the commentary, the PDA may display or highlight it, thus calling the attention of the user to the area in question.

During the presentation, the PDA displays a VCR-style control panel and a slide bar to signal the length of the video clip and its actual position in the timeline (Fig. 3). At any given moment, the user is free to pause, fast forward, rewind, and even stop the presentation by tapping on the appropriate control panel button. This enables the visitor to control the pace of the presentation, select the information he is most interested in, and review sections that most attracted his attention.

Fig. 3. Snapshot of the multimedia guide playing a video

The visual part of the presentation is in the form of an animation, which was constructed and synchronized with the audio part by exploiting concepts of the language of cinematography. These include shot segmentations, camera movements, and transition effects, which are further explained in (Chap. 2). In building the presentations, we defined as a shot a sequence of camera movements applied to the same image. Transitions between images are used to affect the rhythm of the discourse and the message conveyed by the video. A cut occurs when the last frame of a shot is immediately replaced by the first frame of the following shot and it is used to suggest continuation. A fade consists in a shot being gradually replaced by another, either by disappearing (*fade out*) or by being replaced by the new shot (*fade in*). Fades suggest interruption of the flow and therefore may be used when, for example, a new topic is introduced.

Two broad classes of strategies used to build the animations were singled out, similar to those exploited in documentaries. These strategies have been developed to guide the authors in designing the presentations. The first class enforces constraints imposed by the grammar of cinematography; e.g., one such strategy prevents zoom-in/zoom-out sequences as these actions may produce a visual incongruence for the viewer. The strategies of the second type, on the other hand, deal with conventions normally used in guiding camera movements in the production of documentaries; e.g., by recommending the use of sequential scene cuts, rather than a fade-out effect, to visually enumerate different characters in a scene. This approach reinforces a visual organization when presenting various information.

Constraints on camera movements alone could suffice to ensure a pleasant presentation, yet they do not impact the effectiveness of the video clip. In order to have a more engaging presentation, the visual part should not only focus on the right detail at the right time, but it should also emphasize the connection between new information and information already provided. In this manner, continuity between the information is built, which in turn facilitates the viewing of the video clip while stimulating the absorption of new information. As can be expected, the strategies in the second class often rely on information about the discourse structure of the audio part of the presentation, such as enumeration of properties, background knowledge, and elaboration of related information.

One way to describe the discourse structure is by recalling the Rhetorical Structure Theory (RST) proposed by Mann and Thompson's seminal work (1987). It analyses discourse structure in terms of dependency trees, with each node of the tree being a segment of text. Each branch of the tree represents the relationship between a node called *nucleus* and a node called *satellite*. The information in the satellite relates to that found in the nucleus in that it expresses an idea related to what was is said in the nucleus. This rhetorical relation specifies the coherence relation that exists between the two portions of text contained in the nodes.

To exemplify, a *Cause* rhetorical relation holds when the satellite describes the event that caused what is contained in the nucleus. With a *Background* rhetorical relation, on the other hand, the second paragraph (satellite) provides background information with respect to the content expressed in the first paragraph (nucleus). The additional information provided by the satellite reinforces what was previously said in the first paragraph and consequently facilitates the absorption of information. In the original formulation by Mann and Thompson, the theory posited 20 different rhetorical relations between a satellite and a nucleus; other scholars have since added to this theory.

To illustrate the connection between rhetorical relations and cinematic elements, consider the text in Fig. 4. It can be visually represented with two shots of the same image (that is, the tournament) linked by a long cross-fade. Technically, using two shots is not necessary, since the image is the same, however the cross-fade helps the user understand that background information is going to be provided. The first image is thus presented while the first paragraph is heard over the audio, then when the audio switches to, in this case, the background information, the image is enlarged to cover the entire panel and finally refocused on the detail once the audio has stopped.

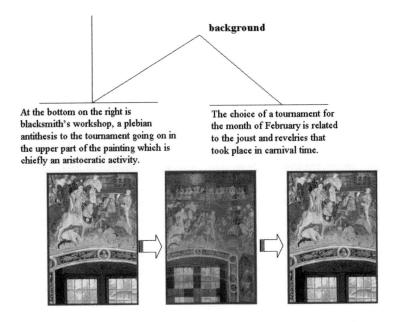

Fig. 4. The "Tournament" example: from the text to the video clip

The guide used for the evaluation employed hand-made video clips. In the context of this work, RST was used as a formalism to guide human authors in choosing the right set of cinematic elements while building a multimedia presentation. Yet since the beginning, RST has been applied in the computer-based text generation field. In the context of the PEACH project, the possibility of generating multimedia presentations from scratch by combining Natural Language Generation techniques with a plan-based generation of camera movements was also experimented with. In that work, presented in (Chap. 2), RST is used to maintain cohesion between the two parts—the verbal and the visual one—of a presentation.

11.4 The User Study

The video guide was designed with the aim of capturing and driving user attention in such a way as to improve appreciation of the actual artwork. A guide is expected to be informative and engaging, without being invasive and/or imposing attentional overhead. The user study focused on some aspects of the attentional demands of audio-video guides, trying to understand whether the use of cinematic techniques could succeed in limiting the overhead costs observed in other cases.

We adopted an information channel model, according to which the device and the fresco are seen as two channels along which information is presented to users, who extract and process it by sampling them. The sampling behaviour and the ensuing fixations on the device or on the fresco are guided by the subjects' mental models of the (statistical) properties of the two channels. The situation is similar, at least in some respects, to that of tasks involving selective attention such as supervisory control or target search (Wickens and Holland 2000). However, whereas in those tasks there is little mutual dependence between the various channels, in our scenario, the dependence is much higher: The presentation comments on and highlights the content of the fresco, and guides its appreciation; hence, cross-channel sampling is not driven (exclusively) by the need to find a target or some information, but, more generally, by the necessity to maintain an appropriate level of synchronization between what the guide is presenting on the device and the contents made available by the fresco. For instance, if the user is watching the device and the guide presents information about the tournament shown in the May panel, we might observe that the user directs her attention towards the relevant part of the fresco. Or, if the user's attention is captured by the fresco's details, then she might feel the need to switch to the device to compare and realign the information she got from the fresco with the video contents of the presentation. In turn, this can trigger further sampling, etc. In the end, cross-channel synchronization seems to be an important factor underlying the sampling behaviour of our subjects, and a major source of attentional demands.

Sampling can be measured by observing the fresco-to-device (FD) and the device-to-fresco (DF) attention shifts performed by subjects. One can hypothesize that attention shifts increase when synchronization is perceived as being more difficult. Such a difficulty, in turn, might be related to various factors: the content of the audio portion of the presentation, the content of the fresco, and what is available on the guide display. Our user study aimed to understand how the patterns of synchronization, measured through attention shifts, were affected by the structural properties of the presentations.

11.4.1 The Control Interface

In order to have a baseline against which to evaluate the synchronization behaviour induced by our cinematic presentation, we built a control version, called the Slide Show guide. It featured the same audio commentaries, but a different visual part, which was organized as a slide-show by taking the initial image of each shot of the presentation, followed by the final image of each camera movement. The images were synchronized in accordance with the audio commentary. Therefore, for each panel of the fresco a cinematic-based video presentation and a corresponding slide-show were available.

As seen, the slide-show and the cinematic guide have the same audio content. Exhibits, about which our guides present information, kept the same conditions. Hence, the only remaining source that could affect synchronization behaviour was the visual part of the presentations. In the cinematic presentation, image changes closely parallel topic changes; camera movement and the other cinematic elements are determined by, and emphasize, the rhetorical structure of the text presented in the audio modality. That is, the cinematic elements provide for a high level of cross-modal (audio-video) integration/cohesion. Moreover, subjects are accustomed to the cinematic language; hence, they can be quite confident in their expectations about what is going on, and what will happen next (high predictability). In the slide-show, on the other hand, the level of cross-modal cohesion and predictability is lower: topic changes are not accompanied by image changes, and the rhetorical structure of the text is not emphasized at the visual level. We expect these differences to affect cross-channel synchronization, making the latter easier in the cinematic presentation than in the slide-show. In terms of attention shifts, this should amount to a lower number of them with the cinematic than with the slide-show guide.

Because of the structure of our presentations, attention shifts can be classified according to the existence/absence of temporal/causal relationship with focal points of the presentation, henceforth referred to as "stimuli". In our presentations, we have: video stimuli (camera movements, transitions, and indicators[2]), audio stimuli (spatial expressions — "at the top...", deictics — "this is …", and comparisons — "like in the last panel …"), and complex stimuli, consisting of various combinations of audio and video ones. The stimuli are of the same number in the two presentations; they are also of the same type, apart from those that in one case contain, and in the other do not contain one or more cinematic element (stimuli of type K). As discussed in the previous sections, the goal of those stimuli is to provide a higher degree of cohesion and coherence both within the presentation (in its two components: the audio and the video part) and between the presentation and what is available on the exhibits. Successful use of these cohesive devices should support better information integration and cross-channel synchronization.

Putting all these observations together, we can formulate our working hypothesis as follows:

---

[2] An indicator is a visual communicative strategy that consists of circling or, in some way, highlighting a detail on an image. Indicators were used in both the cinematic and the slide-show presentations.

Hypothesis: the number of attention shifts is affected both by the type of presentation and by the presence/absence of stimuli. In particular, it is higher with the slide-show and in the absence of stimuli.

11.4.2 Design

Of the subjects, 33 were assigned to the *Cinematic* (C) condition and 33 to the *Slide-Show* (S) condition. Age, sex, education and previous knowledge of the fresco were balanced across the two conditions. All the subjects were casual visitors at Torre Aquila that chose to take part at the experiment. The dependent variables were (a) the number of attention shifts performed and (b) fixation times on the device and the fresco.

The age of the participants ranged from 17 to 64 years, the average being 36 (SD = 12.56). Of the subjects, 18 were male and 28 female. In terms of education, 9% of the subjects had a primary school degree, 53% a high school degree, and 38% a university degree. The declared familiarity with high-tech facilities (Internet, e-mail, Office, CD-ROMS) was high for more than 50% of our sample. The remaining subjects had either no familiarity with Office and Internet (13%), or had never used e-mail (15.5%), or CD-ROMS (21.7%). Acquaintance with PDAs was limited to 35% of the subjects. As to the familiarity with technological tools available in museums, most of the subjects had used audio-guides (70%), and/or tools such as multimodal platforms, kiosk or "special" audio-guides (54%). Only 4,3% of our subjects declared to never have visited cultural places, 15.2% visit them at least once a year, 28.3% from 2 to 5 times a year, 26.1% from 6 to 10; the remaining 26.1% visit museums more than 10 times a year. Self-declared previous knowledge of Torre Aquila frescos varied uniformly between no knowledge at all and very good knowledge.

11.4.3 Procedure

Participants were tested individually at Torre Aquila, each session lasting approximately 20 minutes. Each subject was first asked to compile a questionnaire to assess demographic information, former knowledge of the fresco, and technological skills.

After a short training phase, each participant interacted freely for the same amount of time with the mobile multimedia guide in the frescoed room; once finished, she was asked to fill in a second questionnaire about her experience. This questionnaire consisted of 21 statements, with which the participants had to express their agreement, by using 10 and 5-point Likert scales.

Each visitor was video recorded during the tour of the fresco. The Anvil tool (Kipp 2001) was used to annotate the video recordings, with respect to the stimuli presented and visitors' reaction in terms of eye shifts.

The association between stimuli and attention shifts was determined according to the following procedure: each stimulus was assigned an "observation" time, consisting of the temporal interval it occupies (from its beginning to its end) plus the following 1-second-long interval. Any attention shifts falling in the observation time of a given stimulus were classified as temporally associated to that stimulus; an attention shift that does not fall in the observation time of any stimulus was classified as a "free" shift.

Notice that, because of the way the association between stimuli and attention shifts was determined, it was possible that more than one shift to be associated with the same stimulus: e.g., when the subjects perform successive attention shifts within the time interval of the stimulus. Finally, in the analysis, we focused on the attention shifts originating from either the device or the fresco and terminating on one of them. We ignored the cases where the subject turns his attention, e.g., from the fresco to a place different that the fresco under consideration, then back or to the fresco. As a consequence, the number of DF and FD shifts are, in general, not identical.

11.4.4 Results

11.4.4.1 Fixation Times

Fixation times were computed on the annotated audio-video files, by distinguishing the periods spent by each subject watching the fresco from the time spent watching the device. The results are reported in Table 1.

Table 1. Fixation times: averages and standard deviations

	Cinematic	Slide Show	Total
Device FT	155.6 (104.8)	158.1 (87.5)	158.8 (95.8)
Fresco FT	278.9 (103.3)	278.8 (86.1)	278.9 (94.4)
Total	434.6 (11.7)	436.9 (6.4)	

A repeated measure ANOVA, with the location of the fixation (fresco or device) as a two-level within factor, and the guide version as a between factor produced no main effect of the Version factor, showing that the two guides do not globally differ as to the total time people spent using them. There was a significant main effect of fixation-location (F(1) = 26.821, p<.001); looking at Table 1, it can be concluded that all the subjects spent more time watching the fresco than the device, a result which suggests that, on average, our multimedia guides did not hinder the appreciation of the "real" artwork. Finally, the absence of a significant interaction between the two factors shows that the time spent looking at the device rather than at the fresco did not depend on the way the information was presented.

11.4.4.2 Attention Shifts

A multivariate analysis of variance was run on attention shifts, with Version as a between factor, and Stimulus as within factor. Table 2 reports the estimated means and standard errors; the results of the tests of within and between effects are reported in Table 3.

Table 2. Attention shifts; estimate means and standard errors from ANOVA1

Stimulus	Version		
	Cinem.	Slide Show	global
Absent	21.5 (1.2)	22.8 (2.2)	22.1 (1.5)
Present	31.9 (3.5)	39.2 (3.5))	35.6 (2.5)
global	26.7 (2.7)	31.0 (2.7)	28.9 (1.9)

Table 3. Significant main effects and interaction from ANOVA1. Within factor: Stimulus; between factor: Version. (* p<.05; ** p<.001)

Effect	F	DF	sig.	Observed power
Stimulus	99.86	1	p < .001	1.0
Stimulus*Version	5.11	1	p < .05	0.605

There is no main effect of the between factor, showing that the total number of attention shifts is not affected by the guide version. Attention shifts are affected by the presence/absence of a stimulus: their number increases when a stimulus is present with respect to when the stimulus is absent (Table 2 for the mean values). This result, by itself, is not relevant, given that we did control for the total time occupied by stimuli with respect to the duration of the presentation. More interesting is the significance of the Stimulus*Version interaction, which is due to a higher increase of attention shifts in the presence of the stimulus with the slide-show guide than with the cinematic one.

Hence, at a global level, the two guides do not seem to differ as to the total amount of attention shifts they give rise to. This result rejects the first part of our initial hypothesis, for there is not a global difference of synchronization behaviour between the two guides. The second part of the hypothesis, on the other hand, is supported: the higher number of attention shifts in the presence of stimuli with the slide-show is evidence in favour of the idea that the way the focal points of the presentation are realized by the cinematic guide is more effective than the way followed by the traditional guide. That is, the camera movements and the explicit textual links the former provide help users towards a better integration of the two informational sources.

11.4.4.3 Looking for Subgroups

The distribution of fixation times reported in Table 1 exhibits a high variance, especially for the sample using the cinematic guide. This suggests that our two (sub)samples could be further divided according to the way the fixation times distribute. To this end, two 2-step cluster analyses were run on the data, one for the cinematic condition and one for the slide-show, with the fixation times on the device and on the fresco as variables. Mean values and standard deviations for the resulting groups are reported in Table 4.

Table 4. Subgroups from the cluster analysis

		Device FT	Fresco FT	No. of subjects
Cinematic	Group1	61.93 (37.53)	372.0 (37.11)D	15
	Group2	233.72 (73.00)	201.44 (70.48)	18
Slide Show	Group1	84.08 (48.62)	351.80 (46.30)	13
	Group2	206.20 (72.20)	231.40 (71.50)	20

Our original two groups of subjects can be further split into two subgroups; the first (Group1) comprises people spending most of their time watching the fresco (14% of the time for the cinematic group and 19% for the slide group); the second (Group2) consists of subjects who divided their attention more or less equally between the fresco and the device. One might attribute this difference to the diverse interest in the two guides and wonder whether this factor could affect the attention shift behaviour we discussed above. To see whether this was the case, we ran a multivariate analysis of variance on attention shifts, with a similar design as the one discussed above, but adding a 2-level Cluster variable (Group1 = subjects who spend few time on the device, Group2 = subjects who equally divide their attention between the device and the fresco) as another between factor. The results are summarized in Table 5; Table 6 reports the estimate means and standard errors.

Table 5. Significant main effects and interaction from ANOVA2. Within factors: Stimulus and Direction; between factor: Version and Cluster. * p<.05; ** p<.001

Effect	F	DF	sig.	Observed power
Stimulus	96.75	1	**	1.00
Cluster	11.77	1	**	.922
Stimulus*Version	5.66	1	*	0.65

Table 6. Attention shifts; estimate means and standard errors from ANOVA2

			Version		
Cluster			Cinem.	Slide Show	Global
Group1	Stimulus	Absent	15.5 (2.9)	15.2 (3.1)	15.3 (2.1)
		Present	23.2 (4.9)	32.8 (5.3)	28.2 (3.6)
	Global		19.3 (3.8)	24.0 (4.1)	21.7 (2.8)
Group2	Stimulus	Absent	26.5 (2.6)	27.7 (2.5)	27.1 (1.8)
		Present	39.2 (4.5)	43.5 (4.3)	41.3 (3.1)
	Global		32.8 (3.4)	35.6 (3.3)	34.2 (2.4)
Global			26.1 (2.6)	29.8 (2.6)	28.0 (1.8)

The Cluster main effect corresponds to a significant difference between Groups1 and Group2 attention shifts which is such that the tendency to spend less time on the device corresponds to a lower number of attention shifts. A part from that, the other factors have the same effects we have discussed above and, what is more important, Cluster does not interact in a significant way with any other factors. Hence, Version and Stimulus effects are the same irrespective of the way subjects divided their time on the device vs. the fresco. This is an interesting result, since it supports the view that the synchronization between the two information channels does not depend on the global time/attention subjects devote to the fresco vs. the device, but on the structural properties of the presentation (presence/absence of stimuli).

11.4.4.4 Discussion of the Results

The data discussed in the previous section provide some evidence in favour of the predictions of our model: the cinematic presentation makes synchronization between the two channels easier, at least in the presence of stimuli, this being related to its higher level of predictability and cross-modal cohesion. If confirmed by further studies, these conclusions would support the idea that cinematic presentation makes life easier for subjects in comparison to the slide-show, fostering a more relaxed approach to the fresco. At the same time, the absence of cross-condition differences concerning fixation times and the prevalence of the fresco-time over the device-time show that neither guide prevents subjects from experiencing the actual artworks. Finally, we found that our sample consists of two subgroups, the first globally devoted low attention to the device, and the second divided its attention in a more balanced way between the device and the fresco. This different attitude did not affect the sampling behaviour, showing that the effects mentioned above are robust and due to the structural differences between the two guides/presentations.

11.4.5 Subjective Evaluation

The dimensions considered in the post-test were: perceived system usefulness, perceived ease of use, and information quality. Each dimension consisted of five items/statements for which the participants had to express their agreement by means of 5-point Likert scales. Scores for each dimension were obtained by summing up those of the composing items.

Table 7. Subjective evaluation of the two guides; estimate means and standard errors from ANOVA3

Version			Useful.	Ease of use	Info quality
Cinematic	Cluster	Group1	19.9 (0.8))	22.3 (0.5)	19.7 (0.6)
		Group2	21.4 (0.7)	22.9 (0.4)	20.5 (0.6)
	Global		20.7 (0.5)	22.6 (0.3)	20.1 (0.4)
Slide show	Cluster	Group1	20.6 (0.8)	22.7 (0.5)	20.3 (0.7)
		Group2	22.9 (0.7)	23.1 (0.4)	20.4 (0.5)
	Global		21.8 (0.5)	22.9 (0.3)	20.4 (0.4)
Global			21.2 (0.4)	22.7 (0.2)	20.2 (0.3)

To ascertain whether the experimental conditions or belonging to one of the two subgroups affected the users' subjective evaluation of the guide(s), we ran a multivariate analysis of variance (ANOVA3), on the usefulness, easy of use and information quality scores, with Version and Cluster-Group as between factors.

Table 7 reports the estimated means and standard errors. As can be seen, the figures were all rather high (maximum value = 25) and with a small standard error.

The multivariate test was negative for both factors and for their interaction. However, the between subject test showed a small effect of cluster on usefulness ($F(3) = 3.284$, $p<.05$, observed power = .724) which, according to Table 7, amounts to a somewhat smaller appreciation of the guides by people in Group1 (mean of Group1 = 20.3; mean of Group2 = 22.1). This small difference is not such that we can make much out of it. However, it signals a possible specific relationship between perceived utility and time spent on the guide that deserves more investigation. More generally, the conclusion is that there were no clear signs that our subjects' attitudes towards the guide varied according to the version they exploited and/or their general tendency to spend more/less time on the device. Finally, no significant correlations were found between any of the indices of sampling behaviour discussed above and the subjective dimensions.

11.5 Conclusion

In this paper, we presented the evaluation of a technique to build multimedia presentations by using cinematic principles.

This technique was developed as part of the design of a mobile guide for museum as described in Chap. 1 and Chap. 2, . The purpose was to reduce the invasiveness of mobile devices in the museum experience. A user study conducted in the Museo del Buonconsiglio in Trento, Italy, compared the cinematic presentations with equivalent slide-show versions. The adopted model considered the device and the fresco as two informational channels that for which an optimum guide/presentation should aim to provide maximal synchronization. Our results support the idea that the cinematic guide is superior to the control (a traditional slide-show) in the presence of explicit coherence enhancing cues (stimuli); since no global differences were observed, it can be concluded that the cinematic guide makes better use of those cues than the control. As to the overall impact on the attentional behaviour, the two guides were similar in the distribution of fixation times between the device and the fresco they gave raise to. They were also similar in that both divided their subjects into those who spent comparatively less time looking the device than at the fresco, and those who had a more balanced behaviour. Interestingly, these differences did not affect the synchronization behaviour of our subjects, lending support to the idea that the superiority of the cinematic guide in supporting synchronization behaviour is rooted in the structural properties of its presentations. In the end, and pending further studies on this topic, we can conclude that our result supports the idea that cinematic guides can be less demanding in terms of attention (cross-channel synchronization behaviour) with respect to traditional multimedia audio-video guides.

A subjective evaluation through a post-test questionnaire failed to relate attitudinal differences to the variables and dimensions addressed in the study. The only interesting point (to which we cannot attached much value due to the overall nonignificance of the statistical results) was the possibility that (lower) perceived utility can be a factor related to the quantity of overall attention (fixation times) devoted to the guide.

12 Innovative Approaches for Evaluating Adaptive Mobile Museum Guides

D. Goren-Bar, I. Graziola, F. Pianesi, M. Zancanaro and C. Rocchi

12.1 Introduction

Adaptivity is a technological approach whereby systems monitor and manipulate personal needs and interests. Because of its very nature, it can be expected that personal differences play an important role in explaining adaptivity acceptance and, more generally, people's attitudes towards it. There are findings in the literature that provide some initial support of this view. For instance, it is often emphasized and recommended that users be left with the feeling of being in control of the interaction (Shneiderman 1998). According to Norman (1998), the feeling of being in control over an interaction is an important component of people's comfort with technologies. Several studies have discussed these issues in the context of adaptive systems (Wexelblat and Maes 1997; Jameson and Schwarzkopf 2002), all of them pointing to the opportunity of increasing controllability over all aspects of system adaptation. While discussing the ways in which learners can be given control over learner-adapted teaching systems, Kay (2001) observes that some users may generally have less desire for control than others. She also suggests that those users might find the exercise of too much control distracting or a waste of time, and negatively react to systems that they find too demanding in these respects. So control is not only a generally crucial issue for understanding the adaptive/nonadaptive continuum, but also seems to be sensitive to personality differences. As a first, rough working hypothesis, one might expect that the more people care about control issues, the more they exhibit a negative attitude/disposition towards, or lower acceptance of, adaptivity.

In a review study on evaluation of adaptive systems, Chin (2001) reported more than 30 papers addressing, in one way or another, the empirical evaluation of adaptive hypermedia/hypertext, student modelling, and other related technologies. Evaluation criteria included both quantitative and qualitative methods.

A partially different approach is to look for insights about the importance of more abstract dimensions in a principled way, and then use prototypes and user evaluations as tools to support the discussion, like in the seminal work of Horvitz (1999).

In all these cases, with the possible exception of Horvitz (1999), the efforts have targeted specific systems, or parts thereof. Less attention has been paid so far to investigating the attitudes and dispositions of (potential) users towards the very idea of adaptivity, or abstract/basic dimensions thereof. Admittedly, the study of the acceptability of adaptation is not an easy task, especially if conducted by having subjects use real systems. Even with low-fi mockups (Preece et al. 2002), in fact, the results are always tied to that particular implementation, and are subject to noise from many intervening factors. Moreover, the fact of being involved in a direct interaction with the system often makes it difficult for the subjects to perceive and assess certain aspects that are of a more holistic nature, such as content adaptation with respect to the history of the interaction.

The studies that investigated personalization and adaptivity in the context of adaptive museum guides shared the same view of the studies described above: a prototype system that implements a specific way of conceiving personalization is studied in a realistic setting and overall user performance or user satisfaction is observed. For example, the GUIDE system (Cheverst et al. 2002) adapts Web-like presentations by adding information about nearby attractions that might be of interest to the visitor of a city. An observational study was conducted to assess visitor acceptance of the prototype as a whole, with interesting findings about the perceived values of the features proposed. The REAL system (Baus et al. 2002) adapts the presentation of route description according to actual user position, the technical resources of the device and the cognitive resources of the user. The HIPPIE system (Oppermann and Specht 2000) proposes personalized tours in a museum by maintaining a model of user interests and knowledge. It was evaluated by domain experts and educators with very positive results.

For the HyperAudio adaptive system, a pervasive survey was conducted to elicit user preferences regarding personalization (Petrelli and Not 2005). The authors mainly focused on user modeling, and concluded that user profiles should be abandoned in favour of visit types as a basis for adaptation in museums.

Gena and Torre (2004) evaluated MastroCARONTE, an adaptive system which provides tourist information onboard cars. MastroCARONTE personalizes tourist suggestions (about hotels, restaurants, and places of interests), the way they are presented, and its own behaviour according to a model of the user (driver interest and capabilities) and a model of the context of interaction (e.g., time, location, and driving conditions).

In the context of the PEACH project, we were interested in studying more holistic aspects of adaptive mobile multimedia museum guides. Specifically, we aimed at assessing two different aspects: (1) visitor attitudes towards several basic dimensions of adaptivity relevant for museum guides and the possible relationships between personality traits and user preferences towards those adaptive dimensions, and (2) the overall experience of the visitor in using an adaptive user guide as a technological aid during the museum visit.

Regarding the first aspect, we assessed visitor attitudes towards adaptive museum guides. A study showed that personality traits relating to the notion of control (Conscientiousness, Neuroticism/Emotional Stability and Locus of Control) have a selective effect on the acceptance of the adaptivity dimensions.

For the second aspect, we investigated several constructs that might be relevant for the evaluation of the overall user experiences. As already noted, the evaluation studies of the systems discussed above adopted usability dimensions as the basis for evaluation. This is somewhat supported by the Technology Acceptance Model (TAM) proposed by Davis (1989, 1993), which states that *perceived ease-of-use* and *perceived usefulness* act as predictors for user intention to adopt a system. Yet, there is now growing acceptance that emotional factors in human–computer interaction may play a nonmarginal role in determining acceptance (see Norman 2004 for a general discussion). In assessing TAM, Davis et al. (1992) observed a positive interaction between usefulness and enjoyment, and they recommended that more investigation be performed to clarify which variables operate through enjoyment and usefulness and which have direct influences on intentions and behaviour. More recently, Venkatesh (2000) investigated emotional response as a predecessor to acceptance in the context of TAM.

In the literature, several dimensions have been proposed to measure emotional attachment. Those that seem more relevant in the context of a museum setting are related to the concept of involvement. The notion of "Flow of Experience" (Csikszentmihalyi and Csikszentmihalyi 1988), for example, relates to several factors that seem relevant for assessing overall experience with a multimodal museum adaptive guide: a sense of control; a merging of action and awareness; a loss of self-consciousness; a distorted sense of time; and the autotelic experience, in which the activity is done because the doing is in itself rewarding.

An alternative approach that combines both TAM and Flow was proposed by Agarwal and Karahanna (2000), introducing the concept of *cognitive absorption* as the main determinant of the two cognitive beliefs of perceived usefulness and perceived ease-of-use. They defined cognitive absorption as a state of deep involvement and as a holistic experience that an individual has with an information technology. They identified five dimensions of cognitive absorption: temporal dissociation, focused immersion, heightened enjoyment, control, and curiosity. While experiencing temporal dissociation, the individual perceives herself as possessing enough time to complete a task, contributing to the perceived ease-of-use of the technology. With focused immersion, all the attention resources of the individual are focused on the particular task, thus reducing the level of cognitive burden or mental workload. Amplified curiosity suggests that interaction with a technology invokes excitement about available possibilities. Such excitement should serve to reduce the perceived cognitive burden associated with interaction. A sense of being in charge and exercising control over interaction should reduce perceived difficulty in task performance. Finally, heightened enjoyment means that enjoyable activities are viewed being less demanding.

Lately, Zhang et al. (2006) suggested that the dimension called *Perception of Affective Quality* of a technology is an important factor regarding acceptance. They defined this dimension as an individual's perception that an object has the ability to change his or her affective state.

We used the affective-based adaptive guide described in (Chap. 1) to look at the responses of 110 visitors in questionnaires that combined usability dimensions from TAM and Computer Satisfaction and Usability Questionnaires (CSUQ) (Lewis 1995) and dimensions concerning involvement as discussed above. This work is a preliminary step towards a model of acceptance of adaptive guides in museums. The data showed that a positive attitude towards technology determines a greater sense of control, a deeper involvement, more easy in using the system, as well as a better attitude towards future uses of the system. We also discovered that, quite surprisingly, older visitors were much more favourable towards future use than young visitors.

12.2 Dimensions of Adaptivity for Mobile Guides

In general terms, adaptivity refers to the capability of a system to maintain a model of some characteristics of its users in order to provide them with information in a way that best suites their needs (Brusilovsky and Maybury 2002).

In this work, we focus on that particular type of adaptation that consists in tailoring information presentation (Jameson 2003). We investigate multimedia presentations, delivered on a PDA, that describe artworks. In our case a presentation includes a verbal comment on a visual animation of parts of the artwork (Alfaro et al. 2004; Rocchi and Zancanaro 2004; Rocchi et al. 2004). Adaptivity therefore refers to the capability of the system to modify the content of a presentation to better suit the needs of a specific user.

Our adaptive presentations are structured around four dimensions: location awareness (Location), follow-ups (FU), content adaptation with respect to user interests (Interest), and content adaptation with respect to history of interaction (History). Location awareness refers to the capability of the system to automatically start a presentation whenever the user approaches a relevant object. The FU dimension consists of the automatic selection of additional material. Interest and History address the addition of more details about a given topic, and the automatic construction of comparisons and cross-references, respectively. These dimensions can be found in many, if not all, the personalized museum guides described above.

12.3 Acceptance of Adaptive Systems—an Attitudinal Study

In this first study,[1] we were interested in investigating the acceptance of a general vision of adaptive information presentation rather than of a specific system. To diminish the risk that usability issues—features of the interface, etc. Would interfere with our goals, we had to avoid subject interaction with any actual or simulated system.

Acceptance of a given object, idea, concept, event, etc., relates to the notion of attitude as used in social psychology: "an individual's disposition to react with a certain degree of favourableness or unfavourableness to an object or behaviour" (Ajzen 1993). Attitudinal studies have been sometimes applied to the investigation of technology acceptance, as in Alpert et al. (2003), where user attitudes regarding adaptation on e-commerce Web sites are investigated. In that work, a mixture of simulation and working prototypes were used to present stimuli concerning the 13 adaptivity

---

[1] For a more detailed description of the study see Goren-Bar et al. (2006).

features identified by the authors as relevant in the e-commerce scenario. In our case, we could not maintain the same set-up. Indeed, our targets were abstract dimensions of adaptivity, and we wanted to avoid subjects having to interact with any form of an actual system.

Adaptivity is an emerging technology. In fact, users might have been exposed to different types of adaptivity, some of them already present in many systems, such as book recommendations or alerts for travel packets. More sophisticated techniques of adaptivity need still to be incorporated into present and future systems. In the museum guide domain adaptive systems are barely implemented. Hence, subjects could not be expected to have, by themselves, any attitude at all towards it. To address these issues, our subjects were presented with stimulus situations (in the form of video clips) that had the purpose of allowing them to form beliefs (hence attitudes) about the subject matter, in a uniform and controlled setting. At the same time, this choice was meant to minimize the biases due to the interaction with a real or simulated system.

Personality is likely to be an important factor affecting the acceptance/rejection of adaptivity. Personality can be addressed and measured by resorting to one of the many factor-based models, which organize it into underlying dimensions or factors. Among these models, much popularity has been gained by the Big Five model (McCrae and John 1992; De Raad 2000; Perugini and Di Blas 2002; Wiggins 1996). In one of its most used versions (Costa and McCrae 1992; McCrae and John 1992), the Big Five posits the following five factors:

- Extraversion—This refers to the quantity and intensity of one's interpersonal reactions, sociability, and emotional expressiveness.
- Agreeableness—This reflects individual differences with respect to cooperation and social harmony. It includes the quality of compassion, altruism, trust, modesty, prosocial attitudes or antagonism in one's interpersonal interactions.
- Conscientiousness—This relates to the way we control and direct our impulses. It includes such traits as orderliness, dutifulness, achievement striving, etc.
- Emotional Stability—This refers to the way we react in response to external stimuli: at one extreme, it covers negative emotions such as anxiety, sadness and irritability. At the other extreme, we find people who are less easily upset and less emotionally reactive (neuroticism).
- Creativity—This consists of openness, proactive seeking, and appreciation of new experiences.

An individual's personality can be characterized in terms of the positions (scores) he or she occupies on those dimensions, which, when taken together, form that individual's personality profile.

Another partially different dimension that we considered is the Locus of Control, LoC (Craig et al. 1984). A locus of control orientation refers to where people feel the control over relevant situations is located (Rotter 1966): when internal, the subject thinks that he or she is the controller; an external LoC, in turn, signals that external events are seen as substantially independent from the subject's influence. Adaptive systems, to which users delegate much of the control of the interaction, can be expected to elicit different attitudes/responses according to whether people perceive important events and their own behaviour to be determined by the external world or by the self (see, for example, Rickenberg and Reeves 2000).

12.3.1 The Study

The study aimed to comparatively assess the attitudes towards the four adaptivity dimensions, through two simulated video museum guides, an adaptive (AD) and a nonadaptive (NAD) one.

The main expectations were that first, subjects would prefer the adaptive video guide over the nonadaptive one in the four dimensions; second, subjects would have an overall preference towards the adaptive video guide; and finally, that subject attitudes towards adaptivity would be affected by their personality traits, in particular those relating to the control issue.

The design was a crossover within study where each participant was exposed to both versions of the system. Half of the visitors started with AD and the other half with NAD. Forty subjects participated in this study, 28 females and 12 males. Most of the subjects were students in psychology at the University of Trento, Italy. The rest were students in humanities or social sciences departments. Most of the students were in their 20s, with an average age of 25.1 and SD=5.76.

For each adaptivity dimension, two videos[2] based on Macromedia Flash presentations were prepared, one illustrating the AD system, and the other the NAD one. In designing these videos, we stressed the contrast between a system to which the human delegates the initiative (AD) and a system that delegates the initiative to the human, letting the user be in control (NAD). Each video featured an animated character moving in Torre Aquila, a room in the Castello del Buonconsiglio (Trento) whose four walls are decorated in the upper part with a cycle of frescos illustrating the

---

[2] The videos can be accessed at http://peach.itc.it/attitudinalstudy05/.

months of year. The character was kept as simple as possible; it was shown at a distance (from high above the ground). To avoid any possible influence of the character's appearance on the subject, no gender, age-related characteristics, or facial expressions were visible to the subjects.

The left side of each video featured a PDA showing the actions performed by the fictional character. The AD system consisted of a simple interface with just two buttons, one to stop the current presentation and the other to request more information on a given topic. The NAD video presented a standard, menu-based interface which allowed selection of a presentation for each fresco. Every action (selection, clicking, stopping, etc.) was shown as performed by a pencil (operated by the character). Figure 1 shows a snapshot of one of the videos used in the test.

Fig. 1. A snapshot of one of the videos used in the test

Each participant was tested individually. Each session was divided into three parts: the pretest, the actual test, and the post-test.

During the pretest, the participants completed a questionnaire on their computer literacy, familiarity with the most common museum technologies, frequency of museum visits, and knowledge of the Torre Aquila. They also filled two personality questionnaires: the Big Five Marker Scales (BFMS) for Italian (Perugini and Di Blas 2002) and the Italian version (Farma and Cortinovis 2000) of Craig's Locus of Control of Behaviour (LCB) scale (Craig et al. 1984).

At the beginning of the test phase, the experimenter informed the subject about the study and explained the differences between the two guides. Then, the subject watched two presentations: AD and NAD, with the order randomized. At the end of the second video, the subject indicated which system she or he preferred, indicated on a 1–5 Likert scale how much they liked them (1=I did not like it at all; 5= I liked it very much). Care was taken that the subjects' scores were consistent with the preference expressed at step a by asking the subject to first score the system that he or she preferred the most and then the other. The subject was then tasked to explain the reasons for his or her preferences, providing pros and cons for each system. Once all dimensions were addressed, subjects were asked which system they preferred overall (Global Preference). The videos for the different dimensions were not randomized, given that they had a natural order.

Finally, the post-test phase was meant to assess the subjects' attitudes towards adaptivity by abstracting even more than before from any specific realization. They had to first, order the four basic dimensions according to their importance, and then choose AD between NAD again, this time considering optimal realizations of the relevant functionalities.

12.3.2 Results

The average age of our sample was 25.1 years (SD=5.76). The means and standard deviations for the raw scores at the BFMS were consistent to those reported by Perugini and Di Blas (2002) for the Italian population. Similarly, the values for the LoC—mean=25.1 and SD=9.9—were consistent with the population mean 27 (SD=9.2) reported by Farma and Cortinovis (2000).

This study was mainly an observational one, meaning that most of the relevant variables were not controlled for. In particular, we did not control for the BFMS or the LoC by setting up the sample in such a way that, e.g., equal numbers of subjects were available for each combination of the independent variables. Rather, we directly measured in our sample the values of the independent variables, along with those of the dependent ones, and then studied their relationships. As a consequence, in most analyses the independent variables (BFMS and LoC) were not treated as factors, but as continuous covariates, limiting our attention to main effects. Interactions were not pursued because they are difficult to interpret with continuous covariates. At the same time, our study has the advantages of all observational studies; in particular, a greater freedom in laying down hypotheses and in testing them, allowing for a more exploratory style of data analysis. This made it possible to gather evidence that people's attitudes differ according to the adaptivity dimension considered, and that personality traits do affect those attitudes.

Table 1 reports the counts of the preferences for each system, on each dimension, together with the average score assigned to the two systems. The last two kinds of data are not available for Global, since we did not ask our subjects to score the two systems at the global level.

Table 1. Preference counts, mean score, and standard deviations for the two simulated conditions on the adaptive dimensions (* $p < .05$)

		Location	Interest	FU	History*	Global
	Freq	27	25	15	3	23
NAD	Mean score	4.05	3.81	3.53	2.98	–
	SD	0.85	0.98	1.04	1.02	–
	Freq	13	15	25	37	17
AD	Mean score	3.58	3.69	3.98	4.52	–
	SD	0.91	1.1	1.04	0.67	–

The choices on the five dimensions are different (Cochran test for related samples: Q=43.022, df=4, p<0.01), showing that at least some dimensions elicit different responses from our subjects. Starting from this, we performed statistical analysis on each dimension. Statistically significant differences between AD and NAD choices could be found only for Location (exact probabilities on binomial test, p<.05; power=.64 with α=.05 and power=.76 with α=.1) and History (exact probabilities on binomial test, p<.001; power>.95 with α=.05). Hence, our subjects tend to prefer NAD on Location and AD on History. The result for Location should be taken with some caution given the low power attained, but this is in accordance with observations in Jameson and Schwarzkopf (2002). The second result is much more robust: interestingly, perceiving and appreciating content adaptation with respect to the history of the presentations is a difficult task, for it involves a typical holistic dimension; however, it seems that subjects managed to do so, with a quite uniform preference for AD over NAD.

As far as our sample goes, neither gender nor other descriptive features, such as computer literacy, have an effect on any relevant adaptivity dimension.

The effect of personality traits (BFMS and LoC) was tested through both discriminant analysis and logistic regression. The results were always concordant. The results of the logistic regressions only are discussed here.

For each dependent variable (preference on Location, Interest, FU, History and Global), we ran a separate logistic regression with the five dimensions of BFMS plus the LoC as independent variables treated as covariates. For each dependent variable, the fitting of the model was first measured through the scaled deviance G2(M0 | M1), where M0 refers to the simplest, constant model (only intercept) and M1 to the full regression model. Only those models where the scaled deviance test was significant at a level p<.05 were retained (Table 2). In particular, the model for History was discarded and not considered any further. Conscientiousness appears to affect Location, Interest, and Global. The sign of the parameters suggests that in all cases, higher values of conscientiousness increase the odds for NAD. Hence, more conscientious people tend to prefer NAD over the AD on Location, Interest, and at a Global level. Stability increases the odds for AD on Interest, so that more emotionally stable people seem to prefer the AD version. The other BFMS traits did not produce any significant effect on any dimensions. Finally, the Locus of Control has an effect on Global, with people having a more external (higher score) LoC favouring the NAD over the AD.

Table 2. Summary of regression analyses results (* p<.05; ** p<.01)

	Extravers.	Agreeabl.	Conscien.	Stability	Creativity	LoC
Location			G^2=3.885*			
			ß= −0.098*			
Interest			G^2=6.141*	G^2=8.837*		
			ß= −0.142*	ß= 0.163*		
FU						
Global			G^2=6.276*			G^2=7.476*
			ß= −0.126*			ß= −0.136*

In summary, the dimensions that seem most sensitive to personality traits are Location, Interest and Global. The most effective BFMS traits are Conscientiousness and Stability. The former strengthens the tendency of subjects to prefer NAD (on Location, Interest, and Global); the second correlates with a tendency to prefer AD (on Interest). Creativity, which we consider as subsuming the more specific trait of personal innovativeness, has no effect on AD vs. NAD preferences. Finally, higher LoC (external locus of control) affects the odds in favour of NAD on Global. An analysis performed by a two-step cluster analysis confirmed the above results.

After the subjects had indicated their preference for one of the two systems, they were asked to explain the reasons for the choice in the form of an open answer, providing as many reasons as they wanted. The explanations the subjects provided were classified into five groups:

1. Easiness. This refers to reasons related to some kind of costs/benefits evaluation, e.g., "it is simpler/easier to use/operate".
2. Transparency (of function). It considers the understandability of the way the system works, for example, "it is easier to understand the way it works/what you have to do".
3. Understandability and memorisability of the contents, for example, "the presentations are more understandable/ easier to remember".
4. Control. This refers to the perceived degree of control over the inter-action the two versions afford to the users, for example, "it allows more/ a better control of the interaction".
5. Similarity to a human guide, for example, "it is like a human guide" (i.e., predictability of system behaviour).

Table 3 reports the results. As can be seen, Control is never mentioned as a reason for choosing AD on any dimensions, but it is among the main reasons for NAD preference, especially on Location and Interest. That is, the subjects (correctly) perceive that NAD allows for a greater control over the interaction, and this is a major reason for preferring it over the alternative, cf. Jameson and Schwarzkopf (2002). On the other hand, a frequent motivation for choosing AD was that its perceived easiness (Location and FU) was highest, and it had higher understandability for its content (History). Among the remaining motivations, "similarity to a human guide" does not seem to play a relevant role. This is of some interest for it shows that the choice between AD and NAD was mostly based on the direct appreciation of the respective strengths and weak-nesses, and was not mediated by indirect comparisons with the human guide. Finally, it is worth noting that more than half of the subjects who preferred NAD on FU did so because they found that the NAD system provided more understandable content ("understandability and memo-risability").

It is worth noting the importance of the control issue: those who choose the nonadaptive version most often do so because of the greater perceived control it provides. On the other hand, ease-of-use and memorisabil-ity/understandability were the main reasons behind the choice of the adap-tive system.

Table 3. Reasons for choice AD vs. NAD

		Easiness	Transparency	Understandability/ Memorisability	Control	Human-like
Location	AD	100%	15%	8%	0%	31%
	NAD	19%	15%	15%	85%	0%
Interest	AD	47%	0%	47%	0%	13%
	NAD	16%	4%	32%	84%	0%
FU	AD	80%	16%	32%	0%	8%
	NAD	47%	20%	60%	40%	0%
History	AD	57%	5%	81%	0%	14%
	NAD	0%	0%	67%	33%	0%

12.4 Dimensions of Acceptance—Testing the *Like-o-Meter*

A museum visit is a personal experience encompassing both cognitive aspects, such as the elaboration of background and new knowledge, and emotional aspects that may include the satisfaction of interests or the fascination with the exhibit itself.

The mobile multimedia guide described in (Chap. 1) encompasses all the adaptivity dimensions outlined above. Given the foremost importance of the control dimension, we put a lot of effort during the design phase on the definition of a widget to help the visitor to feel in control of the adaptation process. The basic idea was to develop a widget that supports the visitor in expressing his or her degree of liking towards the current presentation, allowing the system to tune the current as well as the future presentations (Goren-Bar et al. 2005a, 2005b). This widget, called *like-o-meter*, is conceived as both an input and an output device. Figure 2 shows a snapshot of the system (for a full description, see Chap. 1).

Fig. 2. A snapshot of the *like-o-meter* interface

12.4.1 The Study

A total of 143 regular visitors of Torre Aquila were invited to test the adaptive multimedia guide: 61 were males and 82 females. Their age ranged from 20 to 79 years (mean=47, median=50, SD=15.874). All were recruited at the entrance of the Museum of the Buonconsiglio and received a free ticket for visiting the castle as a reward for participating in the experiment. The data of 33 visitors were discarded because they did not completely fill in the questionnaires. The data analyzed below is then based on the questionnaires and the observations on the remaining 110 visitors (49 males and 61 females with average age of 45—median=47, SD=15.534).

Two questionnaires were used in the study. The first questionnaire was aimed at assessing the dimensions of attitude towards art (four items) and attitude towards technology (six items). The second questionnaire was aimed at assessing their experience in using the multimedia guide along diverse dimensions (all as nine-point Likert scales). The dimensions investigated were measured on many different scales and they were then combined and factorized in the following four dimensions:

- Control: obtained by combining items from perceived quality of information, perceived spatial orientation, and control with a combined reliability of 0.797.

- Involvement: obtained by combining items from flow, involvement, perceived time distortion, and perceived presence with a combined reliability of 0.904.
- Easiness: obtained by combining items from easiness to understand, ease of use, and clarity of feedback with a combined reliability of 0.890
- Intention to Use: obtained by combining items from the TAM usefulness with a combined reliability of 0.800.

Additionally, two four-choice questions were aimed at assessing the degree of understanding of the interface and the use of the like-o-meters ("when you are interested/not-interested in a topic presented by the guide, what did you do: (a) you pressed the smiling face; (b) you moved to another fresco; (c) you pressed the sad face; (d) you did nothing") combined in a binary measure called Correct Use (true if the users select answers a and c respectively, false otherwise). Both questionnaires were in Italian.

Each visitor who chose to participate in the experiment was tested individually at the end of the visit. Each received a short description of the system and was left free to interact with the system in Torre Aquila. After the visit, she or he was asked to fill the two questionnaires. She or he could then enjoy his or her free entrance to the rest of the castle.

12.4.2 Results

The study was conceived as an exploratory study on the usage of an adaptive guide. We chose to use age, sex and attitude towards technology as factors. Age and attitude towards technology have been transformed in a two level factors. The age groups were obtained by splitting the ages according to the median value—younger visitors with age less than or equal to 47 and older visitors with age of 48 or higher. Attitude towards technology was considered positive when scored above 0.4 (on a normalized scale from 0 to 1) and negative when scored less.

The dependent variables used were:

- *Control*: how much the visitor felt in control of the interaction with the system relating to the ability of finding information, of localizing the fresco presented, and so on.
- *Involvement*: how much the visitor felt involved with the guide encompassing the feeling of presence and perceived time distortion.
- *Easiness*: how much the visitor felt the system was easy to use, comprising most of the usability dimensions.
- *Intention to use*: this is the intention to use the system in the future as predicted by a TAM model of perceived usefulness of the system

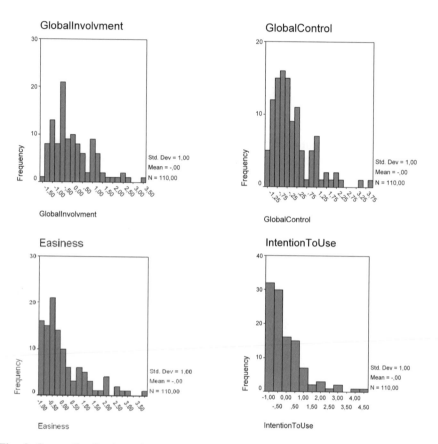

Fig. 3. Score distributions for all visitors on the four studied dimensions: Involvement, Control, Easiness, and Intention to use

All the variables were standardized on distributions with mean 0 and standard deviation 1. Greater scores indicate disagreement. Figure 3 shows the distributions of the scores of the four dimensions of the entire sample. It is worth noting that all show clear left asymmetries, indicating a general agreement on all the dimensions. That is, our visitors generally felt in control of the system, had good involvement, found it quite easy to use and had a propensity to use it again in the future.

12.4.2.1 Effect of Factors on Post-test Measures

All the four dependent variables failed the Shapiro-Wilk test for normality. We then used the nonparametric Kruskal-Wallis test.

Using the Bonferroni correction for multiple tests (We used the probability 0.0166 as a significant level of 0.05 since we performed three tests.), some significant differences were found (Fig. 4).

Test Statistics[a,b]

	GlobalInvolvement	GlobalControl	Easiness	IntentionToUse
Chi-Square	8.254	1.715	2.814	6.678
df	1	1	1	1
Asymp. Sig	0.004	0.190	0.093	0.010

a. Kruskal-Wallis test
b. Grouping Variable: AgeGroup

Test Statistics[a,b]

	GlobalInvolvement	GlobalControl	Easiness	IntentionToUse
Chi-Square	1.368	0.185	3.534	0.102
df	1	1	1	1
Asymp. Sig	0.242	0.667	0.060	0.749

a. Kruskal-Wallis test
b. Grouping Variable: Sex

Test Statistics[a,b]

	GlobalInvolvement	GlobalControl	Easiness	IntentionToUse
Chi-Square	34.981	11.271	15.739	8.870
df	1	1	1	1
Asymp. Sig	0.000	0.001	0.000	0.003

a. Kruskal-Wallis test
b. Grouping Variable: AttituteToardTech (dual)

Fig. 4. Kruskal-Wallis test for all visitors on the four studied dimensions: Involvement, Control, Easiness and Intention to use with grouping variables: Age, Sex and Attitude towards technology

In particular, regarding age group, significant differences emerge with respect to involvement and intention to use and along all the four dimensions studied for attitude towards technology.

Young visitors' average score for intention to use is 0.24 while for older visitors is −0.23. Therefore, the latter have more propensity towards future use of the system. Average scores for attitude towards technology are shown in Table 4. As expected, a positive attitude towards technologies leads to greater agreement on each dimension.

Table 4. Average scores for attitude towards technology on the four studied dimensions: Involvement, Control, Easiness and Intention to use

	Global_Involvment	Global_Control	Easiness	IntToUse
Positive	-0.46	-0.31	-0.32	-0.32
Negative	0.65	0.43	0.44	0.44

12.4.2.2 Relationships Among the Factors and the Correct Use of the System

Correct Use is a binary measure that indicates whether the subjects understood how the like-o-meter works (i.e., if you like the presentation, press the smiley face; if you do not, press the sad face). We wanted to test whether there is a relationship among this variable and the variables used as factors in the study, namely age group, sex, and attitude towards technology.

We used a fitted loglinear model using backward elimination. The best model comprises AgeGroup*CorrectUse + AgeGroup*AttitudeToward-Tech which means that there is a relationship between age and the correct use of the system as well as between age and attitude towards technology. Namely, young visitors use the system in a correct way more often (Fig. 5 top, $\chi^2=6.003$; df=1; sig. < 0.05), and they more often have a positive attitude towards technology (Fig. 5 bottom, $\chi^2=10.595$; df=1; sig. < 0.05) with respect to older visitors.

AgeGroup * CorrectUse Crosstabulation

Count

		CorrectUse		Total
		N	Y	
AgeGroup	younger	13	41	54
	Older	26	30	56
Total		39	71	110

AgeGroup * AttitudeTowardTech (dual) Crosstabulation

Count

		AttitudeTowardTech (dual)		Total
		Negative	Positive	
AgeGroup	younger	23	31	54
	Older	41	15	56
Total		64	46	110

Fig. 5. Distributions of correct use and attitude towards technology by age

In summary, the second study aimed at evaluating the users' experience while using the multimedia guide. A total of 110 regular visitors of the museum evaluated the guide. The results were encouraging. They generally felt in control of the system, had good involvement, found it quite easy to use and expressed their intention to use it again in the future. We also found that a positive attitude towards technology is related to a greater agreement on each dimension (control, involvement, ease of use, and intention to use in the future), meaning that probably this attitude enabled the visitors to be more open to the experience this new technology has to offer during the visit at the museum.

The surprising results were that although young visitors in our sample had generally a more positive attitude towards technology than older visitors and they used the system in a correct way more often (specifically understood better the like-o-meter) the older visitors expressed a greater tendency towards their intention to use the guide in the future. We might speculate that being older visitors less acquainted with new technologies and less skilled to operate properly new systems, they were surprised by the good experience they've got while using it. Their tendency towards using the guide in the future is in fact a very encouraging result, indicating that this type of technology can be used by the museum public in general and not especially by young people with technological background as might be expected.

12.5 Conclusions

This chapter presents two empirical studies aimed at assessing dimensions of acceptance towards adaptivity in mobile museums guides with a holistic perspective.

The first study investigated the relationships between attitude towards adaptivity and personality traits. The study showed that personality traits relating to the notion of control (Conscientiousness, Neuroticism/Emotional Stability, and Locus of Control) have a selective effect on the acceptance of the adaptivity dimensions. The study also confirmed importance of the control issue: Those who choose the nonadaptive version most often do so because of the greater perceived control it provides.

The results of the first study informed the design of the affective-based adaptive guide presented in (Chap. 1). The same guide was then used as the object of the second study aimed at investigating some dimensions beyond usability as evaluation tools for technology designed for cultural heritage appreciation.

The second study tested the adaptive guide with more than 100 visitors to Torre Aquila, using a combination of items taken from several questionnaires and factorized along four dimensions: (perception of) Control, Involvement, Easiness, and Intention to use. The results showed that a positive attitude towards technology leads to greater agreement on each dimension. We also found surprisingly that the older visitors had a greater propensity towards future Intention to use, although young visitors in our sample had generally a more positive attitude towards technology than older visitors and they used the system in a correct way more often.

The two studies, although quite extensive, left open many questions that deserve further investigation. Regarding the first study, one topic left untouched concerns the relationships between attitudes and behaviour. This is a difficult one, involving both subtle theoretical and methodological issues. In our case, things are made even more difficult by the fact that we are studying a new technology. At present people do not have any attitude towards adaptivity simply because it is not commercially available. We tried to circumvent this problem by exposing our subjects to stimulus situations portraying a fictional character using the technology. Moreover, we attempted to maintain even the indirect exposure to implementation aspects as low as possible, giving priority to the assessment of the way specific functionalities/dimensions are perceived. Given this picture, the difficulty of studying the attitude/behavior relationship is even stronger. Still, this investigation is of the utmost importance, not only for obtaining a better understanding of the way people relate to adaptivity, but also for providing more general insights that can help drive development and take-up of future technologies

Regarding the second study, dimension of involvement proved a valuable measure for assessing the guide. Nonetheless, we still lack a theoretical basis to link it to acceptance. The data collected during the study will be the basis for building such a model.

Part VI
Future Research

13 Intelligent Interfaces for Groups in a Museum

O. Stock, A. Krüger, T. Kuflik and M. Zancanaro

13.1 Introduction

Cultural heritage appreciation is an ideal area for exploring new concepts in intelligent user interface research and dealing with a high-profile educational entertainment issue. Furthermore, it is wide open for the introduction of novel technology, as presented earlier in this book.

At the same time, we must be aware of the fact that technology often introduces new bottlenecks created by its specific features. For example, in our specific case we can see that individual-oriented presentations are very good for a single visitor, but may overlook the social aspect of a visit—a very important element which may not at all benefit from the technology. The social aspect may be hindered by the fact that each person is busy listening or interacting with his or her own device's specific presentations and may be disconnected from the others. Another striking case of a bottleneck introduced by technology is the preparation of material for adaptive multimedia. Experience shows that it is very difficult for cultural sites to produce enough content material even for much simpler technology. Content is costly and quality assurance is not easy. When material must be prepared for flexible multimedia presentation, the process tends to require novel expertise, methodologies, and tools for the preparation of the material. Preparation of content for more sophisticated uses makes things much more complex.

Intelligent museum technology was originally conceived for a mobile cultural heritage setting, such as a visit to a museum or to a historical city. Various research projects have been conducted, aiming at sophisticated and adaptive presentations for the individual. They attempt to do away with traditional presentations that are intrinsically the same for all, or for large groups of visitors. We should note the irony of such efforts: most of the times people come to visit such places in groups. Will intelligent interface technology be able to help and even exploit this fact in order to achieve the end goal: namely, a better way of learning, getting interested, and enjoying the experience?

This theme includes various aspects, such as: group modelling, technology for mobile group exploration (including stationary and mobile devices), user adapted interaction within groups, technology-induced conversation after the visit, technology for reflective and collaborative activity in a museum, and integration of technology for the individual and for the group. Some of these aspects have been initially tackled in the PEACH project and the results are presented in chapters of this book.

Another theme of research is concerned with the bottleneck caused by contents. One possibility is abandoning the concept of contents prepared for the visitor by experts and embracing the view of the more liberal-active role provided by a large group: autonomous contributions within a community of visitors. The main problem is then one of selection and possibly of adaptation of the presentation material.

Still another topic concerns the import/export of user models from one situation to another. It is a challenge to define a methodology so that models that were developed in previous cultural experiences can be taken into account to initialize the model of the visitor in the new situation. In the case of groups, the import/export process will be even more complex as the previous experiences may have been not only subjectively different, but also objectively different, and may have concerned different sites.

The affective dimension in the museum experience is important and recent original work brings it into technology see Chap. 1 this volume and Lim et al. (2005). If we focus on children in the museum, the engagement dimension is even more critically linked to fun and play than with adults. Children are almost always part of a group, either a small group that includes their parents or possibly other adults with a guidance role, or they are part of a group of visitors of the same age, in which case their active role within the group is a key factor to make use of in their cultural development.

In the following pages, we discuss some of the themes of our new research activity and look at related implications.

13.2 Technology for Groups in a Museum

As we have seen in this book, various projects, including PEACH, have introduced technology for individual presentations. The visitor has a small portable device, such as a Personal Digital Assistant (PDA) and can receive information relevant to the particular site.

The technology typically takes advantage of a localization system (for instance, based on devices that generate an infrared signal from fixed positions, or based on triangulation through emitters/receivers of wireless digital signals, or based on very sensitive GPS systems, which also work inside buildings).

The interesting thing is that the system knows the profile of a visitor, where the visitor has been, what his or her path through the physical site was and what was presented to him or her. The system can also know the visitor's path in the more abstract "information space". Furthermore, visitor preferences can be inferred from visitor behaviour. More generally, a dynamic user model can be built during the course of the visit. This opens up the possibility of offering a presentation tailored specifically to the individual visitor. The presentation then has the possibility of exploiting different modalities (for example, spoken language and graphics on the PDA screen, or pictures, or dynamic videos to produce a personalized documentary).

So far, most of the efforts devoted to enhancing the museum visit experience have focused on the individual visitor. However, it is known that people visit museum mainly in groups. Petrelli and Not (2005) report that only 5% of visitors come to a museum alone, while 45% come in organized groups, 20% with friends and 30% with children. Groups may visit a museum with or without a human guide. Usually, large groups follow a guided tour, while small groups (families, groups of friends) explore the museum on their own. They follow their own path, at their own pace and thus may benefit from a museum visitor guide that can support the overall group in addition to individuals. An important aspect of the museum visit is the social aspect of interaction among the group members as part of the whole museum visit experience. Individual museum visitor guides do not encourage interaction; on the contrary, they even discourage it.

The Sottovoce project (Aoki et al. 2002) proposed something a limited system: a multimedia mobile guide that supports pairs visiting a museum together. The guide does not involve adaptivity nor intelligent presentations, but basically allows the couple to be synchronized and, potentially, to move in harmony.

As pointed at in Chap. 7, this volume, an interesting theme for the introduction of presentation technology in museums involves the adoption of multiple devices. This may entail, for example, combining a personal, wearable device, with the possibility of having a portion of a presentation delivered on a large, high quality display. In this case, the goal is to facilitate seamless transition from one device to another one, enabling coherent presentations across devices (see also Rocchi et al. 2004).

As is better explained later in this chapter, this is also the starting point for work oriented toward groups. Krüger et al. (2002) introduced the theme of dealing with presentations on a big, fixed screen to groups of visitors, complemented with additional information provided on small personal devices. The idea is that the "cocktail party effect" enables subsequent presentations on multiple media at the same time. Furthermore, a common presentation may be complemented by notes delivered on an individual device, perhaps with dynamic adaptations that take into account the interests of the majority of the audience. Both of these concepts could be further elaborated in very promising directions.

13.2.1 The Social Aspect

An accepted definition for "Group" is the one introduced by Johnson and Johnson (1991). A group is a collection formed by two or more people that (1) interact; (2) are interdependent; (3) define themselves and are defined by others as a group; (4) share norms concerning matters of common interest and participate in a system of interlocking roles; (5) influence each other; (6) find the group rewarding; and (7) pursue common goals. In the case of a museum visit, the roles are not always clearly defined and the nature of the group can vary.

Groups that are simply assembled on the spot (such as visitors that happen to be at a site at the same moment when a public presentation is being given) may still have occasional interactions, but normally these depend on the personalities and attitudes of the individuals. For this latter case, the use of technology can be along the lines experimented in COMRIS (Geldof 1999).

Another way of looking at groups is to consider them to be virtual communities. From a technology point of view, they appear similar to other Web-based virtual communities, except for the role of (1) mobility (shared also with cell phone based communities) and fine positioning, and (2) the specific aspect of cultural heritage oriented presentations, that poses an accent to the quality, style and individual taste of the presentation. All this is worthwhile research material, as we shall see shortly.

Let us turn our attention to members of a small group visiting a cultural site, in the technological setting of an "active environment". They can be equipped with personal presentation devices. Each person may decide on his or her own what to do and how to proceed at any moment. All presentations are personalized on the basis of a user model that starts with an initial profile and evolves dynamically throughout the visit. The development of the personal user model takes into account the visitor's actions, both toward the system and in the physical environment, as well as the current visit history. Three types of interactions can be provided on an individual device:

1. Basic, infrastructural information and interface (including communication infrastructure) specific for awareness of the state of and communication with other individuals in the group.
2. Presentations of the exhibits for the individual members of the group, taking into account the complex context of the group.
3. General interaction with the system oriented to the combination of individual and joint communication with the overall system.

The case of a structured group, like a classroom, is different still. In this case, we have a common task and roles that may be established for accomplishing the specific task. One view for the intervention of technology is to offer a game, such as a treasure hunt, that imposes certain subtasks that involve observing exhibits or acquiring information considered important by the museum curator. Another possible avenue, discussed later in this chapter, is to emphasize the constructive role of the group in preparing material to be used by themselves and other visitors. In this scenario, the group acts as a structured group and there may be well defined subtasks, but individuals are still able to use personal initiative in preparing material. The group members are led to collaborate at the overall group level in order to produce better material from the quality/quantity point of view. The role of technology is important for both the mobile cultural experience—in this case, with an emphasis on helping collect material—and for the group collaboration experience, where the material must somehow be negotiated and integrated by group members.

13.3 Group Modelling

Modelling an individual visitor in the museum scenario is a challenging task. The system may not have any information about the visitor. But the system may need information to quickly and nonintrusively build a model that enables adaptation and delivery of information according to visitor preferences. Underlying technologies include tracking and monitoring user movement in space, inferring user preferences from previous knowledge and current behaviour, predicting the user's visit plan, and acting in support of it.

Current research on Ubiquitous User Modelling (see Berkovsky et al. 2006) will enable us to provide a better starting point for the visitor by initiating an individual user model for a specific visit, based on previous experiences.

Further to the challenges posed by individual modelling, group modelling presents its own set of questions. What is a group model? What are the relationships between the group model and the individual user models? What are the relationships among group member models and how do they evolve?

Group modelling has only recently begun to draw attention (Masthoff 2004), mainly in the area of Interactive TV (ITV), where group modelling is needed for practical implementation. Current research efforts focus on modelling groups to support the selection of television programs relevant to the whole group. Groups are modelled by combining the individual user models of their members so as to provide an integrated model representing common group preferences, as inferred by the user modelling algorithm. Various approaches for combining individual models exist, as can be seen in the work of Masthoff that compares 11 different strategies for integrating individual user models for group modelling in selecting TV programs for a group of viewers. Another example is the work of Kay and Niu (2005), which suggests using several strategies in parallel in order to optimize the selection or the modelling for the whole group. A few additional works regarding group modelling include MusicFX (McCarthy and Anagnost 1998), an implementation of a system that selects music for a group of people in a fitness centre which tries to support group preferences by integrating individual preferences. An initial formalization of group activity is provided in (Hadad et al. 2005).

The museum visit scenario we envisage is more complex than the ITV example, and more ambitious than the SottoVoce project. In our scenario, there is a group of individuals which visits a museum together. Information can be conveyed to the visitors in different ways. One way is as a group presentation, addressing the whole group. In this case, prior work on group modelling discussed above becomes relevant. Another way is individually, as has been done in numerous projects, including PEACH. As discussed later in this paper, visitors may receive group presentations on a large screen that suits the group, but not necessarily each of the group members. At the same time, group members may deviate from the group presentation, or need integration, and can thus receive personal presentations on their personal device.

Addressing the challenge of successfully supporting a group museum visit requires combining and integrating the individual personalized support with the overall more abstract group activity.

The interaction between individuals and between them and the whole group poses a different challenge than group modelling and user modelling. Unlike ITV scenarios, where the whole group is modelled based on somehow integrating the models of its individual members, in the museum visit scenario there is an ongoing and evolving interaction between visitors and exhibition presentations, among visitors themselves, and between the visitors and the group. The underlying notion motivating our work is that the individual can move at his leisure with few constraints as far as time and space is concerned. This requires the individual user models to interact with each other and with a more abstract group model continuously.

Underlying technologies for group support include those mentioned above for the individual visitor. In addition, a group model must integrate the individual user models and apply additional techniques for optimizing the overall group experience. This may sometimes require compromising on individual preferences. It is necessary to model the overall spatial distribution of the group members, and what appears to be their involvement and attention level (for instance, through feedback mechanisms such as the *like-o-meter,* see Chap. 1 this volume). Also needed is a view of the whole group's path through the physical and information spaces.

Interaction among group members visiting a museum enhances the "museum visit experience" and may be even more important than learning (Hood 1983). Hence, a group of visitors is more than the sum of its individuals. Supporting groups of visitors in a museum requires both supporting individual group members in their individual activity and supporting the whole group by creating opportunities for interaction and discussion of the museum experience.

13.3.1 Adaptive Technology for Awareness and Basic Direct Interaction Among Visitors

From a technological point of view, the basic elements for direct social awareness and interaction for a single visitor are:

1. Visualization of the position of the other members of the group.
2. Information about the overall level of enjoyment of the members of the group (available from the individual user model which incorporates behaviour observation and explicit feedback, as said above).

3. Messages to other members of the group—mostly coded messages for informing the others about a point of interest, including an automatic presentation of the point on the map; messages for setting a meeting at the sender location with an indication about how to reach it from the current position; messages for stating that it is time to meet at the entrance and so on. Similarly, virtual *post-it*s can be left at given sites with comments that can be received by other individuals.

Awareness of the state of the other members of the group may be realized by showing their locations or relative distances on the map on the PDA interface. Various techniques exist for displaying spatial information synthetically on a small screen, some of which were introduced for military applications. As for the level of enjoyment of the other members of the group, a colour-based indicator for each one or even an overall group indicator may work well. Of course, spatial (and less exclusively emotional information) are relevant when individuals explore the physical area autonomously. This is particularly important in a large museum, or in the outdoors. It is also important for giving more autonomy to children.

Providing group members with a means of communication may encourage interaction during the visit. Messages to other members of the group can have a form similar to SMS messages, but the important concept is that they occur in an environment where the system has abundant knowledge of the context. Therefore, technology for interaction within groups can be adaptive and a coded message can take a different form at the destination than at the origin. The system knows the positions of the message sender and the position of the receiver (or the receivers), it knows the configuration of the museum, and may also have additional information about its state. For instance, it may know that certain areas of the museum are currently overcrowded and had better be avoided. The system has user models available and they can be important for integrating a message with information oriented toward personal preferences. Or the system may decide about the best timing for delivering the message to each particular individual. Messages can then be automatically integrated with multimedia material, both for giving directions (for instance about how to reach a location) or for helping recognize an exhibit in a room.

Another type of messages is space bound, and is inspired by the familiar concept of post-it notes. Leaving a virtual post-it is a means of employing the social attitude of visitors and getting them more involved. Visitors in a historical city could even get in touch with the local community (as studied in Campiello, see Agostini et al. 2002). In our context, even post-its without free text could be flexible. For instance, they can integrate dynamic information, such as a reference to a specific part of a presentation recommended to other visitors, or, if a pointing device such as the camera described in (Chap. 3 this volume) is integrated, they could display a detail of an exhibit as an indication for further presentations. But, the greatest opportunity for involving visitors is the use of free text for leaving notes, thoughts, and all kinds of messages. This concept is relevant to Mobile Guide 2.0 (Sect. 13.6).

Yet, there is a specific issue here in relation to the modality of input. Normally, we do not wish to have speech input in front of an exhibit. The idea needs collaboration from the museum administration to see if it is possible to introduce booths, or other areas that prevent noise pollution. An alternative is relying on SMS technology or on fixed keyboards at given booths.

The time dimension may be particularly important. When time is limited, a small group may be in a better position for exploiting the remaining time than single visitors. Common to all visitors is that they should not miss the museum's major attractions, suggested by the curators, taking into account their interests. As we know, there is nothing like the emotion of seeing the actual artefact. But at the same time, especially if this site is not well-known to the visitors, the group may better explore the site by moving in different individual directions. Using personal messages and explicit recommendations by other members of the group can be useful for making the best use of the remaining time. Another aspect is "in the hands" of the system: it can provide presentations that are (partially) complementary to the ones provided to other members of the group, in order to widen the area of information covered in the presentations. The system would have to rely on subsequent information sharing, especially when the group members are together after the visit. A more ambitious view of this theme is discussed in the subsequent section on conversations within groups.

Finally, comprehensive personal reporting is important. We have discussed automatic reporting for the individual in (Chap. 4 this volume). In order to support group activity, a comprehensive account of the group museum experience should be provided, and it may include relevant points of communication within the group.

Having briefly discussed basic infrastructural technology that can help the user stay in contact with other members of the group, in the following we deal with other themes for advanced technology for groups in a museum. The group context is exploited specifically in view of advanced concepts of intelligent presentations.

13.4 Conversations Within Groups

In the following, we discuss how presentation technology can help expand conversations within a group. We are interested in presentations that are meant for a group of people moving in a space. We emphasize the fact that they are not only a collection of individuals, but people who will communicate during the visit and possibly afterwards. They will share emotions, provide and follow advice, integrate the acquired information, and discuss their points of view. After all, the goal is for people to get more interested in the subject, and, ideally, come back to the site again. Thus, we consider groups of people who have a social relationship, such as a family, or groups that come together with a specific learning goal, such as a class. Most likely, these groups will interact after the visit.

The level and quality of conversation among small groups of visitors to a museum during the visit, or immediately after, is a fundamental indicator of the success of the museum presentation. Furthermore, provoking conversation is per se a desirable goal within the process of learning. In a book presenting a theory supported by extended ethnographic studies Leinhardt and Knutson (2004) state:

> In the social-cultural way of looking at things, learning means less that an individual "owns" certain knowledge—in the sense of having a valuable possession—and more that an individual can participate in a particular group or world in an active way. Socio-cultural theory emphasizes the idea that meaning emerges in the interplay between individuals acting in social contexts and the mediators—tools, talk, activity structures, signs, and symbol systems—that exist in that context. Individuals both shape and are shaped by these mediators; a unique aspect of humans is our propensity to invent and to invent with the instruments of our own development.

They see learning as a combination of identity, including everything that has to do with personal background, and the learning environment, that must be brought together in an explanatory engagement. The most important factor in learning as a group activity is learning through conversational elaboration.

By observing behaviour in different museum settings, they conclude that:

> The more the museum designers made available intellectual and physical supports for the core ideas of the exhibitions and the more they were used, the more there was evidence of learning. Conversation was a cognitive tool for learning. When groups coordinated explanatory conversation

that reflected the contents in an exhibition by analyzing its components, comparing or contrasting objects or activities, the more they seemed to learn. Conversational activity, as measured by explanatory engagement, was the most influential factor in learning."

So, conflict in ideas and negotiation are part of the process.

What can the role of technology be within this perspective? In this section, we discuss a view of presentations by the system.

Presentations about exhibits on display can be adapted for individual visitors (personalized). In contrast to what occurs with a single presentation, now when the system is aware of the state of all the members of the group there are two ways of adapting the presentation. The first is adapting *for* the group and can be realized following the suggestions given in the specific section in this chapter. The second is adapting *in* the group. The system can prepare a presentation $P_{i,t1}$ for the individual x_i at time t_1 and when appropriate, prepare a presentation $P_{j,t2}$ for a different individual x_j with information that will complement $P_{i,t1}$.

The actual narration in the specific presentation $P_{i,t1}$ must now take into account the fact that not everything will be told. A basic tool of narration is to build an expectation in the audience and then at a later time, release this tension by fulfilling the expectation (or possibly contradicting it, giving a surprise effect). Ideally, the answer to this expectation is in the hands of some other member of the group, so that later interaction will be needed and prove satisfactory.

The system can also exploit social roles (e.g., something different can be expected from a parent than from a child in a subsequent interaction). If needed, especially with children, a motivating game can be used for favouring subsequent interaction.

Two aspects are essential for adaptation:

- Reasoning on the interests, the state and location of the members of the group, if possible on the knowledge related to objects on display, and certainly on the material that has been presented or is going to be presented to the other members so that the group of agents that support the group of individuals can negotiate the "distributed" presentations.
- Preparing individual presentations on the basis of the preceding point. The multimodal narration structure for the individual, tested in our PEACH environment, will have to be adapted.

Research on this topic can find inspiration in the theatre world. Laurel (1991) proposed a similarity between theatre and human–computer interfaces in general. In our context, we are much more specific. We can say that in (traditional) theatre, a message is allocated by the author to a number of different actors, each one playing a role, and the audience has access to the whole presentation (including, of course, the interaction among actors). In our group presentation view, the situation can be considered similar to theatre, except for the fact that members of the audience mostly have access to just one actor (combined with moments in which they can have a collective presentation, for instance on a large shared device). The visitors have a partial picture, with expectations of information material not completely fulfilled. They are somehow led to integrate the material by interacting with each other.

13.5 Shared Devices for Group Presentations

One major problem in the PEACH scenario is that the number of Virtual Windows (see Chap. 7 this volume) available in a museum will always be significantly lower than the number of visitors. This is due to both economic and practical reasons. It is, therefore, worthwhile to find methods which allow several users to use a stationary system at the same time. Novel projection and display technologies, as well as new interaction metaphors, can be combined to enhance sharing of personal and public devices in a museum visit. In the following, we present a few solutions, some which have already been tested and initially implemented.

13.5.1 Voting Mechanisms for Public Presentations

To support multiuser interactions, we adopt the metaphor of a remote control. Users interact with the Virtual Window by pressing buttons displayed on their mobile device. Using wireless LAN technology, this interaction is communicated via a server to the Virtual Window. This server also selects the content to be presented on the Virtual Window, based on the user interaction history. The user can choose different presentations from a list sorted in order of highest interest.

When another user approaches the Virtual Window, the presentation lists of all users in front of the Virtual Window are combined to form a new list, which holds only items that are of interest to all users. If this list happens to be empty, then very general presentations of interest to most visitors to the museum are included in the list. As soon as the running presentation is finished, the newly generated list is shown on each mobile device and on the Virtual Window (Fig. 1).

At this point, each user chooses a presentation on the mobile device. After a first user has chosen a topic, a countdown is started on the Virtual Window. Each user may make a decision until the countdown is finished or until each user has made his or her choice. In order to avoid situations in which there is no definite voting result, each user is assigned a different weight in the voting process. These weights are given according to the order in which the users appear in front of the Virtual Window. In doing so, the voting results become unambiguous and early arriving users are given the most controlling power regarding presentation selection. In each constellation, all user voting weights sum up to 1. Even though the user who arrived first at the Virtual Window has the most power, it is still possible to outvote him or her if several other users agree on a different topic.

Fig. 1 Multiuser interaction using a voting mechanism

13.5.2 Private Annotations to Public Presentations

Instead of forcing users to agree on topics, we have tested a version of the system which combines personal devices and stationary presentation systems in order to provide presentations that fit the interests of all users sharing one presentation system. The idea is to have a general presentation on the stationary device and to fill in personal presentations on the user's personal devices whenever the actual topic of the "root-presentation" does not fit the interests of the user (this approach is discussed in detail in Kruppa et al. (2005). While the focus of the presentation on the stationary device is on general information of a particular topic, presentations on the personal mobile devices present in-depth information related to topics mentioned in the general presentation, but are tailored to the individual interests of group members. The presentations presented to each user on his or her mobile device are chosen automatically based on the user model derived during the museum visit. Users are free to stop a presentation on their personal device at any time, which will then result in an update of the user model of that particular user. Since the "root-presentation" on the stationary device continues while the individual presentations run on the users' personal devices, this presentation method might put a high cognitive load on the users. This is due to the fact that they have to concentrate on the presentation on their personal device while still listening to (and perhaps also seeing) the presentation running on the stationary presentation system. However, empirical studies with this type of presentation system have shown that users are capable of concentrating on their individual presentations without being distracted by the "root-presentation". A critical point within these multi-device presentations is the moment when users must switch their attention from one device to another. The aforementioned user study showed that a Migrating Character can help guide user attention from one device to another by migrating between the different presentation devices.

13.5.3 Group Presentation with Novel Projection Technologies

Besides using PDAs for information presentation and Virtual Windows, novel types of projectors can be used which can either provide large-scale presentations for groups or graphical overlays on real exhibits. By incorporating both fixed and steerable projectors into a museum setting, high flexibility can be achieved. A steerable projector consists of a standard projector mounted on a moving arm that can be controlled by a computer. This setting allows for using any unoccluded surface in a room for projection purposes (Pinhanez 2001). Figure 2 exemplifies a setup in the Hecht Museum at the University of Haifa, Israel (Baus et al. 2006). It illustrates two possible applications for a steerable projector. In the first application, the steerable projector can augment the exhibit with additional details. In the example of an exhibition on Phoenician writings, in which the engravings are not easily readable nor understood, a projection of a schematized image of a scroll with accurate translations next to the real object may greatly enhance visitor experience.

Fig. 2. A steerable projector used to highlight or augment specific items of the exhibits can be used to provide tailored information to groups of visitors

Moreover, the projector can point out (by using arrows) specific interesting parts and characters on the stone, which would not be perceived by most visitors without such help. In the second application, the fixed projector can highlight and enhance large items, such as an ancient ship representation, by highlighting specific parts on the wall where the ship is illustrated and augmenting the schematic drawing with additional relevant information for group members and individual visitors. Both technologies share the high potential to support group interaction by allowing visitors to access information through a common medium, while preserving the possibility of obtaining individual information.

13.6 Mobile Guides 2.0

Content preparation for a mobile, adaptive, and location-aware multimedia guides can be very expensive. Furthermore, conceptually, there may be new directions that deviate from the traditional. Experience with the first period of the Web's existence and its critical rethinking can provide inspiration for a possible novel class of mobile guides.

After the dot-com bust of 2001, Internet experts started to look at the true success stories—like Google, Amazon, and eBay, just to name few—with the aim of understanding the "secret" of success in the Web era. O'Reilly (2005) identified a set of characteristics that new Web applications should have to survive after the "turning point" he called Web 2.0. Among these characteristics, there are some that might prove interesting to exploit in the future generation of multimedia mobile guides for museums.

The most important characteristic that brings together the Web 2.0 applications is that they all, to some extent, rely on the notion of collective intelligence. The Web application that most radically obeys this principle is Wikipedia, which is based on the notion that an encyclopedia entry can be added by any Web user, and edited by any other.

Today multimedia guides are based on the idea of visitors as receivers of information previously prepared by content experts, usually museum curators. Even for adaptive guides, the content and the relations among the different pieces of information are carefully prepared in advance. This makes sense since museums are first of all repositories of knowledge developed through careful filtering of information elaborated by scholars in decades, if not centuries. Yet one can observe assessments of the quality of Wikipedia and make some considerations relevant to the museum domain. In fact, a recent *Nature* investigation (Giles 2005) showed that Wikipedia is almost as reliable as Britannica. If a participation model works for an encyclopedia, why should it not work for museums?

To some extent, visitor participation in the process of content creation during a museum experience can be sustained by the concepts of Inquiry Learning. Inquiry learning developed from constructivist philosophy, which claims that knowledge exists in the process of building and discovering and not necessarily in the products (Rorty 1991). From this point of view, learning is a process in which the student is active in gathering the information, processing it, and connecting it to pre-existing knowledge by interpreting it and turning it from information to knowledge (Salomon, 2000).

Can we imagine a museum mobile guide that allows visitors to produce content as well as being exposed to content? Certainly, there are specific aspects of the guide that do not need to be realized as a mobile version of Wikipedia. As we came to understand in the course of the PEACH project, a museum experience is a unique emotional experience and should not be limited to mobile access to information. A mobile guide should first and foremost provide hints for looking at the objects displayed while rousing visitor desire to seek additional information later on. What kind of information should the visitors of a museum be willing to provide for others' consumption? Not so much reference information, which can be easily— and more reliably—provided by curators or automatically extracted by an encyclopedia. Rather, they should provide links or connections among knowledge elements. As we know well, a link is not merely the connection between two pieces of information; rather it means justification and elaboration and is a piece of knowledge of its own.

The process of connecting information can take place in three different ways: (i) in the very location of the exhibit, using the mobile guide as an input device (ii) in special places in the museum; or (iii) through the Web once the visit is over, or before it starts, possibly at home.

The first possibility is at the same time the richest and the most challenging. The style of interaction supported by the guide must be carefully designed in order to enrich rather than detract from the museum experience. The problem is to offer an appropriate input (voice, "SMS" and so on) and intelligent editing environment.

The second possibility entails allowing visitors—or special groups of visitors, such as school classes—to collaborate in providing information. This could push Mobile Guide 2.0 a step forward, towards being the ultimate tool for inquiry learning. In this scenario, a group of visitors interacts in the museum by accessing the information provided by the curators as well as material provided by other groups who have visited previously and produced the material. The results of their elaboration are fed back into the information system of the museum.

Finally, the possibility of re-elaborating information from home may open new scenarios of co-presence and remote collaboration. From one point of view, it would be pretty similar to the possibility offered by Wikipedia, but with the difference that the re-elaborated information will then be accessible at physical locations in the museum.

A very important issue is specific to the situation we envisage: style of presentation. As opposed to the encyclopedia example, in the museum visit context we want the presentation to speak to us in the right style. We would like a companion that is not only competent, but pleasant as well. Some people may like structured and precise information about the artefact on display. Others may prefer anecdotic narratives. The system should also be sensitive to the language appropriate for the age group of the visitors.

Thus, the problem of selection is potentially complex. We may have thousands of annotated links: new material of various sorts to be accessed in relation to many different characteristics.

Two types of solutions can be investigated: (i) a proactive role on the part of the system, using adaptive filtering to hide information that is deemed less relevant to the given visitors, or selecting the most appropriate style for the situation (this may require the use of sophisticated techniques, including, for instance, text processing for *genre* recognition) or (ii) relying again on participation by allowing visitors themselves to mark the specific links as interesting or useless. Of course, a combination of the two may prove to be a viable solution.

Enabling visitors to a museum to be both the users and providers of information will radically change the way in which museums are experienced. However, it cannot be expected that all visitors will provide information, just as not all Wikipedia users edit entries in the online encyclopedia. As for all the other Web 2.0 applications, the difference between success and failure lies in the ability to trigger the network effect—that is, that a critical mass of contributing users will make additional users want to contribute. How can a network effect be generated? There are no clear-cut rules, but several strategies have been proposed by experts.

The first strategy is to offer products with both a point and a network value. The former is the value of the product for a given user independently of the number of people in the network; the latter is the value of the product that increases when the network effect takes place. The point value of a Mobile Guide 2.0 could be the information produced by appealing experts. Let's imagine a tour at the Musée Cluny, dedicated to the Middle Ages, following Umberto Eco's footsteps. The very same architecture can then be used to allow other people to annotate or link up this information.

Finally, it is clear that in order to be successful, any attempt to build a Mobile Guide 2.0 should go beyond the confines of the lab as soon as possible. Visitors need to feel the network effect before they can be interested in the actual use of the system. Without many people who really update the system, it will be impossible to reach that effect. For bootstrapping, perhaps schools could be encouraged to use the system as part of their didactic activity. Other ideas can be borrowed from market studies in the electronic age.

13.7 Groups of Children

Children love to play together and they learn more easily when in a group. At present, very few technologies are specifically designed to support such co-located interactions. Out-of-the-classroom activities, such as museums visits, provide rich learning opportunities. Unfortunately, they often become unique events, detached from the activities that occur within the classroom. Furthermore, the standard resources available in schools provide limited means for children to recall and elaborate upon the museum experience once back in the classroom. As demonstrated by experiences like Story Table (see Chap. 8 this volume) new technologies for co-located interaction can enrich learning opportunities.

In order to foster productive learning, technology-based means for capturing aspects of the experience for later use in the classroom are essential. Furthermore, creative group activities may result in (computer-based) objects, samples, and media elements that can be brought back to the classroom and then used when reporting and reflecting upon the visit.

Dynamic and interactive representations of narrative structures provided by computational media could allow children to associate and communicate their experience in new and interesting ways.

To support such a scenario, technology should be designed to serve three purposes:

1. *Augment the experience* by allowing children in small groups to creatively and collaboratively engage in the shared endeavour of making, collecting, or configuring objects.
2. *Represent the experience* by allowing each individual child to collect a computational representation of the objects engaged with in the small group.
3. *Share the experience* through computational representations that allow manipulability in support of remembering, articulating, and sharing the learning experience.

The traditional "one computer–one user" setting maps poorly with children's social interaction in most situations (Rizzo et al. 2003), where several children want to, and often do, participate in the activity simultaneously. In creative learning activities with noncomputational materials, such as wood, clay and sand, children in groups usually act upon the material all at once, allowing for joint, as well as individual constructions. Constraints embedded in the material are blended with the children's own social rules, which change over time. We see a strong potential for exploring how children's everyday social practices in these kinds of situations may be incorporated into activities with computational media. We envision that the engagement in such activities can be further enhanced if children can incorporate their own personal artefacts, such as homemade drawings, which thereby may "come to life" in the virtual world.

In this respect, the museum is a privileged setting for experimentation since it is not merely a container of artefacts, but rather an active promoter of cultural heritage values that need to be further elaborated. The elaboration may take place "through" the museum instead of "in" the museum. We envision specially equipped rooms—let us call them Story Rooms—inside the museum for re-elaborating the material "discovered" in the museum. Being inside the museum rather than in the school may help the children shift from the museum's rooms—where they can "collect" material by means of adaptive multimedia guides—to the Story Room where the material can be shared and augmented.

13.8 Conclusions

In this chapter we discussed various research themes, all bound to a common point of interest: groups in a museum. Most museum visits are group-based, either large groups, like classrooms, or small groups, like a family or a group of friends. If we blur the time dimension, the notion of a group can even be extended to include people who do not visit the site at the same moment. The group aspect has been widely studied in sociology, museology and education. In contrast, in the technological research field, most activity up to now has dealt with the individual. Notable advances have been made in the concepts of personalized and context-aware presentations, and in giving reality to the concept of active cultural objects and active museums, including the work conducted in the PEACH project. While there is much potential for further advancement in technology for the individual, we believe that energy should also be put into novel ideas and prototypes for groups of visitors. Here we have not considered obvious cases, such as the introduction of games (such as a treasure hunt), or activity based on specific roles of participants. Instead, we have emphasized concepts like communication within a museum, group-aware presentations (both for a mobile and stationary setting), means for inducing conversation in the group, touching upon a revolution in content preparation, and upon special tools for joint "cultural" activity among children. Initial research in some of these directions was conducted within PEACH; other initial research was part of a Collaboration Project between ITC-irst and the University of Haifa. Further research in this direction is at the core of a substantial novel project that will be see collaboration between ITC-irst, the University of Trento, the University of Haifa, and Bar Ilan University.

References

Abowd G, Atkeson C, Hong J, Long S, Kooper R, Pinkerton M (1997) Cyber-guide: A mobile context-aware tour guide. Wireless Networks 3:421–433

Abowd G, Mynatt E. (2000) Charting past, present, and future research in ubiquitous computing. ACM Transactions on Computer-Human Interaction 7:29–58

Adelson EH, Freeman WT (1991) The design and use of steerable filters. In: IEEE Transactions on PAMI, IEEE, Los Alamitos (CA),13(9):891–906

Agarwal R, Karahanna E (2000) Time flies when you're having fun: Cognitive absorption and beliefs about information technology usage. MIS Quarterly 24(4):665-694

Agostini A, De Michelis G, Divitini M, Grasso MA, Snowdon D (2002) Design and deployment of community systems: reflections on the Campiello experience. Interacting with Computers 14:689-712

Aiello M, Busetta P, Donà A, Serafini L (2001) Ontological overhearing, in intelligent agents VIII. In Proceedings of the Workshop on Agent Theories Architectures and Languages (ATAL2001), Seattle, Springer, Berlin Heidelberg New York, LNAI 2333

Ajzen I (1993) Attitude theory and the attitude-behavior relation. In: Krebs and Schmidt (eds) New Directions in Attitude Measurement. de Gruyter, Berlin

Albertini A, Brunelli R, Stock O, Zancanaro M (2005) Communicating user's focus of attention by image processing as input for a mobile museum guide. In: Proceedings of the 10th International Conference on Intelligent User Interfaces—IUI 2005, San Diego, CA, pp 299–301

Alfaro I, Nardon M, Pianesi F, Stock O, Zancanaro M (2004) Using cinematic techniques on mobile devices for cultural tourism. Information Technology and Tourism 7:61-71

Alfaro I, Zancanaro M, Nardon M, Guerzoni A (2003) Navigating by Knowledge. In Proceedings of the 8th International Conference on Intelligent User Interfaces—IUI 2003, Miami, FL, pp 221–223

Alison D, Gwaltney T (1991) How people use electronic interactives: information age—people, information and technology. In Bearman D (ed) Proceedings of the 1st International Conference on Hypermedia and Interactivity in Museums. Archives and Museums Informatics Technical Report, Pittsburgh, pp 62–73

Alpert SR, Karat J, Karat CM, Brodie C, Vergo JG (2003) User attitudes regarding a user-adaptive e-commerce Web site. User Modeling and User-Adapted Interaction 13(4):373–396

Ambach J, Perrone C, Repenning A (1995) Remote exploratoriums: combining networking and design environments. Computers and Education 24:163–176

Ananny M (2002). Supporting children's collaborative authoring: Practicing written literacy while composing oral texts. In: Proceedings of Computer-Supported Collaborative Learning. Boulder, Colorado, January

Andrè E (2000) The generation of multimedia presentations. In: Dale R, Moisl H, Somers H (eds) Handbook of Natural Language Processing. Marcel Dekker, New York, pp 305-327

Andreatta C, Lecca M, Messelodi S (2005) Memory-based object recognition in digital images. In: Proceedings of the 10th International Fall Workshop—Vision, Modeling, and Visualization, Erlangen, Germany, pp 33–40

Andreatta C, Leonardi F (2006) Appearance based paintings recognition for a mobile museum guide. In: Proceedings of the 1st International Conference on Computer Vision Theory and Applications—VISAPP 2006, Setubal, Portugal, 2:138–142

Aoki PM, Grinter RE, Hurst A, Szymanski MH, Thornton JD, Woodruff A (2002) Sotto voce: exploring the interplay of conversation and mobile audio spaces. In: Wixon D (ed) Proceedings of the SIGCHI Conference on Human Factors in Computing Systems: Changing Our World, Changing Ourselves. ACM, New York, pp 431–438

Aoki PM, Woodruff A (2000) Improving electronic guidebook interfaces using a task-oriented design approach. In: Boyarsky D, Kellogg WA (eds) Proceedings of the Conference on Designing Interactive Systems: Processes, Practices, meThods, and Techniques, ACM, New York, pp 319–325

Arijon D (1976) Grammar of the Film Language. Hastings House, New York

Bailey J, Weippert H (1991) Educational computing challenges for early childhood educators. Australian Journal of Early Childhood, 16 (3): 28–33

Barbaranelli C, Caparra GV, Rabasca A (1998) Big Five Questionnaire Children. Organizzazioni Speciali. Firenze

Bares W, Grégoire J, Lester J (1998) Real-time constraint-based cinematography for complex interactive 3D worlds. In: Proceedings of the 10th National Conference on Innovative Applications of Artificial Intelligence, AAAI 98, IAAI 98. AAAI/ MIT Press, Menlo Park, pp 1101–1106

Baribeau R, Rioux M (1991) Influence of speckle on laser range finders. Applied Opt. 30:2873–2878

Baribeau R, Rioux M, Godin G (1991) Color reflectance modeling using a polychromatic laser range sensor. In: IEEE Trans. Pattern Anal. Mach. Intel. IEEE, Los Alamitos (CA), 14(2): 263–269

Bateman JA (1995) KPML: The KOMET-Penman (multilingual) development environment, release 0.8. Technical report, Institut für Integrierte Publikations- und Informationssysteme (IPSI), GMD, Darmstadt, Germany

Baus J, Krüger A, Kuflik T (2006) Seamless combination of shared and personalized information presentation to groups of visitors in active museums. Proceedings of ABIS 2006, Saarbrücken, Germany

Baus J, Krüger A, Wahlster W (2002) A resource-adaptive mobile navigation system. In: Proceedings of the 7th International Conference on Intelligent User Interfaces (IUI 2002) San Francisco, CA, pp 15–22

Baxter III WV, Sud A, Govindaraju NK, Manocha D (2002) GigaWalk: Interactive walkthrough of complex environments. University of North Carolina at Chapel Hill, Technical Report TR02-013

Bellotti F, Berta R, de Gloria A, Margarone M (2002) User testing: A hypermedia tour guide. IEEE Pervasive Computing, IEEE, Los Alamitos (CA), 1:33–41

Benelli G, Bianchi A, Marti P, Not E, Sennati D (1999) HIPS: Hyper-interaction within physical space. In: Proceedings of IEEE Multimedia Systems 99, International Conference on Multimedia Computing and Systems, Florence. IEEE, Los Alamitos (CA), pp 1075–1078

Beraldin JA, Blais F, Rioux M, Cournoyer L, Laurin D, MacLean SG (2000) Eye-safe digital 3D sensing for space applications. Opt. Eng. 39(1): 196–211

Beraldin JA, Blais F, Rioux M, Domey J, Gonzo L, Simoni A, Gottardi M, Stoppa D (2001) VLSI laser spot sensors for 3D digitization. In: Proceedings of ODIMAP III, Sept 20–22, pp 208–213

Beraldin JA, Picard M, El-Hakim S, Godin G, Latouche C, Valzano V, Bandiera A (2002) Exploring a Byzantine crypt through a high-resolution texture mapped 3D model: Combining range data and photogrammetry. In: Proceedings ISPRS/CIPA International Workshop Scanning for Cultural Heritage Recording, Corfu, Greece, pp 65–72

Beraldin JA, Rioux M, Blais F, Cournoyer L, Domey J (1992) Registered intensity and range imaging at 10 mega-samples per second. Opt. Eng. 31(1):88–94

Berkovich M, Date J, Keeler R, Louw M, O'Toole M (2003) Discovery point: enhancing the museum experience with technology. In: Cockton G, Korhonen P (eds) Conference on Human Factors in Computing Systems. ACM, New York, pp 994–995

Berkovsky S (2005) Ubiquitous user modeling in recommender systems. In: Ardissono L, Brna P, Mitrovic A (eds) Proceedings of the 10th international conference on user modeling, Springer, Berlin Heidelberg New York

Berkovsky S, Kuflik T, Ricci F (2006) Cross-technique mediation of user models. Proceedings International Conference on Adaptive Hypermedia and Adaptive Web-Based Systems (AH-2006), Dublin, pp 21–30

Bernardini F, Martin IM, Rushmeier H (2001) High-quality texture reconstruction from multiple scans. In: IEEE Trans Visualization and Computer Graphics. IEEE, Los Alamitos (CA), 7(4): 318–332

Bertamini F, Brunelli R, Lanz O, Roat A, Santuari A, Tobia F, Xu Q (2004) Olympus: An ambient intelligence architecture on the verge of reality. In: Proceedings of the 12th International Conference on Image Analysis and Processing—ICIAP 2003, Mantova, Italy, pp 139–144

Black A, Lenzo K (2001) Flite: A small fast run-time synthesis engine. In: Proceedings of the 4th ISCA Tutorial and Research Workshop on Speech Synthesis. ISCA Archive. http://www.isca-speech.org/archive/ssw4. Accessed Jan. 2007

Black, A. and K, Lenzo. Flite: A small fast run-time synthesis engine. In: Proceedings of the 4th Speech Synthesis Workshop (ICSA), Scotland, 2002

Bohnenberger T, Jacobs O, Jameson A, Aslan I (2005) Decision-theoretic planning meets user requirements: Enhancements and studies of an intelligent shopping guide. In: Gellersen H, Want R, Schmidt A (eds) Pervasive Computing: Third International Conference. Springer, Berlin Heidelberg New York, pp 279–196

Bornstein MH (1985) The Bear Family. Cognitive coding handbook. Unpublished Manual. National Institute of Child Health and Human Development. Bethesda (MD)

Brajovic V, Mori K, Jankovic N (2001) 100 frames/s CMOS range image sensor. In: ISSCC Dig. of Tech. Papers, pp 256–257

Bresciani P, Penserini L, Busetta P, Kuflik T (2004a) Agent patterns for ambient intelligence. In: Proceedings of the 23rd International Conference on Conceptual Modeling (ER 2004), Shanghai, China. Springer, Berlin Heidelberg New York, LNCS 3288, pp 682–695

Bresciani P, Giorgini P, Giunchiglia F, Mylopoulos J, Perini A (2004b) Tropos: An agent-oriented software development methodology. Journal of Autonomous Agents and Multi-Agent Systems (JAAMAS), 8(3):203–236

Brooke J (2004) SUS—A quick and dirty usability scale. Downloadable at http://usabilitynet.org/trump/documents/Suschapt.doc. Accessed Jan. 2007

Brunelli R (2004) Low resolution image sampling for pattern matching. In: Proceedings of the International Conference on Computer Vision and Graphics (ICCVG) 2004, Warsaw, Poland, pp 962–967

Brunelli R, Mich O (2000) Image retrieval by examples. In: IEEE Transactions on Multimedia. IEEE, Los Alamitos (CA), 2(3):164–171

Brusilovsky P (2001) Adaptive hypermedia. User Modeling And User-Adapted Interaction 11: 87–110

Brusilovsky P, Maybury MT (2002) From adaptive hypermedia to the adaptive Web. Communications of the ACM, New York, 45 (5):30–33

Busetta P, Donà, A, Nori M (2002) Channeled multicast for group communications. In: Proceedings of the 1st International Joint Conference on Autonomous Agents and Multiagent Systems (AAMAS 2002), Bologna, Italy. ACM, NEW YORK, pp 1280–1287

Busetta P, Merzi M, Rossi S, Legras F (2003) Intra-role coordination using group communication: A Preliminary Report. In: Proceedings of International Workshop on Agent Communication Languages (ACL2003), Melbourne, Australia, Springer, Berlin Heidelberg New York, LNAI 2922: 231–253

Busetta P, Serafini L, Singh D, Zini F (2001) Extending multi-agent cooperation by overhearing. In: Proceedings of the Sixth International Conf. on Cooperative Information Systems (CoopIS 2001), Trento, Italy, Springer, Berlin Heidelberg New York, LNCS 2172, pp 40–52

Butz A (1997) Animation with CATHI. In: Proceedings of the 14th National Conference on Artificial Intelligence and Ninth Innovative Applications of Artificial Intelligence Conference, AAAI 97, IAAI 97. AAAI/ MIT Press, Menlo Park, pp 957–962

Butz A, Schneider M, Spassova, M (2004) Searchlight—A lightweight search function for pervasive environments. In: Ferscha A, Mattern F (eds) 2nd International Conference on Pervasive Computing, Springer, Berlin Heidelberg New York, LNCS 3001, pp 351–356

Cahill L, Evans R, Mellish C, Paiva D, Reape M (2000) Towards a reference architecture for natural language generation systems. Technical Report, Information Technology Research Institute, Brighton, UK, August

Calder J, Melengoglou AC, Callaway C, Not E, Pianesi F, Androutsopoulos I, Spyropoulos CD, Xydas G, Kouroupetroglou G, Roussou M (2005) Multilingual personalized information objects. In: Stock O, Zancanaro M (eds) Multimodal Intelligent Information Presentation, Springer, Berlin Heidelberg New York, pp 177–201

Callaway C (2003) Integrating discourse markers into a pipelined natural language generation architecture. In: Proceedings of the 41st Annual Meeting of the Association for Computational Linguistics, pp 264–271, Sapporo, Japan

Callaway C, Kuflik T, Not E, Novello A, Stock O, Zancanaro M (2005a) Personal reporting of a museum visit as an entrypoint to future cultural experience. In: St. Amant R, Riedl J, Jameson A (eds) Proceedings of the 2005 International Conference on Intelligent User Interfaces. ACM, New York, pp 275–277

Callaway C, Lester J (1997) Dynamically improving explanations: A revision-based approach to explanation generation. In: Proceedings of the 15th International Joint Conference on Artificial Intelligence, Nagoya, Japan, pp 952–958

Callaway C, Lester J (2002a) Narrative prose generation. Artificial Intelligence 139(2):213–252

Callaway C, Lester J (2002b) Pronominalization in generated discourse and dialogue. In: Proceedings of the 40th Meeting of the ACL, Philadelphia, PA, July, pp 1241–1248

Callaway C, Not E, Novello A, Rocchi C, Stock O, Zancanaro M (2005b) Automatic cinematography and multilingual nlg for generating video documentaries. Artificial Intelligence 165:57–89

Callaway CB, Daniel BH, Lester JC (1999) Multilingual natural language generation for 3D learning environments. In: Proceedings of the 1999 Argentine Symposium on Artificial Intelligence, Buenos Aires, Argentina, pp 177–190

Carr B Goldstein IP (1977) Overlays: A theory of modeling for computer aided instruction. AI Memo 406, MIT Press, Cambridge, MA

Castro J, Kolp M, Mylopoulos J (2002) Towards requirements-driven information systems engineering: The Tropos project. Information Systems. Elsevier, Amsterdam, The Netherlands, (27): 365–389

Cesari E, Venuti P (1999) The Projective Bears Family. Workshop of the 16th International Conference on Rorschach and Projective Techniques. Amsterdam 19–24 July

Chang CC, Lin CJ (2001) Training v-support vector classifiers: theory and algorithms. Neural Computation 13(9):2119–2147

Cheverst K, Davies N, Mitchell K (2002) The role of adaptive hypermedia within a context-aware tourist guide. Communications of the ACM Special Issue on adaptive Web-based Systems and Adaptive Hypermedia 45(5):47–51

Cheverst K, Davies N, Mitchell K, Friday A, Efstratiou C (2000)
Developing a context-aware electronic tourist guide: Some issues and experiences. In: Proceedings of CHI 2000, The Hague, The Netherlands, pp 17–24

Chin DN (2001) Empirical evaluation of user model and user-adaptive system. User Modeling and User Adapted Interaction 11(1–2):181–194

Chippendale P (2005) Real-time skin labeling in active camera images. In: Proceedings of the 2nd Joint Workshop on Multimodal Interaction and Related Machine Learning Algorithms—MLMI 2005, Edinburgh, UK

Chippendale P, Tobia F (2005) Collective calibration of active camera groups. In: Proceedings of the International Conference on Advanced Video and Signal-Based Surveillance—AVSS 2005, Como, Italy, pp 456–461

Christianson DB, Anderson SE, He LW, Salesin D, Weld DS, Cohen MF (1996) Declarative camera control for automatic cinematography. In: Proceedings of the 13th National Conference on Artificial Intelligence and Eighth Innovative Applications of Artificial Intelligence Conference. AAAI, Menlo Park, pp 148–155

Cigliano E, Monaci S (2003) Multimuseum: A multichannel communication project for the National Museum of Cinema of Turin. In: Proceedings of Museums and the Web 2003. Charlotte, NC

Claassen W (1992) Generating referring expressions in a multimodal environment. In: Dale R, Hovy E, Rosner D, Stock O (eds) Aspects of Automated Natural Language Generation. Springer. Berlin Heidelberg New York

Clark H, Carlson T (1982) Hearers and speech acts. Language. 58(2): 332–373

Cline D, Egbert PK (1998) Interactive display of very large textures. In: Proceedings IEEE Visualization 1998. IEEE, Los Alamitos (CA), pp 343–350

Cohen PR, Levesque HJ (1990) Performatives in a rationally based speech act theory. In: Proceedings of the 28th conference of the Association for Computational Linguistics, Pittsburgh, Pennsylvania, pp 79–88

Cohen PR, Levesque HJ (1991) Teamwork, Technical Report 504, AI Center, SRI International, Menlo Park, CA

Cohen-Or D, Chrysanthou Y, Silva CT, Durand F (2003) A survey of visibility for walkthrough applications. In: IEEE Trans. Visualization and Computer Graphics. IEEE, Los Alamitos (CA).

Collins RT, Lipton AJ, Fujiyoshi H, Kanade T (2001) Algorithms for cooperative multisensor surveillance. In: Proceedings of the IEEE. 89(10):1456–1477

Cosi P, Tesser F, Gretter R, Avesani C (2001) Festival speaks Italian. In: Dalsgaard P, Lindberg B, Benner H, Tan Z (eds) Proceedings of EUROSPEECH 2001 Scandinavia, 7th European Conference on Speech Communication and Technology, 2nd INTERSPEECH Event. ISCA Archive. http://www.isca-speech.org/archive/eurospeech_2001. Accessed Jan. 2007

Cosi P, Cinzia A, Tesser F, Gretter R, Pianesi F (2002) A modified "PaIntE" model for Italian TTS. In: the Proceedings of IEEE Workshop on Speech Synthesis, Santa Monica, California

Cosi P, Tesser F, Gretter R, Cinzia A (2001) Festival speaks Italian. In: Proceedings of EuroSpeech 2001, Aalborg, Denmark

Costa PT, McCrae RR (1992) NEO PI-R: Professional manual. Psychological Assessment Resources, Odessa, FL

Craig A, Franklin J, Andrews G (1984) A scale to measure locus of control of behaviour. British Journal of Medical Psychology, 41:397–404

Crowley J, Berard F, Coutaz J (1995) Finger tracking as an input device for augmented reality. In: Proceedings of the International Workshop on Automatic Face and Gesture Recognition, Zurich, pp 195–200

Crowley K, Leinhardt G, Chang CF (2001) Emerging research communities and the World Wide Web: analysis of a Web-based resource for the field of museum learning. Computers and Education 36:1–14

Csikszentmihalyi M, Csikszentmihalyi IS (1988) Optimal Experience: Psychological Studies of Flow in Consciousness. Cambridge University Press, New York

Dale R (1990) Generating Recipes: An overview of epicure. In: Dale R, Mellish C, Zock M (eds) Current Research in Natural Language Generation, Academic, London

Daniel B, Bares W, Callaway, C. and Lester, J. (1999) Student-sensitive multimodal explanation generation for 3D learning environments. In: Proceedings of the 16th International Conference on Artificial Intelligence, Orlando, FL, pp 114–120

Davis FD (1989) Perceived usefulness, perceived ease of use, and user acceptance of information technology. MIS Quarterly 13(3):319–340

Davis FD (1993) User acceptance of information technology: system characteristics, user perceptions and behavioural impacts. International Journal of Man-Machine Studies 38(3):475–587

Davis FD, Bagozzi RP, Warshaw PR (1992) Extrinsic and intrinsic motivation to use computers in the workplace. Journal of Applied Social Psychology 22(14):1111–1132

De Raad B (2000) The Big Five Personality Factors: The Psycholexical Approach to Personality. Hogrefe and Huber, Göttingen

Debevec P, Taylor CJ, Malik J (1996) Modeling and rendering architecture from photographs: A hybrid geometry and image-based approach. In: Proceedings of SIGGRAPH 96, pp 11–20

Debevec PE, Malik J (1997) Recovering high dynamic range radiance maps from photographs. In: Proceedings of SIGGRAPH 97, pp 369–378

Dey A, Salber D, Abowd G (2001) A conceptual framework and a toolkit for supporting the rapid prototyping of context-aware applications. Human-Computer Interaction Journal 16:97–166

Dietz PH, Leigh DL (2001) DiamondTouch: A multiuser touch technology. In: Proceedings of ACM Symposium on User Interface Software and Technology (UIST). November.

Dix A, Rodden T, Davies N, Trevor J, Friday A, Palfreyman K (2000) Exploiting space and location as a design framework for interactive mobile systems. ACM Transactions on Computer–Human Interaction. ACM, New York, 7(3): 285–321

Dockstader S, Tekalp AM (2001) Multiple camera tracking of interacting and occluded human motion. In: Proceedings of the IEEE 89(10):1441–1455

Doucet A, de Freitas N, Gordon N (2001) Sequential Monte Carlo in Practice. Springer, Berlin Heidelberg New York

Dumont R, Pellacini F, Ferwerda JA (2001) A perceptually-based texture caching algorithm for hardware-based rendering. In: Proceedings of the 12th Eurographics Workshop on Rendering, pp 246–256

Efstratiou C, Friday A, Davies N, Cheverst K (2003) A platform supporting coordinated adaptation in mobile systems. In: Proceedings of the 4th IEEE Workshop on Mobile Computing Systems and Applications. IEEE, Los Alamitos, pp 128–137

Eisenstein SM, Leyda J (1948) The Film Sense. Faber and Faber, London

Elhadad M (1992) Using argumentation to control lexical choice: A functional unification implementation. Ph.D. Thesis, Columbia University

El-Hakim SF (2002) Semi-automatic 3D reconstruction of occluded and unmarked surfaces from widely separated views. In: Proceedings ISPSRS Comm. V Sym. Corfu, Greece, pp 143–148

El-Hakim SF, Brenner C, Roth G (1998) A multi-sensor approach to creating accurate virtual environments. ISPRS J. for Photogrammetry and Remote Sensing, 53(6):379–391

Faig W (1975) Calibration of close-range photogrammetric systems. Photogrammetric Engineering and Remote Sensing, 41(12):1479–1486

Falk JA, Dierkening LD (2000) Learning from museums visitor experiences and the making of meaning. Altamira, Walnut Creek

Farma T, Cortinovis I (2000) Un Questionario sul "Locus of Control": Suo Utilizzo nel Contesto Italiano (A questionnaire on the "Locus of Control": Its use in the Italian context). Ricerca in Psicoterapia, Edizioni La Vita Felice/Tempo Libro, Milano Vol. 2.

FIPA (Foundation for Intelligent Physical Agents) (2002). FIPA Agent Communication Language Specifications. http://www.fipa.org/repository/aclspecs.html. Accessed Jan. 2007

Fleck M, Frid M, Kindberg T, Rajani R, O'Brien-Strain E, Spasojevic M (2002) From informing to remembering: deploying a ubiquitous system in an interactive science museum. Pervasive Computing 1(2):13–21

Franke UJ (2001). Managing Virtual Web Organizations in the 21th century: Issues and Challenges. Idea Group Publishing, Pennsylvania, 2001

Friedman DA, Feldman YA (2004) Knowledge-based cinematography and its applications. In: López de Mántaras R, Saitta L (eds) Proceedings of the 16th European Conference on Artificial Intelligence, ECAI 2004. IOS, pp 256–262

Gamma E, Helm R, Johnson R, and Vlissides J (1995) Design Patterns: Elements of Reusable Object-Oriented Software. Addison-Wesley

Gelb D, Malzbender T, Wu K (2001) Light-dependent texture mapping. HP Labs Tech Report: HPL-98-131(R.1)

Geldof S (1999) Templates for wearables in context. In: Busemann S, Becker T (eds) May I speak freely? Proceedings of the Workshop on NLG, KI-99, Bonn, Germany

Gena C, Torre I (2004) The importance of adaptivity to provide onboard services: A preliminary evaluation of an adaptive tourist information service onboard vehicles. Applied Artificial Intelligence, Special Issue on AI in Mobile Systems 18(6):549–580

Giles J (2005) Internet encyclopaedias go head to head. Nature 438:900–901

Gleicher M, Masanz J (2000) Towards virtual videography. In: Proceedings of the 8th ACM International Conference on Multimedia 2000. ACM, New York

González-Castaño FJ, García-Reinoso J, Gil-Castiñeira F, Costa-Montenegro E, Pousada-Carballo JM (2005) Bluetooth-assisted context-awareness in educational data networks. Computers and Education 45:105–121

Goren-Bar D, Graziola I, Pianesi F, Rocchi C, Stock O, Zancanaro M (2005a) I like it—Affective control of information flow in a personalized mobile museum guide. In: Innovative Approaches to Evaluating Affective Interfaces Workshop, CHI 2005, Portland, Oregon

Goren-Bar D, Graziola I, Pianesi F, Zancanaro M (2006) The influence of personality factors on visitor attitudes towards adaptivity dimensions for mobile museum guides. User Modeling and User Adapted Interaction. 16(1):31–62.

Goren-Bar D, Graziola I, Rocchi C, Pianesi F, Stock O, Zancanaro M (2005b) Designing and redesigning an affective interface for an adaptive museum guide. In: The 1st International Conference on Affective Computing and Intelligent Interaction, Beijing, China

Grinter RE, Aoki PM, Hurst A, Szymanski MH, Thornton JD, Woodruff A (2002) Revisiting the visit: Understanding how technology can shape the museum visit. In: Churchill E, McCarthy J (eds) Proceedings of the 2002 ACM Conference on Computer Supported Cooperative Work. ACM, New York, pp 146–155

Grote B, Stede M (1999) Ontology and lexical semantics for generating temporal discourse markers. In: Proceedings of the 7th European Workshop on Natural Language Generation, Toulouse, France, May

Guidon B (1997) Assessing the radiometric fidelity of high resolution satellite image mosaics. ISPRS J. Photogrammetry and Remote Sensing. 52(5):229–243

Hadad M, Armon G, Kaminka G, and Kraus S (2005) Supporting collaborative activity. Proceedings Twentieth National Conference on Artificial Intelligence (AAAI-05)

Halliday MAK (1973) Explorations in the functions of language, London: Arnold

Halliday MAK, Hasan R (1985) Language, context and text: Aspects of language in a social-semiotic perspective. Deakin University Press, Geelong, Vic. Australia

Halper N, Oliver P (2000) CamPlan: A camera planning agent. In: Butz A, Krüger A, Olivier P (eds) Proceedings of the AAAI Spring Symposium Workshop on Smart Graphics. AAAI, Menlo Park

Halpern JY, Moses YO (1990) Knowledge and common knowledge in a distributed environment. Journal of the Association for Computing Machinery, 37:549—587

Haritaoglu I, Harwood D, Davis LS (2000) W^4: Real-time surveillance of people and their activities. In: IEEE Transactions on PAMI 22(8):809–830

Harvey T. and Carberry S. (1998) Integrating text plans for conciseness and coherence. In Proceedings of the 17th International Conference on Computational Linguistics and the 36th Annual Meeting of the Association for Computational Linguistics, Montreal, Canada, pp 512–518

Hatala M, Kalantary L, Wakkary R, Newby K (2004). Ontology and rule based retrieval of sound objects in augmented audio reality system for museum visitors. In: Haddad H, Omicini A, Wainwright RL, Liebrock LM (eds) Proceedings of the 2004 ACM Symposium on Applied Computing, ACM, New York, pp 1045–1050

Heckmann D, Schwartz T, Brandherm B, Schmitz M, von Wilamowitz-Moellendorff M (2005) GUMO–the General User Model Ontology. In: Ardissono L, Brna P, Mitrovic A (eds) Proceedings of the 10th International Conference on User Modeling, Springer, Berlin Heidelberg New York

Hongjing W, Houben GJ, De Bra P (1998) AHAM: A reference model to support adaptive hypermedia authoring. In: Proceedings of the Conference on Information Science, Antwerp, pp 51–76

Hood MG (1983) Staying away: Why people choose not to visit museums. Museum News 61:50–57

Horvitz M (1999) Principles of mixed-initiative user interfaces. In: Proceedings of CHI 1999, ACM SIGCHI Conference on Human Factors in Computing Systems. ACM, New York, pp 159–166

Isard M, Blake A (1998) Condensation—Conditional density propagation for visual tracking. In: International Journal of Computer Vision 29(1):5–28

Iwasawa S, Ohya J, Takahashi K, Sakaguchi T, Kawato S, Ebihara K, Morishima S (1999) Real-time, 3D estimation of human body postures from trinocular images. In: Proceedings of IEEE International Workshop on Modelling People, Kerkyra, Greece, pp 3–10

Jameson A (2003) Adaptive interfaces and agents. In: Jacko J, Sears A (eds) Human-Computer Interaction Handbook. Erlbaum, Mahwah, NJ pp 305–330

Jameson A, Schwarzkopf E (2002) Pros and cons of controllability: An empirical study. Brusilovsky P, Conejo E. (eds) Adaptive Hypermedia and Adaptive Web-based Systems: Proceedings of AH2002, Malaga, Spain pp 193–202

Johnson D, Johnson F (1991) Joining together: Group theory and group skills. Prentice Hall, Upper Saddle River, NJ

Johnson D, Johnson R (1999) Learning Together and Alone: Cooperative, Competitive, and Individualistic Learning. Allyn and Bacon, Boston

Kaminka G, Pynadath D, Tambe M (2002) Monitoring teams by overhearing: A multi-agent plan-recognition approach. Journal of Artificial Intelligence Research, 17:83–135, Morgan Kaufmann

Kang SB (1999) Survey of image-based rendering techniques. In: SPIE Vol. 3641, Videometrics VI, pp 2–16

Karp P, Feiner S (1993) Automated presentation planning of animation using task decomposition with heuristic reasoning. In: Proceedings of Graphics Interface. ACM, New York, pp 118–127

Karuppiah D, Zhu Z, Shenoy P, Riseman E (2001) A fault-tolerant distributed vision system architecture for object tracking in a smart room. In: Proceedings of the 2nd International Workshop on Computer Vision Systems—ICVS 2001, Vancouver, Canada, pp 201–219

Kay J (2001) Learner control. User Modeling and User-Adapted Interaction 11(1–2):111–127

Kay J, Kummerfeld B, Lauder P (2002) Personis: A server for user models. In: De Bra P, Brusilovsky P. Conejo R (eds) Proceedings of Adaptive Hypertext 2002. Springer, Berlin Heidelberg New York

Kay J, Kummerfeld B, Lauder P (2003) Managing private user models and shared personas. In: Berardina N, Cheverst K, Kruger A (eds) In: Proceedings of Workshop on User Modeling for Ubiquitous Computing. Available online: http://www.di.uniba.it/~ubium03/, pp 1–11. Accessed Jan. 2007

Kay J, Lum A, Niu W (2005) A scrutable museum tour guide system. In: Butz A Kray C, Kruger A, Schmidt A, Prendinger H (eds) 2nd Workshop on Multi-user and Ubiquitous User Interfaces, memo no. 85, Sonderforschungsbereich 378, University of Saarland Press, Saarbrücken, Germany, pp 19–20

Kay J, Niu W (2005) Adapting information delivery to groups of people. Proceedings of the UM Workshop on New Technologies for Personalized Information Access, Edinburgh

Kay J. (2001) Learner control. User Modeling and User-Adapted Interaction 11:111–127

Kennedy K, Mercer RE (2002) Planning animation cinematography and shot structure to communicate theme and mood. In: Proceedings of the 2nd International Symposium on Smart Graphics, pp 1–8, Hawthorne, New York, June 11–13, 2002

Kipp M (2001) Anvil—A generic annotation tool for multimodal dialogue. In: Proceedings of the 7th European Conference on Speech Communication and Technology (Eurospeech). Aalborg, September

Klusch M, Sycara K (2001) Brokering and matchmaking for coordination of agent societies: A survey. In: A. Omicini, F. Zambonelli, M. Klusch, and R. Tolksdorf, (eds), Coordination of Internet Agents: Models, Technologies, and Applications, Springer, Berlin Heidelberg New York, pp 197–224

Kolp M, Giorgini P, Mylopoulos J (2001) A goal-based organizational perspective on multiagents architectures. In: Proceedings of the 8th International Workshop on Agent Theories, Architectures, and Languages (ATAL-2001)

Kray C, Baus J (2003) A survey of mobile guides. HCI in mobile guides. In: Workshop of Mobile HCI, Udine

Krüger A, Kruppa M, Müller C, Wasinger R (2002) Readapting multimodal presentations to heterogenous user groups. Notes of the AAAI-Workshop on Intelligent and Situation-Aware Media and Presentations, AAAI, Alberta, Canada

Krüger A, Butz A, Müller C, Stahl C, Wasinger R, Steinberg K, Dirschl A (2004) The connected user interface: realizing a personal situated navigation service. In: Vanderdonckt J (ed) Proceedings of the 9th International Conference on Intelligent User Interfaces. ACM, New York, pp 161–168

Kruppa M, Heckmann D, Krüger A (2005) Adaptive multimodal presentation of multimedia content in museum scenarios. KI—Zeitschrift für Künstliche Intelligenz Jan:56–59

Kruppa M, Krüger A, Rocchi C, Stock O, Zancanaro M (2003) Seamless Personalized TV-like presentations on mobile and stationary devices in a museum.
In: Trant J, Bearman D (eds) ICHIM03: Proceedings of the International Conference on Hypermedia and Interactivity in Museums, CD-ROM Proceedings,
Paris, ISBN: 1-885626-33-9

Kuflik T, Busetta P, Pensierini L, Bresciani P, Zancanaro M (2004) Personalized
information delivery in dynamic museum environment by implicit organizations of agents. Workshop on Environments for Personalized Information
Access, Gallipoli, Italy, pp. 22–33

Kumar S, Huber MJ, Cohen PR (2002a) Representing and executing protocols as
joint actions. Proceedings of the 1st International Joint Conference on
Autonomous Agents and Multiagent Systems (AAMAS 2002), Bologna, Italy,
pp 543—550

Kumar S, Huber MJ, Cohen PR, McGee DR (2002b) Toward a formalism for
conversation protocols using joint intention theory. Computational Intelligence, 18(2)

Kumar S, Huber MJ, McGee D, Cohen PR (2000), Levesque HJ (2000) Semantics
of agent communication languages for group interaction. In: Proceedings of
the 17th International Conference on Artificial Intelligence, pp 42–47

Laegsgaard E (1979) Position sensitive semiconductor detectors. Nuclear Instru-
mentation and Methods, 162:93–111

Lanz O (2004a) Automatic lens distortion estimation for an active camera. In:
Proceedings of the International Conference on Computer Vision and Graphics—ICCVG 2004, Warsaw, Poland, pp 575–580

Lanz O (2004b) Occlusion robust tracking of multiple objects. In: Proceedings of
the International Conference on Computer Vision and Graphics—ICCVG
2004, Warsaw, Poland, pp 715–720

Lanz O, Manduchi R (2005) Hybrid joint-separable multibody tracking. In:
Proceedings of the 2005 IEEE Computer Society Conference on Computer
Vision and Pattern Recognition -CVPR 2005, San Diego, California,
1:413–420

Laurel B (1991) Computers as Theatre. Addison-Wesley, Reading

Lavoie B, Rambow O (1997) A fast and portable realizer for text generation systems. In: Proceedings of the 5th Conference on Applied Natural Language
Processing

Laws E (1998) Conceptualizing visitor satisfaction management in heritage settings: An exploratory blueprinting analysis of Leeds Castle, Kent. Tourism
Management 29:545–554

Lee P, Simoni A, Sartori A, Torelli G (1994) A Photosensor array for spectropho-
tometry. In: Proceedings EUROSENSOR 94, Toulouse, pp 449–452

Leinhardt G, Knutson K (2004) Listening in on museum conversations. Altamira,
Walnut Creek

Lewis JR (1995) IBM computer usability satisfaction questionnaires: Psychomet-
ric evaluation and instructions for use. International Journal of Human-
Computer Interaction 7(1):57–78

Lim MY, Aylett R, Martyn Jones C (2005) Affective guide with attitude. Proceedings 1st International Conference on Affective Computing and Intelligent Interaction, Beijing

Lin CB, Young SSC, Chan TW, Chen YH (2005) Teacher-oriented adaptive web-based environment for supporting practical teaching models: A case study of "school for all". International Journal of Computers and Education 44: 155–172

Long S, Aust D, Abowd G, Atkeson C (1996) Cyberguide: prototyping context-aware mobile applications. In: Tauber MJ (ed) Conference on Human Factors in Computing Systems. ACM, New York, pp 293–294

Lucas BD, Kanade T (1981) An iterative image registration technique with an application to stereo vision. In: Proceedings of the 7th International Joint Conference on Artificial Intelligence—IJCAI81, Vancouver, BC, Canada, pp 674–679

Luyten K, Coninx K (2005) ImogI: Take control over a context aware electronic mobile guide for museums. 4th workshop on HCI in mobile guides, available online: http://www.mguides.info/. Accessed Jan. 2007

Malciu M, Prêteux F (2000) A robust model-based approach for 3D head tracking in video sequences. In: Proceedings of the 4th IEEE International Conference on Automatic Face and Gesture Recognition—FG 2000, Grenoble, France, pp 169–175

Mamei M, Zambonelli F, Leonardi L (2002) Cofields: Towards a unifying approach to the engineering of swarm intelligent systems. In: Proceedings of 3rd International Workshop on Engineering Societies in the Agents' World—ESAW 2002, Madrid, Spain, pp 68–81

Mancini C, Buckingham Shum S (2004) Towards "cinematic" hypertext. In: De Roure D, Ashman H (eds) Proceedings of the 15th ACM Conference on Hypertext and Hypermedia, Hypertext 2004. ACM, New York

Mann WC, Thompson S (1987). Rhetorical structure theory: A theory of text organization. In: Polanyi L (ed) The Structure of Discourse, Ablex

Marti P, Rizzo A, Tozzi G Diligenti M (1999) Adapting the museum: A non-intrusive user modeling approach. In Kay J (ed) Proceedings of the 7th International Conference on User Modeling, Springer, Berlin Heidelberg New York, pp 311–313

Massari N, Gonzo L, Gottardi M, Simoni A (2004) A fast CMOS optical position sensor with high subpixel resolution. In: IEEE Trans. Inst. and Meas. 253:116–123

Masthoff J (2004) Group modeling: Selecting a sequence of television items to suit a group of viewers. User Modeling and User-Adapted Interaction 14(1):37–85

Matsuyama T, Ukita N (2002) Real-time multi-target tracking by a cooperative distributed active vision agents. In: Proceedings of the 1st International Joint Conference on Autonomous Agents and Multiagent Systems—AAMAS 2002, Bologna, Italy, pp 829–838

McCarthy J, Anagnost T (1998) MusicFX: An arbiter of group preferences for computer-supported collaborative workouts. In: Proceedings of the 1998

ACM Conference on Computer Supported Cooperative Work, Seattle, pp 363–372

McCrae RR, John OP (1992) An Introduction to the Five-Factors Model and Its Applications. Journal of Personality 60:175–215

McKeown K, Barzilay R, Evans D, Hatzivassiloglou V, Klavans J, Sable C, Schiffman B, Sigelman S (2002) Tracking and summarizing news on a daily basis with Columbia's NewsBlaster. In: Proceedings of the 2002 Human Language Technology Conference, San Diego, CA

McKeown KR (1985) Text Generation: Using Discourse Strategies and Focus Constraints to Generate Natural Language Text. Cambridge University Press, Cambridge

McLean K (1996) Planning for People in Museum Exhibitions. Malloy Lithographing, Ann Arbor, Michigan

Mehta B, Niederee C, Stewart A (2005) Towards cross-system personalization. In: Stephanidis C (ed) Proceedings of the 3rd International Conference on Universal Access in Human-Computer Interaction. Lawrence Erlbaum, Mahwah, New Jersey

Metz C (1974) Film Language: a Semiotics of the Cinema. Oxford University Press, New York

Myers B (2001) Using hand-held devices and PCs together. Communications of the ACM. ACM, New York, 11:34–41

Nardon M, Pianesi F, Zancanaro M (2002) Interactive documentaries: First usability studies. In: Proceedings of the 2nd Workshop on Personalization in Future TV. Held in conjunction with 2nd International Conference on Adaptive Hypermedia and Adaptive Web Based Systems. Online: http://itv.eltrun.aueb.gr/topics/ah02tv02/. Accessed Jan. 2007

Niederee C, Stewart A, Mehta B, Hemmje M (2004) A multi-dimensional, unified user model for cross-system personalization. In Ardisono L, Semeraro G (eds) Proceedings of Workshop on Environments for Personalized Information Access, Università degli Studi di Bari, Bari, pp 34–54

Nielsen J (1993) Usability Engineering. Academic, Boston

Norman DA (1998) The Invisible Computer. MIT Press, Cambridge MA pp. 23–50, 185–202

Norman DA (2004) Emotional design: Why we love (or hate) everyday things. Basic Books, New York

Not E, Petrelli D, Sarini M, Stock O, Strapparava C, Zancanaro M (1998) Hypernavigation in the physical space: adapting presentations to the user and to the situational context. The New Review of Hypermedia and Multimedia 4:33–45

Not E, Zancanaro M (2000) The macronode approach: Mediating between adaptive and dynamic hypermedia. In: Proceedings of the International Conference on Adaptive Hypermedia and Adaptive Web-Based Systems, Trento, August

Novello A, Callaway C (2003a) Multilingual generation for museum applications. In: Proceedings of the Italian Association for Artificial Intelligence, Pisa, Italy

Novello A, Callaway C (2003b) Porting to an Italian surface realizer: A case study. In: Proceedings of the 9th European Workshop on Natural Language Generation, Budapest, Hungary

Oberlander J, O'Donnell M, Mellish C, Knott A (1998) Conversation in the Museum: Experiments in dynamic hypermedia with the intelligent labelling explorer. The New Review of Hypermedia and Multimedia, vol. 4

O'Donnell M (2000) RSTTool 2.4—A markup tool for rhetorical structure theory. In: Proceedings of the International Natural Language Generation Conference 2000, pp 253–256

Oike Y, Ikeda M, Asada K (2003) 640 x 480 Real-time range finder using high speed readout scheme and column parallel position detector. In: Symp. VLSI Circuits Dig. of Tech. Papers, pp 153–156

Oppermann R, Specht M (1999) A nomadic information system for adaptive exhibition guidance. In: Bearman D, and Trant J (eds) Cultural Heritage Informatics 1999: Selected Papers from ICHIM 99, Archives and Museum Informatics, Pittsburgh, PA, pp 103–109

Oppermann R, Specht M (2000) A context-sensitive nomadic information system as an exhibition guide. In: Proceedings of the Handheld and Ubiquitous Computing 2nd International Symposium, HUC 2000 Bristol, UK pp 127–142

Oppermann R, Specht M, Jaceniak I (1999) HIPPIE: A nomadic information system. In: Gellersen H (ed), HUC 1999: Proceedings of the 1st International Symposium on Handheld and Ubiquitous Computing, Springer, Berlin Heidelberg New York, pp 330–333

O'Reilly T (2005) What is Web 2.0. Design Patterns and Business Models for the Next Generation of Software. O'Reilly Network.http://www.oreillynet.com/pub/. Accessed Jan. 2007

Paquet E, Peters S (2002) Collaborative virtual environments infrastructure for e-business. In: Proceedings International Conference on Infrastructure for e-Business, e-Education, e-Science and e-Medicine on the Internet—SSGRRw02, January 21–27, L'Aquila, Italy, CD

Pareto L, Lundh Snis U (2005) Reaching out to new visitors: Designing location-aware auditory technology to increase accessibility and augment the experience of museum visits. In: Proceedings of IRIS 28, Available online: http://www.hia.no/iris28/files/authors.htm. Accessed Jan. 2007

Penserini L, Bresciani P, Busetta P, Kuflik T (2005) Using TROPOS to model agent based architectures for adaptive systems: A case study in ambient intelligence. In: Proceedings of the IEEE International Conference on Software—Science, Technology and Engineering (SwSTE) 2005, IEEE, Herzliyah, Israel

Penserini L, Spalazzi L, Panti M (2004) A P2P-based infrastructure for virtual-enterprise's supply-chain management. In: Proceedings of the 6th International Conference on Enterprise Information Systems (ICEIS 2004). INSTICC-Institute for Systems and Technologies of Information, Control and Communication, 4:316–321

Perugini M, Di Blas L (2002) Analyzing personality-related adjectives from an eticemic perspective: The Big Five marker scales (BFMS) and the Italian AB5C taxonomy. In: B. De Raad and M. Perugini (eds) Big Five Assessment. Hogrefe and Huber, Göttingen, pp 281–304

Peterson C, McCabe A (1983) Developmental Psycholinguistics: Three Ways of Looking at a Child's Narrative. Plenum, New York

Petrelli D, Baggio D, Pezzulo G (2000) Adaptive hypertext design environments: Putting principles into practice. In: Brusilovsky P, Stock O, Strapparava C (eds) Proceedings of the International Conference on Adaptive Hypermedia and Adaptive Web-Based Systems. Springer, Berlin Heidelberg New York, pp 202–213

Petrelli D, Not E (2005) User-centred design of flexible hypermedia for a mobile guide: Reflections on the hyperaudio experience. User Modeling and User-Adapted Interaction 15(3–4):303–338

Pham TL, Schneider G, Goose S (2000) A situated computing framework for mobile and ubiquitous multimedia access using small screen and composite devices. In: Proceedings of the ACM International Conference on Multimedia. ACM, New York

Phung SL, Bouzerdoum A, Chai D (2002) A novel skin color model in YCbCr colour space and its application to human face detection. In: Proceedings of the 9th International Conference on Image Processing—ICIP 2002, Rochester, NY, 1:289–292

Pinhanez,CS (2001) The everywhere displays projector: a device to create ubiquitous graphical interfaces. In: Abowd GD, Brumitt B, Shafer S (eds) UbiComp 2001 Proceedings of the 3rd International Conference on Ubiquitous Computing. Springer, Berlin Heidelberg New York LNCS, pp 315–331

Potonniee O (2002) Ubiquitous personalization: A smart card based approach. In: Proceedings of the 4th Gemplus Developer Conference, Gemplus Research Publications. Availab le online: http://www.gemplus.com/smart/rd/publications/pdf/Pot02per.pdf. Accessed Jan. 2007

Power R, Doran C, Scott D (1999) Generating embedded discourse markers from rhetorical structure. In: Proceedings of the 7th European Workshop on Natural Language Generation. Toulouse, France

Preece J, Rogers Y, Sharp H (2002) Interaction Design: Beyond Human–Computer Interaction. Wiley, New York

Press WH, Teukolsky SA, Vetterling WT, Flannery BP (1992) Numerical Recipes in C, 2nd Edition. Cambridge University Press

Proctor N, Tellis C (2003) The state of the art in museum handhelds. In: Bearman D, Trant J (eds) Proceedings of Museums and the Web Conference, Archives and Museum Informatics, Pittsburgh, PA, pp 227–237

Pulli K, Abi-Rached H, Duchamp T, Shapiro LG, Stuetzle W (1998) Acquisition and visualization of coloured 3-D objects. In: Proceedings International Conf. Pattern Recognition, pp 99–108

Raptis D, Tselios N. Avouris N (2005) Context-based design of mobile applications for museums: A survey of existing practices. In: Tscheligi M, Bernhaupt R, Mihalic K (eds) Proceedings of the 7th international Conference on Human Computer Interaction with Mobile Devices and Services, ACM, New York, pp 153–160

Ravelli L (1996) Making language accessible: Successful text writing for museum visitors. Linguistics and Education 8:367–387

Reiter E (1994) Has a consensus NL generation architecture appeared, and is it psycholinguistically plausible? In: Proceedings of the 7th International Workshop on Natural Language Generation, pp 163–170

Reiter E (1995) NLG vs. Templates. In: Proceedings of the 5th European Workshop on Natural Language Generation

Reiter E, Dale R (2000) Building Natural Language Generation Systems. Cambridge University Press, Cambridge

Reynolds CW (1987) Flocks, herds, and schools: A distributed behavioural model. In: Computer Graphics 21(4):25–43

Rich E (1979) User modeling via stereotypes. Readings in intelligent User Interfaces 3(4): 329–354

Rich E (1983) Users are individuals: Individualizing user models. International Journal of Man–Machine Studies 18(3):199–214

Rickenberg R, Reeves B (2000) The effects of animated characters on anxiety, task performance, and evaluations of User interfaces. In: Proceedings of the ACM SIGCHI Conference on Human Factors in Computing Systems, CHI 2000. ACM, New York, pp 49–56

Riedijk FR, Smith T, Juijsing HJ (1993) An integrated optical position sensitive detector with digital output and error correction. Sensors and Actuators A, 32:1–6

Rioux M (1984) Laser range finder based on synchronized scanners. Applied Opt. 23, pp 3837–3844

Rizzo A, Decortis F, Marti P, Rutgers J, Thursfield P (2003) Building narrative experiences for children through real time media manipulation. In: Blythe MA, Monk AF, Overbeeke K, Wright PC (eds) Funology: From Usability to Enjoyment. Kluwer, Norwell, pp 189–199

Rocchi C, Stock O, Zancanaro M, Kruppa M Krueger A (2004) The museum visit: Generating seamless personalized presentations on multiple devices. In: Vanderdonckt J, Nunes NJ, Rich C (eds) Proceedings of the 2004 International Conference on Intelligent User Interfaces. ACM, New York, pp 316–318

Rocchi C, Zancanaro M (2003) Adaptive video documentaries. In: Ashman H, Brailsford T, Carr L, Hardman L (eds) Proceedings of the 14th ACM Conference on Hypertext and Hypermedia. ACM, New York, NY, pp 36–37

Rocchi C, Zancanaro M (2004a) Template-based Adaptive Video Documentaries. In: Baus J, Kray C, Porzel R (eds) Proceedings of Artificial Intelligence in Mobile Systems. pp 79–83

Rocchi C, Zancanaro M (2004b) Rhetorical patterns for adaptive video documentaries. In: Proceedings of Adaptive Hypermedia Conference, Eindhoven, The Netherlands, pp 324–327

Rocchini C, Cignoni P, Montani C, Scopigno R (2002) Acquiring, stitching and blending diffuse appearance attributes on 3D models. The Visual Computer, 18:186–204

Rorty R (1991) Objectivity, Relativism, and Truth. Cambridge University Press, New York

Rossi S (2006) Communication and overhearing for modeling and monitoring group interactions. PhD Thesis, University of Trento

Rossi S, Busetta P (2004) Towards monitoring of group interactions and social roles via overhearing. Proceedings of the Eighth International Workshop on Cooperative Information Agents (CIA 2004). Erfurt, Germany, September 2004. Springer, Berlin Heidelberg New York, LNAI 3191:47–61

Rossi S, Kumar S, Cohen PR (2005) Distributive and collective readings in group protocols. In: Proceedings of the Nineteenth International Joint Conference on Artificial Intelligence IJCAI-2005. pp 971–976

Rotter JB (1966) Generalized expectancies for internal versus external control of reinforcement. Psychological Monographs 80(1)

Rushmeier H, Taubin G, Gueziec A (1997) Applying shape from lighting variation to bump map capture. In: Proceedings Eurographics Rendering Workshop. pp 35–44

Ryokai K, Vaucelle C, Cassell J (2003) Virtual peers as partners in storytelling and literacy learning. Journal of Computer Assisted Learning. 19(2):195–208

Salomon G (2000) Technology and education in the age of information [in Hebrew: Tehnologia vehinukh be'idan hameida]. Haifa University and Zmora-Bitan, Haifa and Tel Aviv

Samis P (2001) Points of departure: Integrating technology into the galleries of tomorrow. In: Bearman D, Garzotto F (eds) Archives and Museum Informatics. Pittsburgh, PA

Santuari A, Lanz O, Brunelli R (2003) Synthetic movies for computer vision applications. In: Proceedings of Visualization, Imaging, and Image Processing—VIIP 2003. Benalmadena, Malaga, Spain, 1:1–6

Sarini M, Strapparava C (1998) Building a user model for a museum exploration and information-providing adaptive system. In: Brusilovsky P, De Bra P (eds) Proceedings of the 2nd Workshop on Adaptive Hypertext and Hypermedia, Report No. 98/12, Computer Science Reports. Eindhoven University of Technology Press, Eindhoven, pp 63–68

Scarlatos Y, Dushkina S, Landy (1999) TICLE: A tangible interface for collaborative learning environments. In: Atwood ME (ed) CHI 99 Extended abstracts on human factors in computing systems. ACM, New York, pp 260–261

Schiele B, Crowley JL (2000) Recognition without correspondence using multidimensional receptive field histograms. In: International Journal of Computer Vision. 36(1):31–50

Schlkopf B, Smola A (2002) Learning with Kernels. MIT Press, Cambridge, MA

Schnadelbach H, Rodden T, Koleva B, Flintham M, Frases M, Izadi S, Chandler P, Foster M, Benford S, Greenhalgh C (2002) The Augurscope: A mixed reality interface for outdoors. In: Proceedings of the ACM Conference on Human Factors in Computing Systems—CHI 2002. Minneapolis, Minnesota, pp 91–96

Scott DR (1999) The multilingual generation game: Authoring fluent texts in unfamiliar languages. In: Proceedings of the 16th International Joint Conference on Artificial Intelligence. Stockholm, Sweden

Searle JR (1969) Speech Acts. Cambridge University Press, London

Semper R, Spasojevic M (2002). The electronic guidebook: using portable devices and a wireless Web-based network to extend the museum experience. In: Proceedings of Museums and the Web Conference. Boston, MA

Shaw J (1998) Segregatory coordination and ellipsis in text generation. In: Proceedings of the Joint 36th Meeting of the ACL and the 17th International Conference on Computational Linguistics. Montréal, Canada

Shaw M, Garlan D (1996) Software Architecture: Perspectives on an Emerging Discipline. Prentice Hall

Shneiderman B (1998) Eight Golden Rules for Interface Design. Designing the User Interface (3rd Edition) Addison-Wesley, Reading, MA

Silberberg T (1995) Cultural tourism and business opportunities for museums and heritage sites. Tourism Management 15:361–365

Smith RG (1980) The contract net protocol: high level communication and control in a distributed problem solver. IEEE Transactions on Computers, C-29(12): 1104–1113

Specht M, Oppermann R (1999) User modeling and adaptivity in nomadic information systems. In: Caenepeel M, Benyon D, Smith D (eds) Proceedings of the i3 Annual Conference: Community of the Future. Available online: http://www.i3net.org/ser_pub/publications/proceedings/i3ac99-proceedings.pdf, pp 65–68. Accessed Jan. 2007

Stede M (1996) Lexical semantics and knowledge representation in multilingual sentence generation. Ph.D. Thesis, University of Toronto

Stock O (2001) Language-based interfaces and their application for cultural tourism. AI Magazine, 22(1):85–97

Stock O (1993) ALFRESCO: Enjoying the combination of NLP and hypermedia for information exploration. In: Maybury MT (ed) Intelligent Multimedia Interfaces. AAAI, Menlo Park, CA, pp 197–224

Sumi Y, Mase K (2001) AgentSalon: Facilitating face-to-face knowledge exchange through conversations among personal agents. In: Müller, JP (ed) Agents 2001: Proceedings of the 5th International Conference on Autonomous Agents. ACM, New York, pp 393–400

Sumi Y, Mase K (2004) Interface agents that facilitate knowledge interactions between community members. In: Prendinger H (ed) Life-Like Characters. Tools, Affective Functions, and Applications. Springer, Berlin Heidelberg New York, Cognitive Technologies Series, pp 405–427

Sycara K, Widoff S, Klusch M, Lu J (2002) Larks: Dynamic matchmaking among heterogeneous software agents in cyberspace. Autonomous Agents and Multi-Agent Systems. 5(2):173–203

Tahara Y, Ohsuga A, Honiden S (1999) Agent system development method based on agent patterns. In: Proceedings of the 21st International Conf. on Software Engineering (ICSE 99). IEEE, Los Alamitos (CA) , pp 356–367

Theobalt C, Magnor M, Schueler P, Seidel HP (2002) Combining 2D feature tracking and volume reconstruction for online video-based human motion capture. In: Proceedings of 10th Pacific Conference on Computer Graphics and Applications—PG 2002. Beijing, China, pp 96–103

Tidhar G (1999) Organization-oriented systems: theory and practice. PhD Thesis, Department of Computer Science and Software Engineering, University of Melbourne Press

Tunnicliffe SD, Beer L (2002) An Interactive Exhibition about Animal Skeletons: Did the Visitors Learn Any Zoology? Journal of Biological Education. 3(36):130–134

Van Gool L, Tuytelaars T, Pollefeys M (1999) Adventurous tourism for couch potatoes. In: Solina F, Leonardis A (eds) Proceedings of Modeling and Using Context, Second International and Interdisciplinary Conference. Springer, Berlin Heidelberg New York, pp 98–107

Van Someren MW (1994) Think Aloud Method: A Practical Guide to Modeling Cognitive Processes. Academic, Boston

Venkatesh V (2000) Determinants of perceived ease of use: Integrating control, intrinsic motivation, and emotion into the technology acceptance model. Information Systems Research 11:342–365

Verdaasdonk H, van Rees CJ, Stokmans M, van Eijck K, Verboord M (1996) The impact of experiential variables on patterns of museum attendance: The case of the Noord-Brabant museum. Poetics 24:181–202

Veron E, Levasseur M (1983) Ethnographie de l'exposition. Bibliothèque Publique d'Information, Paris

Wahlster W, Kobsa A (1989) Dialog-based user models. In: Kobsa A, Wahlster W (eds) User Models in Dialog Systems. Springer-Verlag Berlin, Heidelberg, New York

Wang L, Kang SB, Szeliski R, Shum HY (2001) Optimal texture map reconstruction from multiple views. In: Proceedings Computer Vision and Pattern Recognition (CVPR01)

Want R, Schilit B, Adams N, Gold R, Petersen K, Ellis J, Goldberg D, Weiser M (1995) The PARCTab ubiquitous computing experiment. Tech. Rep. CSL-95-1, Xerox Parc, Palo Alto, CA

Wechsler D (1986) Wechsler intelligence scale for children—revised; Italian Version (V. Rubini and F. Padovani eds), Organizzazioni Speciali Firenze

Weiser M (1991) The computer for the 21st century. Scientific American. 265: 94–104

Wenders W (2001) On Film. Faber and Faber, London

Werner T, Zisserman A (2002) New technique for automated architectural reconstruction from photographs. In: Proceedings 7th Europe. Conf. Computer Vision, 2:541–555

Wexelblat A, Maes P (1997) Issues for Software Agent UI. Unpublished manuscript, available from http://web.media.mit.edu/~wex/. Accessed Jan. 2007

White M, Caldwell T (1998) EXEMPLARS: A practical, extensible framework for dynamic text generation. In: Proceedings of the 9th International Workshop on NLG. Niagara-on-the-Lake, Ontario

Wickens CD, Holland JG (2000). Engineering Psychology and Human Performance. Prentice Hall, Upper Saddle River, NJ

Wiggins JS (1996) The Five-Factor Model of Personality. Guilford, New York

Williams L (1983) Pyramidal parametrics. Computer graphics. In: Proceedings of SIGGRAPH 83. 17:1–11

Woodruff A, Aoki P, Hurst A, Szymanski M (2001) Electronic guidebooks and visitor attention. In: Bearman D, Garzotto F (eds) Proceedings of the International Cultural Heritage Informatics Meeting. Archives and Museum Informatics, Pittsburgh, PA, pp 437–454

Wooldridge M (2002) An Introduction to Multiagent Systems. Wiley, New York

Yang FJ, Kim JH, Glass M, Evens M (2000) Lexical usage in the tutoring schemata of CIRCSIM-tutor: Analysis of variable references and discourse markers. In: Proceedings of the 5th Annual Conference on Human Interaction and Complex Systems. Urbana, IL

Yoshimura S, Sugiyama T, Yonemoto K, Ueda K (2001) A 48k frames/s CMOS image sensor for real-time 3-D sensing and motion detection. In: ISSCC Dig. Of Tech. Papers. pp 94-95

Zhang P, Li N, Sun H (2006) Affective quality and cognitive absorption, extending technology acceptance research. In: Proceedings of the 39th Hawaii International Conference on System Sciences (HICSS-39 2006), Kauai, Hawaii

Authors

Adriano Albertini, albertini@itc.it
ITC-irst, Trento, Italy

Ivana Alfaro, alfaro@itc.it
ITC-irst, Trento, Italy

Claudio Andreatta, andreatta@itc.it
ITC-irst, Trento, Italy

Angelo Beraldin, angelo.beraldin@nrc-cnrc.gc.ca
NRC-CNRC, Ottawa, Canada

Paolo Bresciani, bresciani@itc.it
ITC-irst, Trento, Italy

Roberto Brunelli, brunelli@itc.it
ITC-irst, Trento, Italy

Paolo Busetta, busetta@itc.it
ITC-irst, Trento, Italy

Charles Callaway, callaway@itc.it
ITC-irst, Trento, Italy

Alessandro Cappelletti, cappelle@itc.it
ITC-irst, Trento, Italy

Paul Chippendale, chippendale@itc.it
ITC-irst, Trento, Italy

Sabry El-Hakim, sabry.el-hakim@nrc-cnrc.gc.ca
NRC-CNRC, Ottawa, Canada

Lorenzo Gonzo, lgonzo@itc.it
ITC-irst, Trento, Italy

Dina Goren-Bar, dgb1717@gmail.com
Ben-Gurion University of the Negev, Israel

Ilenia Graziola, graziola@itc.it
ITC-irst, Trento, Italy

Giuseppe Iandolo, iandolo@itc.it
ITC-irst, Trento, Italy

Antonio Krüger, krueger@cs.uni-sb.de
DFKI, Saarbrücken, Germany

Michael Kruppa, krueger@dfki.de
DFKI, Saarbrücken, Germany

Tsvi Kuflik, tsvikak@mis.haifa.ac.il
University of Haifa, Israel

Oswald Lanz, lanz@itc.it
ITC-irst, Trento, Italy

Marianna Nardon, nardon@itc.it
ITC-irst, Trento, Italy

Elena Not, not@itc.it
ITC-irst, Trento, Italy

Loris Penserini, penserini@itc.it
ITC-irst, Trento, Italy

Fabio Pianesi, pianesi@itc.it
ITC-irst, Trento, Italy

Michela Prete, prete@itc.it
ITC-irst, Trento, Italy

Cesare Rocchi, rocchi@itc.it
ITC-irst, Trento, Italy

Franca Rossi, frarossi@itc.it
ITC-irst, Trento, Italy

Silvia Rossi, srossi@itc.it
ITC-irst, Trento, Italy

Massimiliano Ruocco, ruocco@itc.it
ITC-irst, Trento, Italy

Alessandro Santuari, santuari@itc.it
ITC-irst, Trento, Italy

Oliviero Stock, stock@itc.it
ITC-irst, Trento, Italy

Francesco Tobia, tobia@itc.it
ITC-irst, Trento, Italy

Paola Venuti, venuti@form.unitn.it
Università di Trento

Francesca Voltolini, voltolini@itc.it
ITC-irst, Trento, Italy

Massimo Zancanaro, zancanaro@itc.it
ITC-irst, Trento, Italy

Index

Cognitive Technologies

Printing: Krips bv, Meppel
Binding: Stürtz, Würzburg